Developing Management Skills

Developing Management Skills

Techniques For Improving Learning and Performance

Margaret Dale

KOGAN
PAGE

First published in 1993

Apart from any fair dealing for the purposes of research or private study, or criticism or review, as permitted under the Copyright, Designs and Patents Act, 1988, this publication may only be reproduced, stored or transmitted, in any form or by any means, with the prior permission in writing of the publishers, or in the case of reprographic reproduction in accordance with the terms of licences issued by the Copyright Licensing Agency. Enquiries concerning reproduction outside those terms should be sent to the publishers at the undermentioned address:

Kogan Page Limited
120 Pentonville Road
London N1 9JN

© Margaret Dale, 1993

British Library Cataloguing in Publication Data

A CIP record for this book is available from the British Library

ISBN 0 7494 0218 0

Typeset by Photoprint, Torquay, Devon
Printed and bound in Great Britain by Biddles Ltd, Guildford and Kings Lynn

Contents

8.   The manager's role   189

9.   Learning organisations   219

| Preface

Developing Management Skills is a sequel to *Assessing Management Skills*, which was written with Paul Iles. The aim of this second book is to take the ideas expressed in the first a stage further. Paul and I worked together on the early stages of this book, recognising that once management skills have been assessed, interest in the skills themselves and the individuals possessing them tends to decline. We suspected that one reason for this was the limited knowledge about what to do next.

Much is written and said about the importance of training, yet in practice, availability of dedicated facilities and resources is as constrained as ever. This apparent scarcity of facilities is contrasted by the millions of opportunities that exist around us all in our everyday jobs. These can be found in the tasks in hand, our colleagues and the wider world in which we operate. This book has been written to help managers and interested others recognise those opportunities and use them productively.

The book concludes by looking at what individual managers can achieve in the context of the wider organisation. It is accepted that individuals acting alone face limitations. Managers can be influential and powerful in helping the development of others, but only if they acknowledge their role and responsibilities for releasing this potential. Much can be achieved from example and by helping others develop. The idea of the 'learning organisation' is spreading; from this the importance of total growth, improvement and development in relation to organisational productivity, well-being and even survival can be seen. Therefore the development of individuals needs to be seen in a wider context – the parts in relation to the whole.

The first book took as its starting point the manager's role in assessing skills. This second book pursues the idea by describing the manager as being responsible for self-development and that of others. The third, if it gets written, will continue this theme further by exploring the manager's role in developing the learning organisation.

Margaret Dale
December, 1992

Acknowledgements

I am very grateful for the help and support given by Lorna, who revised the script and corrected the bad English; Chris and Jennie, who read the draft and provided useful feedback; and by Mick, who gave the accountant's perspective. Most of all, my appreciation is due to Roger. This book would not have been written without his generously given ideas, care and encouragement.

1
Introduction

This book is aimed at managers, trainers and other personnel practitioners, as well as others who are interested in developing their own skills and those of their colleagues. It intends to provide practical guidance on ways of helping development happen at work. It will not be a theoretical discourse, although appropriate concepts will be used – rather, it is intended to give the reader some ideas on how to make the best use of the opportunities that already exist, and how to create new ones by translating training concepts and theories into developmental action.

It is a matter of concern that there are occasions when, after investment in training has been made, the training is not translated into practice. There may be a number of good reasons why this happens, but in many cases it is due to a failure by managers to enable individuals to apply their learning. In other cases the investment is not made in the first place, and individuals are left to grow on their own. Again this may be due to a number of reasons, a common one being the apparent shortage of funds.

One purpose of this book is to demonstrate that the cost of investment in training and learning need not be high in monetary terms. The book also aims to show how, by following a few basic principles, managers can make the best return on that investment, helping others to develop in a purposeful way to the mutual benefit of themselves, and their employers.

There are many detailed and practical texts on training. These provide sound guidance on how to organise training activities both on and off the job, and give some of the background needed to understand the learning processes and particular requirements of adults in the work context. Other complementary sources are the texts on self-development. These will be drawn upon when further information would be helpful, as they provide practical guidance on how managers can develop their own skills and abilities.

PRACTICAL SUPPORT FOR LEARNING

It seems that there is a shortage of practical support for managers to help them turn everyday work into a rich environment in which development can occur both for themselves and for others. This books aims to make good this shortage by focusing on ways in which job-related and on-the-job activities can be used as positive opportunities for learning. While it is possible for the individual to achieve much alone, having a manager who is committed to making the principles of development work and who is able to provide both support and practical help can make a world of difference. This book is for those who want to enhance their own learning and that of others. Tips, check-lists, case studies and examples of what can be done will be used to show what others have found possible – it is hoped that these ideas and the materials suggested will indicate the full scope of what is possible, enabling managers to devise their own approaches to suit their own situations and people.

THE MEANING OF WORDS

It may be useful, at this point, to explain exactly what we mean by the term 'development'. Development is the process of growth or advancement, making or becoming bigger or fuller, or more elaborate or systematic, or coming to maturity. All of these concepts imply adding on to something that is already in existence. These definitions are different from those of training, education, and even learning.

Education and learning

Training and education are processes that are done to a third party. You are trained to do a job or to perform a task. Education may equip you for life by being a transformation process that you go through, but essentially, when you are educated you are given knowledge of subjects, ideas and concepts and are taught how to use them. It is possible to test the levels of knowledge and compare the standards attained between people. Learning and development are different – the individual is more in control of the processes, and they are more dependent on the individual's starting point. It is not possible to be 'learnt'.

Reg Revans (1980), the father of action learning, said:

> training systems intended to develop our young may do little more than to make them proficient in yesterday's techniques . . . . But all managers will be caught up by the currents of change and swept into new unknowns never before encountered . . . . In such conditions, nobody can say what programmed knowledge those in such predicaments may need . . . . In such exploration of the unfamiliar too great a reliance upon inappropriate programmed knowledge may become a fatal weakness . . . . We may structure our argument from the outset by identifying the acquisition of programmed knowledge as P, and of questioning insight as Q, so writing the learning equation:

$$L = P + Q.$$

Learning is a complex process that is totally unique and internal to the individual. It requires both the input of 'P' and the experience and skills of 'Q'. The same experience and the same piece of knowledge can have totally different meanings to two people, to equally good effect. The development of the skills may require the same programme to be followed; the content will be the same and the skills demonstrated will show the same behaviour patterns to those watching. However, the ways in which the watcher and listener learns the skills and knowledge will differ. Behaviour patterns will vary and the interpretation of the content will be used to form a knowledge base unique to each individual learner. The cognitive processes used during learning are idiosyncratic and the existing levels of knowledge and acquired skills, even among the young, will not be the same. Those engaged in the evaluation of training, particularly development, assessment and the accreditation of prior experience and learning, know how fraught and difficult this task is. The development of skills and the acquisition of insight into self, others and processes can stem from so many different stimuli that it is nearly impossible to determine an ideal sort of structure for training and education.

Competence and skill

It is fashionable at the moment to talk about *competencies* or *competence*. Occupational standards or competence statements have been or are being produced for most jobs to form a basis of training and vocational qualifications. They purport to embody the knowledge and skills required for successful completion of a job.

The method used to identify types of competence concentrates, by default, on outcomes of behaviour. Some concerns about this methodology have been expressed in the personnel management, training and development journals. However, it would not be helpful to enter into the debate at length here, as managers wishing to gain practical guidance may be side-tracked. Some of the issues that affect development at work will be considered later.

One of the major problems arises from the use of words that have similar but different meanings. When the idea to develop a profile of a competent manager was first proposed, reference was made to work being done in America by the McBer Organisation and Boyatzis for the American Management Association (Boyatzis, 1982). The American meaning of the word 'competency', in this context, is 'the difference between an average and a superior performer'. 'English' 'competence' means 'someone who is capable, or adequately qualified or effective'. The National Council for Vocational Qualification's definition is 'the abilities to perform the activities within an occupation'. Each of these are legitimate definitions for use when discussing development, but they can have different implications.

To avoid confusion, the word *skill* will be used, taken to refer to task-related behaviour that can be acquired through learning and improved with practice and help. An *ability* is a mental or physical trait, a *talent* is something born within an individual that distinguishes that person, (for example being able to produce life-like cartoons or use humour during presentations). It is possible to learn and develop talents, but they tend to be more difficult than skills to acquire or change, as they are deeply embedded as part of a person's individuality. This is the reason why some people are good at doing a particular task while others, no matter how hard they try, are never able to perform adequately.

Example 1.1

Public speaking, for example, requires skills of delivery and communication and an ability to project oneself with a degree of self-confidence. The former may be learnt and improved with practice, but without the latter, the speech will never be really good.

Both skills and abilities affect an individual's performance, but it is the acquisition, application and development of skills which should command the manager's attention. The concern here is with the development of the skills needed for effective performance of the job in the employing organisation, now and in the future. The development of personal abilities needs also to be taken into consideration, but the limited scope for changing this aspect of an individual's personality should be taken fully into account.

Personal growth is an important element of the development process and, of course, personality factors have a major impact on individual performance. In some situations, therefore, influencing personality factors may be a necessary part of individuals' development at work. The limitations and special considerations that have to be given to this area of development work will be discussed at the appropriate point later. Knowledge, attitudes and value systems will be considered in relation to the contribution, positive and negative, that they make to learning.

Defining skills

Having established the importance of precise definition of the word 'skill', the same degree of precision will be applied to the definition of the skills themselves. It would be reasonable, however, to ask whether the time taken to do so is time well spent. Some of the skills may seem to be so well known, and their meaning so precise, that there is no point in defining them closely – or is there?

Example 1.2

Is a skilled communicator someone who speaks fluently; or someone who is concise and precise; or someone whose writing follows the principles of plain English; or someone who produces flowing, well-argued essays? All of these people can be skilled communicators in certain settings. In others, however, they may be deemed inadequate for the job.

The need for definition and precision is more important when describing interpersonal skills. In this area the assessment of effective performance is even more dependant on organisational factors. There is greater scope for imprecision, as the words are jargon, have several different meanings in common use, and have very different implications in practice. A 'skilled leader' will be a very different beast in a voluntary organisation to one in a mass production factory. In Mager's (1984) parable of the Fuzzy:

Once upon a time in the land of Fuzz, King Aling called in his cousin Ding and commanded, 'Go ye out into all of Fuzzland and find me the goodest of people, whom I shall reward for being so good.'

'But how will I know one when I see one?' asked the Fuzzy.

'Why, the person will be sincere', scoffed the king, and whacked off a leg for her impertinence.

So, the Fuzzy limped out to find a good person. But soon she returned, confused and empty-handed.

'But how will I know one when I see one?' she asked again.

'Why, the person will be dedicated', grumbled the king, and whacked off another leg for her impertinence.

So the Fuzzy hobbled away once more to look for the goodest of all people. But again she returned, confused and empty-handed.

'But how will I know one when I see one?' she pleaded.

'Why the person will have an empathetic understanding of her own self-actualizing potential', fumed the king, and whacked off another leg for her impertinence.

So the Fuzzy, now on her last leg, hopped out to continue her search. In time, she returned with the wisest, most sincere and dedicated Fuzzy in all of Fuzzland, and stood the person before the king.

'Why, this person will not do at all', roared the king. 'Too thin, too thin to suit me.' Whereupon, he whacked off the last leg of the Fuzzy, who fell to the floor with a squishy thump.

The moral of this fable is that – if you can't tell one when you see one, you may wind up without a leg to stand on.

Another way of saying the same thing is: 'If you don't know where you are going, how will you know when you get there?'

This approach to skill definitions helps to assess skill level and can indicate areas in which improvements can be made. Some of the techniques that can be used to define skills are described in detail in our previous book, *Assessing Management Skills*. The simplest approach is to answer Mager's question: 'How do you know one when you see one?'. The example given above demonstrates how the skills of communication can be defined differently depending on how they are to be used and the organisational expectations of a skilful communicator. This question, while being simple to ask (very little preparation is needed), is not simplistic. Considerable thought is needed if the answer is to be satisfactory and clear in its meaning.

Other people can be involved who will bring their own perspectives and meanings, enriching the final definition. The process of involvement may in itself also be beneficial. Considerable debate can be generated, and disagreements and misunderstandings brought into the open. The resultant definitions of skills will be jointly owned, and a common meaning established. Answering a simple question can, in fact, be a valuable contribution to building a team. The definitions, being richer, and jointly owned, should be more robust and clearer in their meaning. However, involving others takes more time than answering questions alone. It also means that if the disagreements and misunderstandings are not resolved, or the conclusions are not shared, other problems may be created.

The dangers of over-definition

There are some dangers in over-precise definition. The approach chosen by the National Council for Vocational Qualification for use in the specification of occupational standards has some strengths, while also exemplifying the weak points of competence definition. The standards can be used rigidly, in a prescriptive way that could stifle rather than enable development. The amount of detail given in the standards, and the fineness of the breakdown, leave little scope for interpretation. This is deliberate and, in some senses, quite right. The poor standard of managerial skills has been seen as a major handicap to Britain's ability to compete effectively in the international market-place. The use of competence statements to define manager skills was seen as a way of increasing and improving those skills. The original intention was to use the definitions to guide development by indicating areas in which managers could acquire new skills and/or build on their existing skills. The way in which the approach has been applied, however, involves a rigidity that is confining. It inhibits flexibility and changes of emphasis by not allowing for individual organisational adjustment. The detailed statements are liable to become outdated. Changing circumstances and altering environmental conditions will mean that skill requirements, emphasis and competence will take on different meanings. These changes are happening constantly and, some would argue, at an ever-increasing speed. The definitions used last year may not be appropriate for this year nor the ones required by effective managers next year, and those deemed to be effective in one organisation may not be so judged in another.

The value of precision

So, when specifying skills, a fine balance has to be made between necessary precision, and over-definition. Enough detail is required to provide direction and guidance for managers as assessors, developers and for their reports, so that any diagnosis is made on the basis of real rather than supposed need. The definition should also contribute to learning and development, by providing an indication of areas in which improvement can be made and growth take place. On the other hand, the specification should not be cast in concrete. As situations change, the definitions must be capable of being reviewed and revised. Levels of organisational and individual competence change as the environment alters and individuals come and go. The demands being placed upon them and the organisation change over time, and expectations are modified as a number of external forces exert their influence. Skill definitions consequently require some room for adjustment and interpretation, but they should not be so general as to be meaningless. This is not easy. Mager's question is full of pitfalls for the unwary Fuzzy!

The definition of skills can also be used to chart a forward course. One of the most difficult aspects of dealing with the future is its degree of uncertainty. A technique for reducing uncertainty is to distinguish between the known, the known but not acknowledged, the unsure, and the really unknown. Defining skills needed for effective performance in the future is a process that can help to distinguish between the known and the unknown, so reducing uncertainty.

Example 1.3

Look forward a year from now and ask, 'What are the critical incidents that will affect whether we are successful? What difficult, almost intractable tasks will face us?'

From the answers generated by such an exercise, it will be possible to go on to analyse what skills will be needed to complete those tasks and to manage the incidents. Some of these will be the skills already known as being necessary for skilful managers. Some may be new. Using a similar process, take the organisation's mission or vision and ask, 'Which skills are required now to realise it, and which will be needed in the foreseeable future?' Such analysis may produce some surprises. It is also likely that they will be fuzzy and, as such, will need to be redefined regularly as the vision is refined.

The method of defining skills outlined above is a demonstration of the skills of managing uncertainty and dealing, constructively, with ambiguity. These, it can be argued, are some of the key management skills needed now for effective performance. However, the other skills used in this process – the analysis of the future, and clarifying, defining and refining situations and performance – are not yet widely acknowledged, despite the valuable contribution they can make.

This process may seem to be long-winded, and a possible detraction from getting on with the pressing jobs in hand. But again, 'if you do not know where you are going, how will you know when you get there?'; and 'how are you going to get there?'

To sum up, the definition of skills can help to express and make explicit the organisation's present view of an effective, competent manager. This allows a reasonably accurate assessment to be made of current levels of performance, and gives indications of where and how performance can be improved. The process of skill definition can contribute to the progress of the organisation by assisting with the refinement of the vision. The clarification of the skills needed to maintain effectiveness for the predicted future also helps the organisation and its employees develop.

THE VALUE OF FRAMEWORKS

A long list of skills which are needed can be overwhelming, making their acquisition a 'Mission Impossible'. It has often been found more useful to create a *conceptual framework* into which the skills can be fitted. For example, we all know broadly what a manager does, but there is no clearly expressed, modern, simple model. Fayol's (1949) description of the functions of management which he gave as planning, organising, staffing, directing and controlling, were a useful guide. Some still find Fayol's model helpful, but it is now dated and it omits some aspects of the modern management role. The NCVQ occupational standards for managers contains what could be called a conceptual framework. The key roles are given as 'manage operations, manage finance, manage people, manage information'. However, these roles reflect the approach used to define them and can be seen as being too concerned with the tasks rather than the role. As noted above, the standards are produced by functional analysis, which is concerned with the outcomes or competent performance, not the skills needed to achieve those outcomes. It has been found that a conceptual framework of the whole role helps people understand what is expected of them in total.

A way of creating one is to use an alternative approach to functional analysis which produces statements of outcome of performance. An example of one such model is the Framework given in Fig. 1.1 The skills are grouped into five domains: 'interacting with the environment, managing the job, developing the organisation, working with others, and knowing self. The focus on skills encourages assessors, assessees, developers and developees to create a model of the whole role which can be easily understood, shared and applied to everyday work.

Being simple, a conceptual framework such as this can provide a shorthand means of communicating the expectations of the role. It is also an image for the future, giving stress to 'knowing where you are going'. It allows the critical skills to be kept to the forefront, priority activities to be identified and other activities to be balanced. In the busy world of modern work, it is very easy to get certain aspects of the job out of proportion and to lose sight of other less pressing but nevertheless equally important aspects of the role. Valuable skills can fall into disrepair through under-use; needed skills may remain unacquired; potential may remain underdeveloped and unrecognised skills be wasted.

The term 'Framework' has been chosen deliberately as the model is intended to provide boundaries to keep the business in check. Some of the activities that rush in to fill the diary can be legitimately excluded if role-holders are clear about their role it helps others share the understanding and this means that role negotiations can be conducted more easily. This can avoid the negative consequences of role confusion which are described in the literature on organisational behaviour.

The Framework takes account of the differences between a senior executive director and a first-line manager. Each of its domains should be reflected in the different managerial jobs, but the skills needed for effective performance have different emphases. Thus the Framework provides guidance on which skills need to be developed as individuals progress through the levels of management, and can help them prepare for future roles. It can also serve as a means of identifying weak, under-used or undeveloped skills, and can draw attention to those that are not currently employed by the organisation or individual.

The value of a conceptual model will be referred to again. The use of such

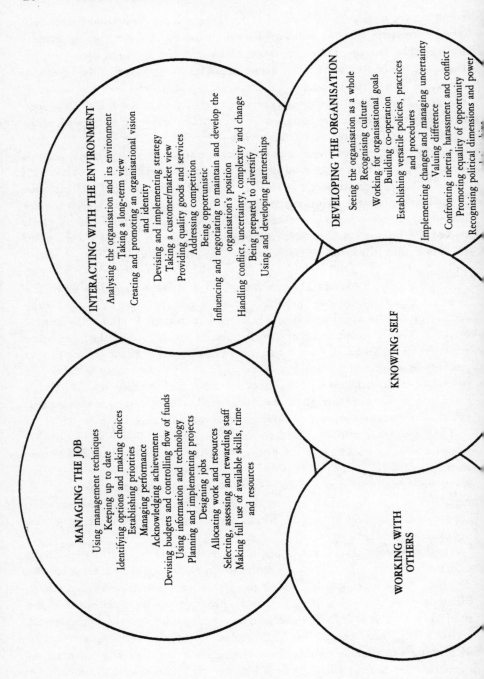

INTERACTING WITH THE ENVIRONMENT

Analysing the organisation and its environment
Taking a long-term view
Creating and promoting an organisational vision
and identity
Devising and implementing strategy
Taking a customer/market view
Providing quality goods and services
Addressing competition
Being opportunistic
Influencing and negotiating to maintain and develop the
organisation's position
Handling conflict, uncertainty, complexity and change
Being prepared to diversify
Using and developing partnerships

DEVELOPING THE ORGANISATION

Seeing the organisation as a whole
Recognising culture
Working for organisational goals
Building co-operation
Establishing versatile policies, practices
and procedures
Implementing changes and managing uncertainty
Valuing difference
Confronting inertia, harassment and conflict
Promoting equality of opportunity
Recognising political dimensions and power

MANAGING THE JOB

Using management techniques
Keeping up to date
Identifying options and making choices
Establishing priorities
Managing performance
Acknowledging achievement
Devising budgets and controlling flow of funds
Using information and technology
Planning and implementing projects
Designing jobs
Allocating work and resources
Selecting, assessing and rewarding staff
Making full use of available skills, time
and resources

KNOWING SELF

WORKING WITH OTHERS

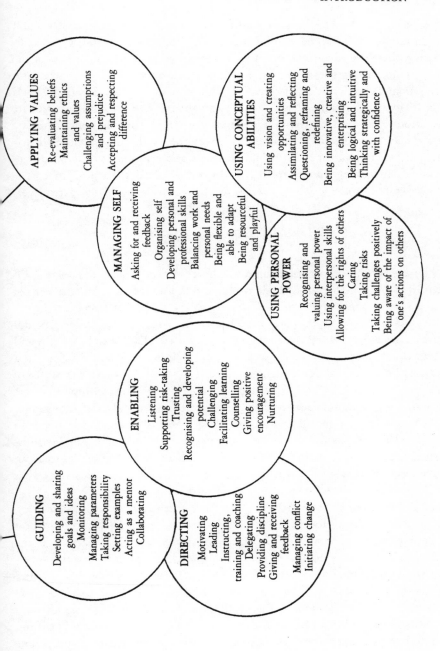

APPLYING VALUES
Re-evaluating beliefs
Maintaining ethics
and values
Challenging assumptions
and prejudice
Accepting and respecting
difference

USING CONCEPTUAL ABILITIES
Using vision and creating
opportunities
Assimilating and reflecting
Questioning, reframing and
redefining
Being innovative, creative and
enterprising
Being logical and intuitive
Thinking strategically and
with confidence

MANAGING SELF
Asking for and receiving
feedback
Organising self
Developing personal and
professional skills
Balancing work and
personal needs
Being flexible and
able to adapt
Being resourceful
and playful

USING PERSONAL POWER
Recognising and
valuing personal power
Using interpersonal skills
Allowing for the rights of others
Caring
Taking risks
Taking challenges positively
Being aware of the impact of
one's actions on others

ENABLING
Listening
Supporting risk-taking
Trusting
Recognising and developing
potential
Challenging
Facilitating learning
Counselling
Giving positive
encouragement
Nurturing

GUIDING
Developing and sharing
goals and ideas
Monitoring
Managing parameters
Taking responsibility
Setting examples
Acting as a mentor
Collaborating

DIRECTING
Motivating
Leading
Instructing,
training and coaching
Delegating
Providing discipline
Giving and receiving
feedback
Managing conflict
Initiating change

models has been found to be useful in different areas of work with managers and so a similar approach can be recommended. The Framework is not promoted as the best or the only such structure. One could almost say that, regardless of the detail, so long as a model is accepted and used as a means of helping your own development as well as that of others, it almost does not matter which one is chosen. The development of the model is a valuable exercise in itself, and its application on a consistent basis across an organisation can reap many benefits. The alternative is akin to shopping in a megastore without a shopping list — potentially very rewarding, as untold treasures and tempters to the palate are discovered; however, the efforts to obtain the goods desired are unfocused, possibly wasted, and the whole exercise is time-consuming (if not expensive).

THE MANAGER'S ROLE

The manager's role and contribution to the development of skills are critical. Of course, it is possible for individuals to develop themselves without the help of their bosses — in some cases, quite effectively. Nevertheless, it is so much better if the boss and the staff work together in a partnership. Developmental opportunities fly around all the time in everyday work. These can be caught and used for the benefit of the people and the job. Helping others to develop their skills can be beneficial for managers as well as their staff, as the skills of developing others (ie training, coaching, mentoring, counselling, etc) are improved and the content may add to the manager's own skills and knowledge. (Intek MacMillan's First Line Manager Programme illustrates this point in practice.) It is also possible for the development opportunities to provide spin-offs such as improvements to operations and create other opportunities that can be extended to other staff and colleagues. In some ways, it is surprising that such a rich process is not a greater part of normal working.

Jobs benefit from the use of development opportunities. As well as enabling existing tasks to be performed better (eg faster, less wasted resources, greater output, etc) alternative ways of doing a job may be found as a result of the acquisition of new knowledge, extending and/or adding to existing skills levels — and applying them. The process of applying the learning means that existing approaches will inevitably be questioned and some things will be done differently. Not for one moment is it suggested, however, that all learning results in change and that change as an end in itself is good. Sometimes learning serves to confirm that current practice is the best for the situation and people involved. At other times it will indicate that current practice may not be the best, but the exploration of the various pros and cons of change may lead to the decision not to change, and this can contain valuable learning. Without the involvement of the boss in the exploration and consideration of the possibilities of change can only be partial and more difficult to implement.

This does not mean that it is not possible to make use of opportunities for learning and development without the involvement of the boss. It does mean, however, that it is more difficult to exploit the full potential of such opportunities and to realise the possibilities for the job. Examples of how the organisation can lose out as a result of managers failing to fulfil this part of their role will be given later. The overall aim of this book is to help managers perform this function adequately. This will be done by highlighting the skills involved with developing others, indicating the sorts of opportunities that exist, ways of making the most of them and how to fabricate new ones.

THE ARRANGEMENT OF THIS BOOK

This book is arranged in a way that is intended to aid the reader's development. After having considered why it is important to define skills, the cost of developing and not developing others will be explored. Realising and maximising opportunities is very much a feature of the current business world. A tough economic climate and the need for economy, efficiency, effectiveness and conservation mean that waste of any kind has to be avoided. All aspects of working life are under scrutiny with cost and pay-off in mind. The utility of any action is a major consideration in decision-making. This applies as much to personal development as to financial investment. The rate of return is another such factor. Consequently the full costs and benefits of engaging in and not engaging in staff development have to be calculated.

Opportunities where development and learning can occur are not always obvious. Yet there are many aspects of human resource management that can be used as developmental opportunities in addition to their other, primary purpose. Some of these will be described and indications of how they can be used to twin effect will be outlined.

The manager, as already indicated, has a key role. Regardless of function and specialism, all managers have responsibilities for the management of their human resources, in addition to their other resources. (The term 'human resources' can have two interpretations. Either the people are seen as units of production, or as unique individuals with aspirations and goals of their own which may be different to those of the manager and/or organisation. The main sense used here will be the latter. However, the former is used when the organizational need for the effective performance of its staff is paramount.) The way in which managers perform their role and carry out their responsibilities for the development of their staff can have a major impact on their performance, working life and growth. The different approaches that can be taken by carrying out this role will be described. Ways in which these approaches can be used and themselves developed will also be explained.

To make the most of the developmental approaches, some basic understanding of the learning and development processes is needed. Unlike the other resources of the organisation, human resources are not inanimate objects, even though in some organisations they may be treated as such. The way in which people learn and develop is peculiar to each individual. Some of the principles of learning theory will be used to explain what is likely to happen as part of the learning process. It is not intended to equip the readers as amateur psychologists, and a little knowledge is recognised as being especially dangerous in this field. This brief exploration is simply intended to help managers avoid some of the more common pitfalls that inhibit development.

Once the basic ground of learning has been covered, some of the techniques and methods that exist for the creation of learning and developmental opportunities will be discussed. Some of these may seem familiar to those with knowledge of training and education. However, the running of training events and courses will not be covered. The emphasis will be given to their use as part of normal working practice.

The provision of useful feedback is a critical part of learning and developing. It is so important that a large section is devoted to how and how not to give feedback to others. Poorly given or badly constructed feedback can do irreparable damage, wrecking an otherwise positive learning experience. How to give feedback in a helpful way will be the main theme. Even messages that, under certain circumstances can be painful and unacceptable, can be used to contribute to development.

Finally, some of the other factors that can damage and inhibit development will be covered. In so many cases, development opportunities are wasted because the individual is not able to put the skills to use or to translate the knowledge gained into practice on everyday activities. Learning, as defined, is evidenced by the application of skills and knowledge. This is not to say that all learning needs to be applied immediately. However, if learners can see no opportunity of using the resulting skills or knowledge, the point of development, inevitably, is diminished in their eyes. Managers can take action to remove some of the barriers, either directly or by helping learners to remove them for themselves. How to do this will be discussed so that managers can identify for themselves what they need to do to support development fully.

The final chapter will deal with the realities of modern business life. The environment is changing constantly. At one time such terms as 'unpredictability' and 'turbulence' were in vogue; now the word 'chaos' is frequently used to describe conditions. How can managers develop themselves and others when such a high degree of uncertainty exists? Some organisations swing from rapid growth to equally rapid decline – see the financial sector for shining examples of both. Others have experienced steady growth, – the leisure industry, for example – while some, such as public sector organisations, have experienced a steady decline. Simply motivating staff in either set of conditions is not easy; encouraging development when staff are under pressure to do more with less (this is true for both states) requires special skills on the part of the manager.

Taking an ethical approach is being seen increasingly as a key element of modern management practice – one which is frequently missing. This may be due to the fact that the rapidly changing economic climate, short-cutting and other bad management practices have led to some people feeling exploited by their employing organisations and managers. The declining influence of trade unions has also enabled managers to look for ways of dealing with staff, singly and collectively, bypassing traditional industrial relations methods. In other cases managers have acquired an increased sense of responsibility for the quality of their employees' working lives. They have also become more aware of the impact of their actions on others. These trends are changing how managers perform their role, so it would be amiss to exclude them from a book that is concerned with a key part of the management role – development learning and growth.

The ideal way of working is for the principles and methods described in this book to form the fundamental part of everyday working – then special consideration would not be needed and anyone who suggested that development is an excessive cost would be regarded as strange. The concept of the 'learning company' is used to show how managers and others with influence in an organisation or a part of an organisation can develop its way of operating, to encourage and foster the development of its members.

This book is intended to be practical, so extensive use is made of examples, case studies and check-lists. Experimentation is an essential part of learning, and some ideas are proposed for you to try. It is possible that some of these will not work. Many developmental opportunities and ways of satisfying need are dependent on the individuals involved, the context of their situation, the desired outcome, and everybody's starting point. Not everything can be guaranteed to work, every time, in every situation. However, even if an approach does not seem to be immediately suitable, it should not be discounted for ever. Sometimes a particular combination of events can mean that an unusual approach will be the best for that particular purpose. Because of this, every effort has been made to avoid being faddy. Many techniques are products of their time, and later appear to have had their day, been forgotten or are now regarded as old-fashioned. But for someone who has not had experience of an approach or idea, the first time they encounter it, it is brand new for them.

Most existing texts focus on the manager's development or the training and development of staff. Here, the emphasis is placed on the value of partnership between manager and others and the collaboration which is needed if the process is to be fully effective. This focus is based on the belief that there is no one given right way, and that the manager does not always know best. So much of development and learning is dependent on factors which are unique to the organisation and people within it. Consequently the ideas are proposed for use, adaption, to be tried out and tested. The examples are drawn from real life – the author's own work and the reported work of others. Where possible, critical appreciation will be made and indications given of the strengths and weaknesses of the different approaches. Efforts will also be made to indicate possible pitfalls and ways in which improvements can be made. While guidance can be provided, there is only one way to find out whether a particular developmental tactic will work. That is to try it out.

By taking a practical approach, it is hoped this book will be of lasting value as a source of reference and a working tool for practising managers who want to improve their own performance, that of their organisation and, most importantly, help themselves and others to develop, learn and keep on growing.

2

What are skills?

INTRODUCTION

The introduction of the National Vocational Qualifications has focused on the need to define and develop job-related skills. A similar emphasis was found during the 1960s in the early years of the Industrial Training Boards, when the focus was placed on the specification of learning objectives. In the interim, it seems that training and development has been less targeted and more concerned with the development of the person as a whole. There is nothing wrong with this approach and much has been achieved by it. However, now there is a requirement for a clearer purpose and the need for development activity to be targeted at organisational or business objectives.

The Handy (1987) and the Constable and McCormack (1987) reports both pointed out that one reason behind the economic failure of this country was lack of managerial skills. This deficiency was handicapping competitive performance in the world markets, was inhibiting the use and development of other skills, and was leaving internal markets and businesses vulnerable to attack. One aspect of this was identified as the low levels of training and development opportunities available and taken up by existing managers. This applied both to the quantity and quality of provision. Most managers received no training at all; those who did usually attended very general, non-specific seminars. Little preparation was being done for future managers; most courses offered were Business Studies, together with Diploma courses in Management Studies (initially introduced by the British Institute of Management to improve the quality of management) and latterly Master of Business Administration courses. These, too, were criticised for being more concerned with academic achievement as assessed by knowledge of theory, rather than with the acquisition and application of skills.

The reports, the subsequent establishment of the Management Charter Initiative and the creation of the National Council for Vocational Qualifications have resulted in a shift from awarding qualifications on the basis of 'what you know' to assessing and certifying 'what you can do'.

This chapter will explore some of the issues implicit in this change of emphasis, and will give practical guidance on how skills can be defined in particular circumstances. Generic skill definitions have their value, and will be discussed, but managers need to be able to define the skills required for their own organisation. This is particularly necessary as changes take place and the different demands placed on individuals require the development of new skills. Consequently, practical ways of defining skills, in specific contexts, will be described and examples of the techniques being used will be given.

WHAT ARE SKILLS?

Skills are aspects of performance that can be learnt and improved with practice. In Chapter 1, the distinction was made between skills and competence. It is important to be clear about the differences, as the words tend to be used interchangeably. The differences may seem small in some situations; in others they are very large. Competency statements are being used increasingly for the accreditation of prior learning, and it is intended that in future they will be built into the assessment of the learning from training obtained from education courses.

Skills used at work need not be subjected to such formal education, as they are individuals' personal abilities that are applied to particular tasks. They are different from talents or traits. The latter, also called attributes, are the aspects of personality that make an individual unique and valuable. Personality traits, it is argued, remain stable throughout an individual's life. They are a product of genetic factors combined with a bit of social conditioning and some experience. The experiences gained during a person's formative years have the most profound effect on their personality and establish the foundations of their character.

While it is said that traits remain stable, changes can and do occur as a result of experience and ageing. This whole area of personal psychology is hotly debated in some quarters and is full of unanswered questions. It would be beyond the scope of this book to go into depth on these issues. However, it has generally been agreed that an individual's personality influences their behaviour and attitudes. Both of these may be modified through experience and/or as a result of deliberate effort on the part of the individual.

Behaviour

Behaviour is the demonstration of personality and attitudes as the individual interacts with the environment and the other people in it. Behaviour can be controlled, or it can be reactive. The control of behaviour is the arena in which skills are exercised. These skills are witnessed and experienced by others and therefore can be assessed. Their acquisition and development can also be assessed, performance levels can be reported upon, feedback given, and additional practice can be arranged if needed.

Attitudes

The way in which people see the world is conditioned by their attitude; how attitudes are formed will be discussed in much more depth later. A person's attitude can influence their willingness to learn. It can also prevent learning taking place. Formed from the combination of experience, social conditioning and personality, attitude can be manifested in behaviour. However, it is possible to both conceal an attitude, or even to act contrary to one's attitude.

Example 2.1

Jane had always been a shy girl. However, while at school she had been excellent at English and after graduation she obtained work in a media company as a copywriter. Her skills were quickly recognised and she was rapidly promoted. Part of her new role meant that she had to represent the company at high-profile publicity events. She hated social events and having to make small talk, but as it was a key part of her job, she learned how to overcome her aversion.

Generally, an individual's attitudes are matched by their behaviour, although sometimes this is not so. At one time it was believed in training circles that if the aim was to change someone's behaviour, the starting point should be their attitude. This belief underpinned much of the early race relations training – it was thought that exposing an individual's prejudices and explaining the negative effects of stereotyping would be sufficient to stop discriminatory behaviour. Later, it was realised that this approach in some cases was seen as threatening and could lead to a hardening of attitudes, rather than bringing about the desired change. Consequently an alternative approach was used which started with behaviour. This approach is based on cognitive dissonance theory, the basis of which is that individuals will change their attitudes if they behave publicly in a way that is contrary to those attitudes originally held.

Example 2.2

The new managing director was a firm believer in appraisal. One of her first acts was to set up a briefing session for all section heads. This was to be followed by two days' training, and then they would be expected to appraise all their first-line supervisors.

'What a waste of time', thought Fred; 'we have far more important things to do.' But, being required to attend, he turned up at the training session. The trainer was not bad, he concluded after the first morning. But Fred had a surprise coming. The afternoon and the following morning were to be spent conducting practice appraisal meetings. The first one Fred ran was bad, confirming his belief. But the second was a lot better, showing a marked improvement; the trainer paid him a compliment. (The first he had received since he couldn't remember when.) He then had to act as an appraisee for one of his colleagues and, to his surprise, actually enjoyed receiving the feedback. He went away thinking 'Perhaps there's something in this after all?'

Personality

Personality change or modification is a different matter to attitude. Individuals' personalities are products of the person and their history. Some organisations consider personality traits for recruitment purposes and use them to help individuals to develop particular aspects of behaviour the organisation believes to be necessary. The justification for exploring traits is based on the belief that the information gathered will help predict how a particular individual will behave in a given set of circumstances. The prediction is based on generally held assumptions about the relationship between particular personality traits and particular behaviour patterns. This can be seen from some of the descriptions used in Cattell's 16PF (personality factor) categories:

- Those generally regarded as being *reserved* tend to be detached and critically aloof; those regarded as being *outgoing* are described as being warm-hearted, easy-going and participating.

- Those *affected by feelings* tend to get emotional when frustrated, are changeable in their attitudes and interests, easily perturbed, get into problem situations and are evasive of responsibilities, tending to give up.

- Those who are *emotionally stable* tend to be emotionally mature, stable, constant in interests, calm, unruffled, do not let emotional needs obscure the realities of a situation, adjust to facts and show restraint in avoiding difficulties.

- Those who are *humble* tend to be obedient, mild, accommodating, conforming and submissive; those who are *assertive* can be independent, stubborn and dominant.

- Those described as being *sober* tend to be prudent, serious and taciturn. *Happy-go-lucky* people are lively, enthusiastic and impulsive.

- People who are described as being *expedient* feel few obligations and disregard or evade rules. On the other hand, the *conscientious* are persistent, staid, moralistic and rule-bound.

WHAT ARE SKILLS? • 31

Influencing personality

It is possible for an individual to learn how to control the manifestations of these traits; this may be especially necessary if they are proving to be dysfunctional for the individual in particular settings. Psychotherapeutic treatment and in-depth counselling are options, but it is not suggested here that managers should begin to go to these depths. However, it is useful to know the rationale that underpins some of the approaches used by organisations. One of the fundamental ethics for the proper use of these techniques is the willing, informed participation of the individual concerned. The increased use of psychometric instruments in organisations for selection and development has caused concern and debate and has led the Institute of Personnel Management to issue a code of practice. The British Psychological Corporation has also endeavoured to set standards regarding their use. The reason for this is to ensure that individuals undergoing the tests are treated with respect and that basic principles regarding confidentiality and use of the information are established.

Whether it is legitimate within the world of work to try to influence and change an individual's personality is a matter for debate and leads on to further ethical considerations. However, influencing and changing individuals' behaviour and developing their use of skills are not contentious issues, as these form part of the employment contract and are implicit in training and development.

So, changing personality is not a topic for further consideration here. Skills development, on the other hand, can be a way of minimising the negative impact of undesirable personality traits and maximising the positive impact of desirable traits:

Example 2.3

The newly created job of sales co-ordinator required someone able to deal with customer complaints in a sympathetic manner. The job also required new sales opportunities to be created from enquiries. One requirement on the person specification therefore was for outgoing characteristics.

An administrative supervisor was the only candidate who satisfied the other requirements on the specification. However, during the selection process, the individual came over as being somewhat detached and reserved. On the grounds that he matched most of the criteria, it was decided to appoint him and provide a programme of planned activities and structured feedback to help overcome these so-called 'personality weaknesses'.

Knowledge

There are two parts to an individual's knowledge bank: that which is known about, and the subconscious. As individuals pass through life they gather and learn facts, perceive facts and acquire other pieces of information that are added to the cognitive store. This forms the memory and is accessed as the individual processes new information and/or prepares to react to a situation or another person. There is general knowledge (ie what can safely be assumed to be known by most people) and job-specific knowledge, which is gained as a result of being educated and/or trained to carry out a particular task or range of tasks. Some job-specific knowledge may be fundamental to being able to carry out a job; other aspects may be desirable. For example, an accountant could be expected to know how to draw up an accurate balance sheet, but a marketing manager would only be expected to be able to read one.

An interesting feature of knowledge banks is that, frequently, individuals are unaware of all that they know. The learning process takes an individual from a state of unconscious incompetence, through conscious incompetence, to conscious competence, to unconscious competence. There is a difference between the thought processes of experts and novices. The latter tend to use mental check-lists to ensure that decisions are being made on sound foundations and that all relevant factors have been taken into account. Experts tend to rely on trial and error (heuristics) and their own 'expert judgement', not necessarily being aware of precisely how they make their decisions.

Because knowledge tends to 'sink' into the subconscious, it is possible for an individual to believe that they 'know' something because they used to know it. 'It's like riding a bike – never forgotten'. Or is it? How many people once knew how to calculate Pythagoras' theorem and can still find the length of the triangle's third side? Knowledge, not used, decays.

Another feature of knowledge is that individuals believe that their own knowledge is fact. It's the same as something being true because it has been in the newspapers. But many 'facts' are no more than one individual's perception of reality, which may be different from that perceived by others.

Example 2.4

John thinks it is pleasantly warm today and, because he enjoys his job, he knows his company is a good employer. But Mary is cold and the company is a rotten place to work. It is too mean to put on the heating. Who is right?

It is this belief in the veracity of one's own view that leads to many an argument at home and at work. The truth, as in the above example, is often that both

people are as right as each other – or as wrong.

As a consequence, when considering the development of experienced, knowledgeable people, it is worth finding out exactly:

- what they do know
- what they think they know but don't know
- what they think they don't know but do know
- what they don't know

Competence

The American approach

The National Vocational Qualifications are described as competence statements. Competency, as applied to job-related behaviour, was the term first used by Boyatzis (1982) for the American Management Association, whose President had asked, in the early 1970s, 'What are the characteristics that distinguish superior performance by working managers?' Two thousand managers in 41 different types of jobs were studied, using the Job Competence Assessment method. This has several steps:

1. A criterion measure of job performance is established.

2. The key components of superior performance are identified, using job element analysis.

3. The distinguishing characteristics are identified, coded and categorised.

4. The characteristics are compared with the elements of superior performance to identify those characteristics that distinguish the two.

5. These characteristics are related back to the criterion measure.

Thus, a competency is defined as an underlying characteristic of a manager *causally related to superior performance* on the job.

The results of Boyatzis' study identified 18 competencies, which grouped into four larger clusters:

1. Goal and action management

2. Directing subordinates

3. Human resources management

4. Leadership.

One of the techniques used to identify these competencies in the study, Behaviour Event Interviewing, will be described in more detail below. It is interesting to note that the project aimed to identify generic skills that could be transferred to any managerial situation. These results are a statement of skills such as:

MANAGING GROUP PROCESS: Ability to stimulate others to work effectively in a group setting.

The British approach

'Competence' was the similar term chosen by the National Council for Vocational Qualifications (NCVQ). However, the meaning implied is very different to that of the AMA's 'competency'. Its definition by the Training Agency (1989) is 'the ability to perform the activities within an occupation or function to the standards expected in employment. It is a wide concept which embodies the ability to transfer skills and knowledge to new situations within the occupational area' (BTEC, 1990). The major difference in the use of the terms is the British omission of any reference to superior performance. The British definition refers to recognisable work activities which are expressed as outcomes. The American statement refers to skills or behaviour needed to achieve the desired output.

Competences are broken down into elements, each of which are recognisable activities, which group into units. Units collate into a statement of competence. The technique used to identify competence is called functional analysis. This elicits the contributions made by individual workers to the organisation by their performance of a job. The functions of individuals are identified and 'broken down until they are described in sufficient detail to be used as [occupational] standards' (Training Agency, 1989). For each occupational area, an Industrial Lead Body has been established which comprises the people who know their industry best. Numerous consultation exercises and validation processes have been carried out to draw up the standards within each industrial group. The standards are intended for use in training and assessing levels of competence on the job. They provide a means of recognising performance in terms of action, behaviour or outcome. The process used to identify competence is similar to that used by Boyatzis, above, ie:

1. The key purpose of the occupational area (job) is described.

2. The question 'what needs to happen for this to be achieved?' is asked.

3. The process is repeated until the functions being identified are reduced to unit of competence level.

There are clear differences in the statements that have emerged from this process and those produced by the AMA project. The British approach has aimed to produce statements which reflect outcome achieved by the efforts of an individual, rather than the inputs made by them in terms of skills. Thus most of the competence statements tend to be task focused:

UNIT II 9   SEEK, EVALUATE AND ORGANISE INFORMATION FOR ACTION
Element II 9.2   Forecast trends and developments which affect objectives.

Personal competence statements have been written to supplement the task-focused ones. These are nearer to the skill focus of the American competencies:

DIMENSION 2.2   RELATING TO OTHERS
2.2.3   Actively build relationships with others. (This includes using behaviour appropriate to the situation.)

DIFFERENT TECHNIQUES USED TO IDENTIFY SKILLS

Behavioural event interviews

This technique is very similar to another, which is known as critical incident technique. Both focus on a specific event or chain of events involving the subjects of the analysis. The subjects are asked to tell the interviewer about an event in which they were effective. Probing questions are used to trace the whole event and the individuals are encouraged to reflect on why certain things were said or done or happened the way they did. The purpose of this is to explore underlying motives, rationalisations or explanations and to unpick the individuals' assumptions. The process is a friendly enquiry looking for behavioural examples.

After the interview, the examples are sorted into critical incidents (ie those that were causal and described using active verbs).

Example 2.5

Interviewer 'Tell me about a major piece of work for which you were solely responsible.'
Interviewee 'I was responsible for a major publicity campaign. It involved commissioning the design of an expensive press advertisement, organising staff to respond to the ad, producing the material to be sent out and dealing with the orders once they had been received.'
Interviewer 'Tell me about the parts that went well.'
Interviewee 'The planning. My team and I sat down right at the beginning and worked through as much of the operation as we could, identifying what would

happen when and what needed to be done in preparation. We didn't use a critical path exactly but nearly did.'

Interviewer 'What were those critical incidents?'

Interviewee 'The main ones were getting in the extra staff and telephone lines and getting the information we needed for the publicity material from other sections.'

Interviewer 'What did you do to get the extra staff?'

Interviewee 'I told my boss that I was going to do it, and did it. That surprised me. I had not done that before and it worked.'

Interviewer 'Why do you think that was so?'

Interviewee 'He *had* to trust me. There was no one else and I suppose I had the strength of my conviction. I knew we couldn't do it any other way. And from then on he let me get on with the whole exercise. I felt that I could have almost anything I said I needed to complete the project.'

Interviewer 'What did that do for you?'

Interviewee 'I suppose it gave me a new sense of confidence that helped me carry myself through when we hit later difficult patches.'

Interviewer 'Such as?'

and so on . . . .

The resulting behaviours/skills identified in this example can be written as:

- to involve appropriate others;
- to plan the *whole* project, as far as is possible;
- to make allowances for unforeseen events;
- to specify, clearly, resource requirements;
- to communicate those requirements clearly and confidently to those who have control of the needed resources

Functional analysis

Functional analysis, as described earlier, is used to identify the function of a job in terms of its outcomes. It is a technique designed specifically for the purpose of developing standards. Mansfield (1989) sets out the essential features as:

- Focusing on *whole work roles*.
- Employing an *outcome* approach – identifying key purposes and functions which draw together activities which have the same purpose and same standards attached to them.
- Taking a *top-down model*, starting from a clear functional statement of the entire occupational area which breaks down into significant roles.

A functional analysis is carried out by drawing together groups of people who are familiar with the occupational area being analysed. The first stage is to define the key purpose of the entire area in terms of outcome. The definition is specified by the use of active verbs or phrases, an object and condition. This model is adopted to ensure that each statement can be applied to all levels within the occupation.

The group of 'experts' then considers the rules for disaggregation, or the process by which the statement will be broken down into smaller components. The rules should be chosen to represent the occupational area and the stage of analysis. They allow a taxonomy of sorts to be constructed which ensures that a complete description of the occupation is made, generates categories that are exclusive and forms a credible reflection of practice within the occupation. Consequently the rules will be different for each area.

The analysis of the key purpose continues until it starts to throw up potential 'units of competence'. These are the categories that represent marketable competences, defined as those which can be taken seriously as tangible job roles by employers. They are categories that are common within the industry and can be used for assessment. They could also be used to form credible qualifications. This process continues until it has reduced the unit into elements and criteria by which performance can be identified.

While this approach is somewhat laborious, the involvement of people from within the occupational area under consideration is a strength. Once the initial consultation has been carried out, the development of the standard statement is largely a desk exercise, translating the opinion of the experts into a common format for public consumption.

A typical example is drawn from the NVQ Level 5 standards in Management 7:

MANAGEMENT II
Key purpose: To achieve the organisation's objectives and continuously improve its performance.
Key role: Managing people.
Unit II 8 Develop teams, individuals and self to enhance performance.
Element II 6.2 Identify, review and improve development activities for individuals.

Performance criteria:

(a) Development objectives and activities are based on a balanced assessment of current competence, potential future competence and career aspirations in line with current and anticipated team/organisational requirement.

(b) Individuals are encouraged and assisted to evaluate their own learning and development needs and to contribute to the discussion, planning and review of development.

(c) Plans contain clear, relevant and realistic development objectives and details of supporting development activities.

(d) Development activities optimise the use of available resources.

(e) Plans are reviewed, updated and improved at regular intervals after discussion and agreement with the appropriate people.

Behaviourally anchored rating scales (BARS)

This technique was developed for use in conjunction with management by objectives. As it was never popularised to the same extent, it has not been so discredited as management by objectives. BARS starts with the same premise as that outlined above for the purpose of the functional analysis. The major difference between BARS and functional analysis is that the latter is carried out for an occupational area as a whole; behaviourally anchored rating scales can be developed for a single job, for one group of staff or for one organisation. The experts can be those people who are carrying out the job, as well as appropriate others.

The process to be followed in constructing a rating scale is typically:

1. The job's purpose or objectives are defined. (This can be done by a manager as part of an appraisal meeting, as part of drawing-up a job description, or for this specific purpose. It would be normal to involve the job-holder, if there is one, and others who have a direct interest in the job in question.)

2. Key aspects or major areas of activity needed to carry out the purpose are specified.

3. Measures of effective performance are identified. (These should be given in behavioural terms. It is this final stage that is critical for the development of a rating scale.)

Those participating in the process are asked to identify incidents that are critical to success or failure. These incidents should be separate aspects of human activity that can be evidenced. It is not good enough to say that a key objective of a manager's role is 'to build a strong team by communicating effectively'. Rather, statements or dimensions of behaviour need to be developed that can be clearly attributable to the actions of the individual concerned, in terms that are meaningful. So in this case it would be better to say, 'the manager holds regular team meetings at which the team objectives and progress towards achieving them are discussed'. Alternatively, dimensions can be identified by specifying what a poor manager does, or what a good manager does not do. For example, 'the manager is confused about the team's objectives and confuses everyone else'.

From these dimensions, rating scales can be built up. At the top of the scale is the superior performance, the best the organisation can reasonably expect. At the bottom comes the lowest level of performance that can be tolerated. The scale is filled out by incremental steps, using as many points as is thought helpful. There is some accepted wisdom on the number of points in such scales. It is common to find five, but with this number there is a tendency to put everyone in the middle. Four leads to big differences between the dimensions, while seven means the gradations are slight, can overlap, and again the centralist tendency is possible. The best number found in practice is six. However, care needs to be taken to ensure that the increments between the points are of about the same size, that they are easily distinguished and valid. The numbers on the scale exist to demonstrate the steps in it, but they are not meaningful in themselves. They are representations of the dimensions which go to build up critical areas of performance.

Trying to construct BARS for all aspects of a job, especially a complex one, would be costly and over-elaborate. Their strength comes from their use in areas which are regarded as being key to effective performance. Another strength of the technique is that it lends itself well to the involvement of those to be assessed. Discussion groups drawn from different levels, sections or interest groups can be organised to debate the distinction between good, middling and poor performance, the scales can be checked by consulting the same or other groups, and they can be validated in trials in the same way. BARS also provide models for development purposes. The gradations indicate what more an individual needs to do to improve on actual performance, as the following example shows.

Example 2.6

Resourceful:
Ability to find other ways of doing things and to act on own initiative.

1. Stops progress by damping others' initiatives.
2. Needs to be told what to do and how to start.
3. Initiates activity but quickly runs out of steam.
4. Initiates and maintains activities.
5. Is imaginative and is resilient under adversity.
6. Initiates imaginatively, is resilient and enables others to develop their ideas.

Repertory grid

Repertory grid is a technique used most frequently by psychologists. It was devised by Kelly (1980) as a means of eliciting 'personal constructs'. Kelly proposed that each person is a natural scientist struggling to make sense of the world. This is done, he suggests, by the establishment of frameworks of belief systems, values, attitudes, experiences, which are used to explain and predict situations. Because they are deeply held assumptions, people are not able to recognise for themselves the framework through which they see their world and the people in it. Kelly devised the repertory grid technique to help individuals explore their constructs. Personal construct theory will be described in more length later. Repertory grids are filled in in five stages:

1. The individual is asked to identify a number of separate items to act as the elements of the grid. These may be people, tasks, situations etc;

2. The individual is asked to compare individual elements against each of the others in groups of three, identifying two which are similar in some way and one which is different;

3. The individual is asked to give the reason(s) for the similarity and the reason(s) for the dissimilarity. These need not be opposites, and care should be taken to avoid superficial or simplistic reasons. These are the constructs;

4. The individual is asked to rank the elements that were not part of the original triad against the constructs as given;

5. The grid is analysed by element and by construct, as in the example below.

Example 2.7

The purpose of the grid is to elicit constructs relating to an effective leader.

The elements chosen are known people who have occupied the role of leader:

Chris	Martin	Tony	Peter	Tom	Irene	1	6
S 2	S 1	D 6	5	4	3	clear	muddled
4	6	S 1	S 2	D 5	3	short-term	vision
6	4	1	D 5	S 2	S 3	moody	placid
D 6	4	S 2	5	S 1	3	impatient	patient
4	S 1	6	D 4	3	S 2	strong	weak
S 1	3	6	2	S 4	D 5	fair	unfair
6	S 1	4	5	S 2	D 3	aims	dreams

(S indicates the two people in the group who are thought to be similar; the D indicates the third who is thought to be different in some way.)

The grid displays the constructs used by the person completing the grid to describe others' behaviour. The constructs held about effective leaders are those rated 1. The people so rated are those thought to be the better leaders in the group. Those rated nearer to 6 are regarded as being less effective.

Goal analysis

This method is complementary to Mager's earlier definition of instructional objectives. He says an objective should express a performance/behavioural statement, the standard to be attained, and the conditions under which that performance will normally be expected. Designed to build on this approach to deal with the intangible areas of performance or attitudes, it helps the analyst to define 'how you would know one when you saw one' (Mager, 1984). The analyst can be a line manager, an interested colleague or trainer, or a personnel professional. No special qualifications are required. The question helps to remove the fuzzies from the description of effective performance.

Goal analysis has seven stages which can be carried out by the analyst alone, or which can involve several interested and informed others:

Stage One

State the attitude in behavioural terms. Everyone to be involved in the process brainstorms and generates a list, such as:

A good leader:

- sets a good example;

- communicates clearly;

- treats staff fairly;

- establishes clear goals and shares them;

- monitors progress.

Stage Two

Identify which statements need further clarification. For example, what does 'sets a good example' mean in practice?

- abides by the standards set for the group;

- develops and maintains good quality working practices.

Stage Three

Sort the list into clusters of similar meanings:

- communicates clearly;
- establishes clear goals and shares them;
- treats staff fairly;
- abides by the standards set for the group;
- monitors progress;
- develops and maintains good quality working practices.

Stage Four

Eliminate any redundant words or phrases, to ensure that the list is clear and concise.

Stage Five

Add, if needed, the behaviours that should not occur.
  A good leader does not

- give contradictory instructions to staff;
- gossip about peers or reports.

Stage Six

View the complete list and ask whether it accurately and reasonably reflects human behaviour. (It is important to stay in the zones of reasonableness.)

Stage Seven

Submit the list to other people, to see if they think it is possible for one person to carry out all the behaviours.

Job analysis

This technique has been left to the end, as it is the one most often described in training and personnel textbooks. The proponents of functional analysis criticise it for not addressing the need to highlight standards. The technique was never intended to do so. Its purpose is to differentiate between the knowledge, skills and attitudes required to carry out, effectively, the different component parts of a job.

Typically, a job is broken down into the key tasks, which are then analysed. This is to enable post holders to be trained to perform all the tasks that make up a particular job. Harrison (1989) gives a full account of how the technique can be used. It tends to be more usefully applied to simpler jobs. Jobs with sophisticated skills or knowledge requirements are likely to result in an analysis which could be simplistic and which misses the essence of the job in an effort to generalise, or one which is too detailed to be of any practical use.

Example 2.8

Job: To prepare a business plan

Task	Knowledge	Skills	Attitudes
1. To develop a view of the future	Forecasts and trends	Create a vision	Forward-looking, realistic
2. To gather needed data	Sources	Data-gathering	Accuracy, thoroughness
3. To discuss with appropriate others	Who to ask or leave out	Consultation techniques	Willing to listen
4. To write plan	Required format	Writing skills	Clarity, conciseness

HOW SKILLS ANALYSIS CAN BE USED

Despite its reported limitations, job analysis, as all the other techniques, has two benefits. The first is the outcome generated by the process of the analysis; the second is the process itself. All the above techniques require discipline and rigour. Knowledge of the principles supporting the technique, its limitations and the background to its development is interesting. The best learning is obtained from using the structured thinking that needs to be used to apply the technique to real jobs. In addition to the primary uses, the techniques can be described below as approaches to problem-solving, and so applied to all other types of problem.

Functional analysis

Its main use is to identify the performance standards of a competent performer. This allows for the assessment of current levels of performance and the recognition of areas where improvements can be made. The competence statements can also be used in the design of training and educational programmes. One of their purposes is to ensure that the contents reflect the needs of the job by enabling skill development, rather than focusing on the transmission of knowledge. The standards also provide a framework for the award of indicators of achievement. They are not qualifications in their own right; rather they provide a means of comparison between the many different qualifications being offered by the multitude of professional and examining bodies. Fletcher's guide (1991) gives a very thorough description of the background to the development of standards, the role of NCVQ and the practical use of statements and qualifications.

As most of the work on the standards has been done at national level, the technique used for their specification is not readily accessible to line managers. However, if there is a need to carry out an analysis at local level, there is no real reason why an organisation cannot set up its own 'industrial lead body' and draw together a panel of its own experts to carry out the functional analysis. This would be particularly appropriate in a developing area of work, or one in which highly specialised skills are required but have not yet been subjected to attention nationally. While many competence standards have been published, especially at levels 1–3, covering most occupational groups, some have yet to be done.

One of the recognised shortcomings of functional analysis is its inability to adapt rapidly to changes in the areas of work. There is some doubt about the national standards' ability to respond to or accommodate newly emerging roles. However, there is no reason why an organisation should have to wait for national initiatives, when the methodology is not the exclusive preserve of the Training, Employment and Enterprise Department. It is possible for organisations to take action internally, to develop their own competence statements, if that is what is required.

BARS

Behavioural anchored rating scales focus attention on to different levels of performance within a confined skill area. In the context of skills development, this technique is potentially more useful than functional analysis as it draws an individual's attention to what can be done to bring about improvement. BARS focus on the input from an individual in terms of behaviour whereas functional analysis is concerned with the outcome of that performance. The competence statements describe the areas in which an individual should be active and therefore give the breadth of a job. BARS can be used to concentrate attention on to those areas considered to be critical for effective performance, and as such can be more limited in scope – they do not need to be comprehensive. The incremental nature of the rating scale allows for assessment to be made against a comparator – the ideal level of performance. The individual can carry out a self-assessment and/or be assessed by appropriate others, who may include the manager, peers, clients – almost anyone in a position to assess the demonstration of that particular skill. The individual, possibly with help, can decide what action needs to be taken to improve that performance.

Example 2.9

Joe had been told that his political antennae were not sharp enough. Several good opportunities had been missed, simply because he had not seen how they could have been realised. The company used rating scales to help with appraisal. Joe was reflecting on his performance and used these scales to help him come to terms with what had happened.

The following statement seemed to be particularly fitting:

Acumen
Recognises the impact opportunities and actions have on other parts of the organisation, especially with regard to resource utilisation and cost.

1. Is unable to distinguish between cause of events and effect of actions and decisions on the organisation and its resources.

2. Sees events and decisions in isolation.

3. Is able to link actions to consequences, but cannot identify own role in the process.

4. Can identify own role but cannot identify ways of controlling events or resource utilisation.

5. Is able to relate actions taken by self and others to consequences, and can identify ways of controlling resource utilisation.

6. Is able to take account of consequences and resource factors (including cost) when analysing opportunities and situations, when making decisions and/or taking action.

Joe decides that, while he knew of the opportunities, he did not recognise their relevance to his area of work. As a result he didn't think that there was any need for him to act, and even if he had, he was not sure what he could or should have done. As a result of his deliberations, he went back to his manager to ask for guidance and some answers to the following specific questions:

1. How could he get hold of information sooner about opportunities such as those he had missed?

2. Would his manager talk through with him whether such opportunities could be advantageous or not, and explain her thinking?

3. How should he have taken advantage of the previous opportunities, and how would he have been able to get hold of the initial capital that would have been needed?

4. What suggestions did his manager have on how he could build up some allegiances, so that other people would tip him off in future and be prepared to help him get the resources needed to exploit opportunities?

Repertory grid

One major weakness with this technique, as described above, is its focus on living people and hence past behaviour. It is not really designed to be a forward-looking tool, as its basis is the elicitation of constructs already established. The technique could be modified, but envisaging the future is not its real purpose. Neither does the technique allow for absolutes, but it does draw attention to role models, both positive and negative. The comparison of similar and dissimilar elements does tend to draw out opposites, even though it need not do so. These can highlight aspects of behaviour that are regarded as undesirable. In example 2.7, the people regarded as poor leaders were seen as being weak, muddled and unfair. The good leaders were fair, clear and forward-looking with aims.

The most useful role that repertory grid can perform is to aid understanding and gain insight. It can be used by a manager to think through what works and what does not work as a way of developing practice. As an alternative to using people as elements, it is possible to use events. This could act, for example, as a way to identify those aspects of an event which were critical, so that features that should be avoided in future and those which should be strengthened can be recognised.

Goal analysis

The strength of this technique is its ability to clarify the intangible and de-fuzz the 'fuzzies'. In this capacity it is particularly helpful for identifying future needs. One of the most difficult aspects of developing skills in an uncertain environment is knowing which aspects of behaviour to work on. The uncertainty of the time makes it hard to work out which skills will and which will not be needed to be effective. Coping in this sort of world is a skill in itself.

Goal analysis provides a mechanism for helping the forward projection of thought. By asking questions such as:

- 'What will the managers be doing next year?'
- 'How will we know if they are being effective?'
- 'What would lead us to think some are failing?'

and applying Mager's technique, it is possible to identify which aspects of behaviour are more likely to be required than others. It will not answer the questions, but will provide a more structured framework for thinking such matters through in the unique context of one organisation in its own environment. It also provides a way of developing one of the skills of dealing with uncertainty – separating what is known from the predictable, from the uncertain, from the unknown.

Job analysis

This technique was developed as an aid for training, which is where its main strength lies. It helps to distinguish the elements that are needed for the design of training programmes and courses. It also provides an indication to the individual as to what is expected of a competent performer across the whole job. This could be daunting, as the technique does tend to produce long lists. This is especially true for more complex jobs and seems almost over-bureaucratic in today's climate. It also tends to be historic and can become rooted in time. Carrying out a job analysis properly can be time-consuming and, as such, may discourage revision.

A good job analysis is closely linked to the job description. There is an increasing move away from precise descriptions, preference now being given to outlines of the role purpose. Job analysis does not fit comfortably with this approach. In any case, for a lot of jobs, the competence statements produced for NVQ purposes will have removed the need for organisations to carry out their own analysis for generic jobs.

WHO CONDUCTS A SKILLS ANALYSIS?

Ideally the people who know the job best – those carrying it out – should be involved at some stage. As well as knowing about the job in question, they have the experience of doing it in practice. However, they can be too closely involved to see the job in its full context. It was because of this potential for myopia that a separate specialism for carrying out job analysis was developed.

Management scientists, work study engineers and O&M staff are not as common as they once were, but the principles behind their role still have some validity. Their job was to provide the 'looking glass', to reflect back the situation. Being detached, they were better able to be objective than staff directly involved with the jobs being analysed. The purpose of this was to help organisations and their managers see themselves as others see them, gathering data from a number of different sources and putting the whole picture back together. The use of experts can be useful, but they can only gather and report back on what they find. It is up to the organisation's managers to make decisions.

The myopia is not confined to job-holders. Managers too can be too close to the job, and may have their own preconceptions, but nevertheless they should have a major role in any analysis, for ultimately they are the ones who decide whether performance is of an acceptable standard, and by which criteria those judgements are made. Regardless of who carries out the analysis, it should be the responsible manager who confirms the end result, be they goals, behavioural rating scales, competence standards, constructs, or knowledge and skills.

A manager can carry out the analysis alone without expert advice, which is the reason the techniques have been described in operational detail. They are sophisticated tools and, in the wrong hands or used the wrong way, can be damaging – but so can any management technique. The most important aspect to remember is that they should be used with integrity and in the knowledge that they do not produce the whole and only truth. The real value of a manager conducting an internal analysis is his or her capacity to involve the people concerned. This can be turned into a team-building activity and is perhaps the best way of securing general acceptance of the outcome. It does not really matter which technique is used, providing the outcome is useful and is helpful for those concerned. A participative approach ensures that:

- the priorities of those directly affected are reflected in the context of the organisation's needs;

- they have an understanding of how the outcome was produced;

- the meaning of the words used is understood and shared;

- they have a high degree of ownership.

This 'ownership' is essential for successful operation of development activities. If criteria or skills are imposed on people without their believing that the criteria or skills have any relevance to them in their jobs or their context, they will not be very motivated to working on their acquisition or development of those skills.

SUMMARY

This chapter has defined the nature of skills, as distinguished from traits, knowledge, attitudes and behaviour. The reasons why it has been necessary to re-emphasise the development of skills in the context of the national economy have been described. A similar approach to that adopted by the National Council for Vocational Qualifications and the Management Charter Initiative was taken by the American Management Association. The differences between the British and American uses of the words 'competency' and 'competence' have been examined. The contrast in meaning has been used to illustrate the difference between outcomes in terms of performance and inputs in terms of skills.

The different ways of analysing skills have been considered and the best uses of the analytical techniques have been explored. Because of the importance of competence statements, space has been taken to describe the steps of both behavioural event interviewing and functional analysis. Other techniques are described to enable line managers to define skills for themselves, to reflect their own organisational needs and contexts. The failure of national standards to take account of these variations is a major criticism of NVQs. The other techniques – behaviourally anchored rating scales, repertory grid, job and goal analysis – are described in a practical way, with examples of how they can be carried out.

Ways in which skills analysis can be used have been discussed, and consideration given to who is best placed to carry out any analysis. If any conclusion has been reached, it is the need to involve the people most directly concerned with the acquisition, development and deployment of the skills – in other words, the post-holders and their managers. This recommendation is based on the need to obtain commitment and ownership, without which, learning and development cannot happen. Involvement may add to the cost of identification, however, and this must be weighed against other costs incurred and losses made as a result of ineffective or poor performance. Ways of calculating these costs will be discussed next. Consideration also needs to be given to the way in which any remoteness resulting from non-participative identification inhibits learning and development. The various aspects of blocks to learning will be described later.

3
Costs and payback of development

INTRODUCTION

This chapter will explore various ways of viewing the costs of engaging in developmental activities and consider the cost of not doing so. All too often, the reason given for not developing staff is the lack of resources – usually money. Time is another common reason. Frequently, these are excuses for other reasons, but the need for adequate resourcing cannot be denied. Effective development requires the proper investment of both money and time. Without some of each, the excuses can become very real blocks which will prevent action from being taken.

It should be appreciated that one of the best forms of development, which takes place as part of the everyday job, does not require vast quantities of either time or money. On-the-job activities do not require course or trainer fees, but they do require time and commitment, and these have a cost attached. Understanding this can be helpful in both justifying the time being spent and demonstrating the benefits of doing so.

Real costs can seldom be calculated accurately, as many are *sunk* or *hidden*. Nevertheless, it should be and is possible to work out how much funding is needed for a training project. It should also be possible to identify any payback. It is regrettable that investing in people's growth has to be seen in such simplistic terms. It can be claimed that such investments should be acts of faith, part of the implicit terms of contract and actions a good employer takes as a matter of course. But in a difficult economic climate, it can also be argued that such spending can be a recipe for business collapse, and collapsed organisations cannot contribute to the growth of their ex-employees very well.

Many well-run training and development units have gone under because they failed to demonstrate, in terms the decision-makers could understand, their contribution to business performance and strategic implementation. Many training and development budgets have felt the 'accountant's knife' early when economies have had to be made. Business decisions are rarely made on acts of faith. Most organisations – profit-making, not for profit, and publicly funded alike – use money and other quantitative measures as a common currency with which to compare options and evaluate results. Development activities are then obliged to establish their worth in these terms. Accountancy techniques can be helpful here. For example, *cost benefit analysis* and *added value* can help to assess the full costs and benefits of development activities. *Rate of return on investment*, an assessment of the *value of assets*, an estimation of benefits likely to be accrued to the individual and the organisation, and the way in which development activities can affect the *rate of depreciation* can all be calculated.

This chapter will discuss how these techniques can be applied to development activities and offer an alternative view to human resource costs.

Investment or expense?

Normally the costs of training and development are those associated with running the training function or buying a place on a course. The scale of these costs is often a major inhibitor and a frequently given reason for not training staff. While cost should be a factor in any decision, expenditure should not be seen in isolation. Training is an investment that has pay-offs and benefits which can be offset against the cost. Sadly, very little guidance is available for managers to help them calculate the true costs involved. Even more lacking is guidance on how to demonstrate the full benefits of engaging in developmental activities. Often budget managers are expected to believe it is a 'good thing' to do. Very few of them, in the hard real world of increased cost sensitivity, are convinced by such arguments alone. Many need the evidence to support acts of faith.

The alternative is to treat training and development expenditure as an *investment*, or a contribution to building up the organisation's resource bank. There have been some significant changes in recent years that have shifted the way in which an organisation's total resource bank is viewed, from both management and accountancy perspectives. The traditional approach, seeing the workforce as a cost, starts from the premise that the organisation is a continuing entity which provides work and rewards for those in need of them. This view stems from a time when labour was in plentiful supply and it was an employer's market. Since then there have been substantial changes in the nature of organisations, the labour market and the expectations of workers. Changes in the economic climate have resulted in a mismatch between supply and demand. Workers, skills and employers may be in the wrong places relative to each other. Organisations, even those previously thought to be stable, can no longer guarantee the security which requires a continual and predictable demand for labour. Many workers are no longer prepared to be treated simply as units of production. They expect more from a job than just salary, despite the high levels and recurrence of unemployment.

Traditional management and accountancy techniques have not fully caught up with these changes. There are, however, some indications of newer approaches that will enable organisations to treat their staff as a resource rather than a cost. These changed approaches require some radical alterations to be made to the traditional techniques used to construct balance sheets and attribute costs. They also require some fundamental questions to be asked.

HUMAN RESOURCES AS ASSETS

The ways in which organisations employ and treat their employees have been affected not only by the changes to the economy, but also by developments in technology. The increased speed and capacity of data transfer and communication systems have resulted in different sorts of skills being required and different ways of working being adopted. Handy (1990), for instance, describes how these changes have affected farming, the most primary of all industries, changing tied farm labourers into computer operators, skilled machine operators and entrepreneurial, self-employed subcontractors.

Increased sophistication and complex technology require 'brain rather than brawn'. The pace of developments and advances in technology and machine applications demand that workers remain up-to-date – they cannot rely on old knowledge and skills. But as staff develop their knowledge base and skills, so they come to recognise their increased contribution and value to their employer. They expect different forms of reward, treatment and opportunities. Physical prowess is no longer the marketable commodity; the knowledge, skills, experience acquired and the ability to learn are all increasing and will continue to be the talents in demand.

Valuing people

The contributions of all its employees and/or members combine to build up the skill and knowledge base of an organisation. This base is as intangible as the value of a brand name, but it is an asset, exactly the same as 'St Michael' is to Marks and Spencer. A value is frequently placed on goodwill during take-overs, mergers and company sales. Why is it not as easy to value the distinctive competency of the human resource in a similar way? This is especially important if the human talents are what provide the organisation with its competitive superiority or its uniqueness.

Parker, Ferris and Otley (1989) describe how staff may be valued. They offer human resource accounting as 'a possible route to the informing of decision-makers who wish to better manage their human resources'. The American Accounting Association Committee on Human Resource Accounting is quoted as defining human resource accounting as 'the process of identifying and measuring data about human resources and communicating this information to interested parties'. It may sound pretty dull, mechanistic stuff on the surface, but beneath the formality of textbook definitions the approach contains some interesting and useful ideas for those who are concerned as much with people and their development, as with corporate viability. These ideas help to shift the current approaches, which see and treat development and training activities as a cost, to seeing them as a means of enriching the organisation and individuals alike.

DEVELOPMENT ACTIVITIES AS INVESTMENTS

The traditional approach is to treat human resources as *units of production*. The labour and associated expenditure represent revenue costs that are attributed to an appropriate activity and offset against income or used to determine price, fee, etc. This approach can be found in production, service, public or private sector operations. Regardless of source, revenue income flows into the organisation from sales, fees and charges, grant or gift. Costs are outgoings which need to be balanced if the organisation is to remain financially viable.

Using the traditional balance sheet as the main means of assessing an organisation's worth in fact under-estimates its real value. Treating staff as an outgoing fails to recognise the ways in which the people contribute and add value to the operations and the general health of the organisation. As monetary measures are the most commonly used indicators, other ways of assessing worth do not provide the shared language or commonality needed by which to compare organisations.

An organisation can choose to view its staff in other ways. One alternative to treating them as units of production is to regard them as *assets*. This enables some of the otherwise intangible aspects of human resource management to be converted into financial terms, without losing some of the qualitative elements. These are essential if staff are to be seen as unique individuals, and sometimes can serve to reinforce their value. Employing monetary values may be the only way to carry out comparative analysis which enables judgements to be made between disparate units of resource.

Utility theory

An alternative to monetary values is available which allows a notional value to be assigned to the resource in question. *Utility theory*, according to Cascio (1987):

> provides a framework for making decisions by forcing the decision-maker to define clearly the goal, to enumerate the expected consequences or possible outcomes of the decision and to attach differing utilities or values to each. Such an approach has merit since resulting decisions are likely to rest on a foundation of sound reasoning and conscious forethought.

Utility theory is normally used as an aid to decision-making. It enables the decision-maker to evaluate the comparative worth of each of the possible courses of action, by constructing a 'pay-off matrix'. The decision-maker is encouraged to identify the choices available and the factors affecting the decision. The possibility of these outcomes occurring can be weighted in terms of desirability and the probability of their achievement, or the degree of risk involved, is assessed. The influence of each of the factors is also weighted. From these multipliers the decision-maker can calculate the utility of each choice.

Example 3.1

Aim: To learn how to implement a new computerised record-keeping system

Choice	Factor			Probability	Utility
	A	B	C	·	(1=low, 9=high)
1	+1	+4	−1	.3	4.7
2	−1	−1	+4	.6	1.2
3	+3	+4	−2	.8	5.4
4	+4	+4	−4	.9	4.4

Choice	Factors (+4 to −4)
1 = Secondment	A = Availability
2 = Course	B = Cost
3 = Reading and experience	C = Time required
4 = Experience alone	

Conclusion:
Reading and experience would seem to be the 'best' way of achieving the stated aim.

Utility theory and some of the other ways of assigning worth allow an organisation's human resource assets to be dealt with differently to other organisational assets. After all, it is the actions of people that add value and provide the utility to the financial and physical resources. Utility is a useful concept, as it contains more than just usefulness. It enables value to be evaluated, while including elements of desirability. Thus comparisons can be made between very different alternatives and aspects of human resource management.

If an organisation's staff are to be viewed as an asset, decisions regarding their deployment and future need to be made in a calculated fashion. Utility theory, it is argued, enables these decisions to be made. Smith (1988) has used this approach to work out the effectiveness of different selection methods

> in the same terms as production managers, sales managers and data processing managers instead of relying on less convincing qualitative statements or the general effects of better selection.

A similar case can be made for the technique for evaluating development choices using average and superior performance as the comparators.

Cascio (1987) goes into greater depth about the different ways in which utility theory can be used to evaluate the usefulness and value of various selection methods. He argues that by improving the selection method, an organisation can take steps to ensure that the quality of those appointed is improved. He also shows how similar methods can be used to demonstrate the comparative worth of different training and development interventions. All his examples use complex equations to calculate the effectiveness of outcomes achieved. Nevertheless, as shown below, they have some use by drawing into the equation:

• an estimate of how long the training or development activity will continue to have an effect on performance;

• the number of people at the receiving end of the activity;

• the true difference in job performance between the average trained and untrained worker. (This can be calculated using the performance ratings obtained by those trained, the ratings of those untrained, together with the standard deviation obtained by comparing the ratings of those trained and those untrained modified by a reliability weighting given to the methods used to assess performance);

• the variability of job performance of the untrained group;

• the per person cost of the activity.

Example 3.2

Imagine an organisation that uses a performance management scheme which combines over a year a re-evaluation of the job with a review of performance to determine training and development needs, an assessment of the individual's readiness for promotion or movement, and some other measures which will be used to assess performance-related pay.

The evaluation process is based on an analysis which combines dimensions of effective performance of the job, in terms of knowledge and skill, and the particular degrees of complexity, responsibility, discretion and decision time needed for each discrete element.

When linked to defined levels of performance, the resultant matrix permits an individual's performance to be rated on each factor and an overall rating to be assigned.

A simplified matrix for a service administrator would appear as below:

Performance level *Job elements:*	1	2	3	4	5	6
Record maintenance • use of spreadsheets and computer database						
Work planning • use of scheduling techniques • maintenance of stock levels						
Customer liaison • verbal and written communication skills • ability to deal with enquiries						
Peer relations • ability to co-ordinate work-loads • willingness to work as a team member etc						

Overall assessment ....
Performance standard key:

1 = requires remedial action to be taken quickly
2 = requires improvements to be made
3 = adequate
4 = above average with potential
5 = ready to extend level
6 = capable of carrying about more advanced work now

(The dimensions would define the identified job elements)

This rating scale can be used to contribute to the utility equation, which can also demonstrate the effectiveness of a work group. The manager's aim is to have a skewed distribution amongst a team of 20 in the service department. It is deemed acceptable in the organisation to have 15 per cent of workers at level 2, 20 per cent at level 5 and 5 per cent at 1 and 6. The rest are expected to be spread in levels 3 and 4.

This approach may seem mechanistic, but the organisation takes a serious view of its responsibilities to its workforce. It has adopted policies aimed at developing a conducive environment, believing that a well-treated workforce is productive and loyal. These policies have paid off. The organisation has been successful and has a reputation for being a good employer. It does not have any problems recruiting or retaining staff. It is also renowned for having staff ready to take up more demanding roles, when needed and at the right time for them.

Since this approach was introduced, the economic climate has had an adverse effect on this, and many other organisations. It operates in a sector that has been competitive in terms of both price and quality. While not aiming to be 'top drawer', the organisation has always tried to provide a quality service to its consumers, at the same time remaining highly competitive on price. The current position is different from any previously encountered. There is a war raging in the sector. Price-cutting and raising consumers' expectations are the main tactics being used. One way in which this particular organisation has responded has been to reduce internal revenue expenditure, working to achieve increased competency and productivity.

A very real dilemma is posed to the organisation's managers. How can they improve competence when the money available to spend on training and development has been reduced? A both/and solution is to argue for more training and development resources while using other ways of enhancing the staff's performance. The rating scale enables utility theory to construct an argument which can be tested and assessed against other investment/cost-reducing decisions.

Utility theory's most common use is to estimate the worth of alternative courses of action. It can help managers put together a case to stand against the other claims being made on an organisation's limited resources. The theory makes it possible to compare and contrast options (including that of doing nothing) and shows how development activities can achieve cost-effective results. Like another technique, it has its flaws. Care needs to be taken to ensure that as much relevant information is included as possible and that a range of outcomes are contemplated. Account should be taken of prejudice when assessing the effect of influencing factors and the probability of the outcome being attained.

The technique does not reduce subjectivity, but allows individual preferences to be clearly shown alongside organisational factors. As with any decision-making technique, it should not be used to make the decision; its proper use is to inform the decision makers and help them structure their thoughts.

VALUATION OF THE HUMAN RESOURCE

Another technique for demonstrating the worth of development activities and the total human resource is to give a value to the knowledge and skills of the workforce. Some workers are regarded as being irreplaceable because their experience has given them 'unique' skills. But how often is this belief tested? Can an individual's special contribution be assessed and valued in tangible and specific terms? The way to answer these questions is to calculate a 'worth' using a process similar to that used to evaluate added value. The knowledge and skills possessed by individual members of the workforce have to be assessed in some way. An audit is helpful, as it provides a means of combining different skills and knowledge into a common format or profile. It is possible to collate the profiles of staff to identify the skills, experience and knowledge available. It also provides a way of finding out which skills exist but are not currently being used, and which are missing.

Skills audit

Once the audit has been completed and profiles drawn up, the ways *can* be identified in which the skills and knowledge add value and contribute to the processes which transform raw inputs into finished outputs.

The inputs are normally:

- money (capital and revenue);

- materials (raw, plus those required for maintenance);

- human power (energy and time).

The value added by each component input can be calculated by assessing its contribution to the value of the output. This may be measured in many ways – as income, profit, numbers of customers served (throughput), examination results of students, discharges from custody or hospital, levels of performance in comparison to other workers, degree of achievement of objectives, etc.

The value assigned to the contribution of the workforce can be quantitative, numeric or financial. Competence statements (or a similar structured categorisation of skills levels) can be used to distinguish between levels of proficiency, providing a means of rating overall performance. A rating scale can easily be developed to show how close a worker or group of workers is to full competence.

The use of measures enables feedback to be obtained. The information gathered is useful for helping to identify where improvements can be made to the process. Having broken down the inputs to component level, the contribution of each to the worth and quality can be assessed. A highly skilled engineer cannot produce quality dies from poor grade steel; similarly, an untrained engineer cannot be expected to produce the dies to the standard required, even with top-quality materials.

Example 3.3

An inexperienced, partially trained, insurance broker's clerk, operating at an ascribed level of 60 per cent competence, costs a total of £6 per hour to employ. A fully trained clerk, with one year's experience and working at 85 per cent competence, costs £9. The inexperienced worker can produce ten quotations per week, while the experienced worker can produce 18 and deal with routine enquiries for information. It is estimated that two hours per week, or 90 hours a year, costing £540 of the trainee's time and £1,080 of the supervisor's, is required to reach 85 per cent competence.

The employment cost of producing the ten quotes is £240 per week, against £360 for the 18 prepared by the experienced clerk. The annual productivity potential of the untrained clerk equals 500 quotes. The clerk costs £12,000 to employ. The trained clerk costs £18,000 and potentially produces 900 quotes. At a training cost of £1,620 and £6,000 extra employment costs, 400 more quotations are produced. Each of the trained clerk's quotes cost £21.80, against the untrained clerk's £24. In addition the trained clerk is able to undertake other duties, such as answering routine enquiries.

The untrained clerk's level of output increases incrementally as skills develop. (A frequent assessment of performance would allow this to be reflected in the calculation, if so wished.)

This technique also provides a useful means of evaluating the effects of a long-term development programme. For instance, the catering business of a metropolitan council faced the threat of closure unless it very quickly reduced its operating loss. The management was restructured to give the unit managers full responsibility for running their own business. It was accepted that they would need training to help them understand the change (previously they had been working chargehands) and assume their new role, which included the management of staff and financial performance. A development programme was constructed using action learning techniques which made use of real-life problems to extend the managers' skill levels. After 18 months an evaluation was conducted. The cost of the programme, in terms of managers' and facilitators' time, was estimated and subtracted from the year-end figures. An estimate of the financial outturn assuming no change was calculated. This was compared to the actual result minus development costs and showed the cost-effectiveness of the programme. Even though other factors had influenced the improvement, the effect and value of the programme was still evident after a number of years.

Qualitative value

If this quantitative approach is not acceptable, a *qualitative* worth can be calculated. Professional and service organisations are more likely to want to assess the intangible features of quality performance. In production and some service organisations, quantitative measures are satisfactory, as they tend to be the more usual forms of currency. But in those organisations where the tradition has been one of a concern with the quality of the output, rather than its measurement, it is difficult to assign an acceptable numerical value to demonstrate the worth of the workforce. Therefore some other forms of assessment are needed.

Example 3.4

A firm of solicitors wants to distinguish between the quality and level of performance of its junior partners as they gain in experience. The assessment is to provide a means of allocating work and calculating charges. To do this, the senior partners decide to use the repertory grid technique to create a development profile that distinguishes between the levels of expertise at different stages of training. Novice, trainee, semi-trained, nearly trained and fully trained are used as elements for the grid. The senior partners and some selected clients are asked to complete the matrix and give the constructs that describe the differences and similarities between the junior partners at each stage of training.

The analysis of the grids is used to create a rating scale. As the complexity and level of difficulty of the different jobs also have been elicited, the composite grid can be used to create a development plan which will enable the more complex and difficult cases to be allocated to the appropriate groups of 'trainees'.

SWOT Analysis

An alternative way to create a human resource audit is to carry out a full *SWOT analysis*. SWOT analysis is typically used in marketing and strategic planning. The usual way of carrying out such an analysis is for an organisation to scan its environment for threats and opportunities. It then turns inside to examine its ability to minimise or negate the threats and maximise the opportunities. Good quality information about the organisation's future and its environment is needed if this operation is to be carried out fully. In human resource terms, this requires a knowledge of the organisation's mission, or long-term goals, the skills needed to achieve these, the appropriate labour market and an assessment of available strengths. The difference between the skills currently held and those needed to achieve the long-term goals is the gap that has to be filled from the external market, developed by the current staff employed, or forgone. A realistic analysis of the labour market can often save time and recruitment costs.

The skills originally thought to be needed and readily available from outside can turn out to be not so common, for several reasons:

- The skills identified as being needed are imaginary and so will never be available (eg the brilliant leader who will solve all the problems).

- The skills are too wide-ranging to be possessed by single individuals.

- Some of the skills are situational or organisationally specific and so cannot be obtained from outside.

It is not uncommon for an organisation to undervalue its own staff's skill levels. (Evidence of this can be seen when an organisation searches long and hard to find a suitable person from outside to fill a vacant post, believing potential internal candidates to be inadequate in some undefined way. A frequent conclusion is for the internal person to be appointed after a lengthy and costly recruitment process has failed and staff have become somewhat disillusioned.) The proper use of SWOT analysis can enable a thorough, impersonal assessment to be made of a staff's skills and to help the organisation's managers recognise, realistically, what is required from outside. This form of analysis can also acknowledge the potential of current staff. If this is done in conjunction with strategic planning, suitable development programmes can be set in place to implement the plan before the organisation starts to fail because of its lack of skills in critical areas.

Distinctive competence

These approaches still, however, have the tendency of seeing staff as units of production, part of the process used to transform inputs into the organisation's outputs. A different way is to treat the human resource as the part of the organisation that creates its *distinctive competence*. This competence is created by those features that give an organisation its advantage or superiority over its competitors. It also comes from the factors that lead consumers to choose that particular organisation's outputs rather than those of others. The concept of distinctive competence is equally relevant to profit-making and not-for-profit organisations, providing that the consumers have some choice between suppliers.

Day and Wensley (1988) provide a model for identifying an organisation's competitive superiority. An essential element is the assessment of the organisation's skill base, including its ability (ie the staff's) to respond quickly to change, as well as their functional capabilities. To assess the different contributions of individuals, groups and functional areas, diagnose gaps and identify their distinctive competence, some means of comparing against competitors or an idealised model of the organisation is required. Techniques such as soft systems methodology and other marketing/strategic choice and decision-making tools are useful. As it is not appropriate to describe them at length here, the interested reader is referred to Rosenhead (1989).

The term 'organisational culture' is now widely used to describe the way history, size, type of business and the influential people who have shaped an organisation over the years combine to create its uniqueness. However, culture should not be seen merely as a product of the past, without appreciating that future culture is being shaped now by the people currently involved with an organisation. Today's escapades and successes become tomorrow's myths, and those responsible become the heroes and villains. Recognising the full contribution people make to the total organisation points to another way of valuing them as precious assets, making a special unique contribution. Taking this perspective suggests they can be assayed in the same way as a brand name or goodwill. Both of these assets are intangible, but nevertheless quantifiable. Why should the human resource not be treated similarly for accountancy purposes?

There are other reasons why it is important to view staff as part of the organisation's distinctive competence, assign a value to the workforce and treat people accordingly. Reference has been made above to increasing shortages of skills as a result of rapid technological advances, changes in the market-place and the effects of economic recession. The increasing ageing of the population will also mean that competent and up-to-date staff will become a much sought-after commodity. If the pool of unemployed remains large and people stay out of work for lengthy periods, their future employability will diminish, whereas competition for skilled, experienced staff will become fiercer. The future of the labour market presents personnel planners with the stuff of nightmares. It will become more critical that organisations treasure the skills and competences of their current staff and invest in them if they are to retain them as up-to-date, available and effectively used assets.

Treating staff as long-term assets allows other aspects of human resource management to be paralleled to other types of investment decisions. Similarities may be drawn between recruitment and selection decisions and those made to purchase high-cost plant or buildings. Recruitment and selection activities are high-cost – just placing an average display advertisement in a national daily newspaper can cost in the region of £1,000. Other costs, such as the production of recruitment literature, printing applications forms, and postage, will be incurred and time spent over a period of several weeks before an appointment is made. The initial set-up costs of an employee can be added to the annual cost of employment. The turnover rate for a particular staff group can be used to find the average length of stay, and other predicted costs may be included so the total amount an individual is likely to cost the organisation during the expected period of the employment contract can be determined.

Example 3.5

It is not unreasonable to expect a manager, earning £15,000 per year, to stay in an organisation's employment for five years. The employment cost for that period will amount to £86,250 (ie annual salary plus employment costs × 5). (The actual total will, of course, alter in line with inflation.) In addition to the initial recruitment costs, other expenditure will be incurred. Training and car/travel costs are obvious examples. Other costs, however, are generated – employees create expense. They have ideas, need secretaries, want desks and equipment, use stationery and telephones, require support facilities and cause problems. All add to the employment revenue costs, and should be taken into account when calculating the total scale of the investment resulting from the decision to employ a member of staff.

Rate of return

It would not be abnormal for an organisation to consider the pay-offs expected from high-level recruitment expenditure. Any other form of high-level expenditure would normally be subjected to detailed scrutiny. One aid to making this sort of decision is the calculation of the expected rate of return. This is made by working out how many sales or how much income can be expected from the turnover achieved by the asset in question. Various financial ratios are used, most of which concern the efficiency of the output's production. Another way to look at the utilisation of assets is to determine the contribution they make to profitability, or the value they add to the output.

Example 3.6

An organisation decided to employ a marketing specialist, as it was dissatisfied with the degree of penetration it had achieved so far in a particular market segment. It employed a recruitment consultant to find suitably qualified candidates. The consultancy fees amounted to 2 per cent of annual salary, which was set at £17,500. In addition, it is estimated that the appointment process would take time worth another £2,500.

The organisation pays a guaranteed bonus of 1 per cent of salary, plus a share in profit which is estimated to be 1.5 per cent of the pay bill. One per cent of salary is allowed for training and development. With other employment costs amounting to 15 per cent, the cost of employing the marketing specialist will be:

	£
Recruitment – time	2,500
fee	3,500
Salary	17,500
Bonus and profit-share	3,375
Training and development	1,750
Total in the first year	£28,625

The organisation expects that the person appointed will stay for four years. Thus an investment of £90,500 will be sunk in the appointment. Other costs are expected, such as office needs, staff support, travel, sickness benefits etc.

Depreciation

If an organisation is to regard its staff as assets in which it has made a capital investment, and is expecting some rate of return from them, the other side of the equation ought to be considered. It is normal practice to depreciate expensive assets over their anticipated life span. For some very major capital purchases, an organisation borrows to fund the initial expenditure and then has to pay back the loan plus its accrued interest. These costs, too, have to be attributed.

Similarities can be perceived between depreciation and the decay of an individual's effectiveness over the period of their employment. Additionally, the cost of paying back the initial investment and the other normal running costs can be equated to the costs of maintaining an individual's level of performance.

Learning curves

Learning curves are used to show how long it takes for individuals to reach acceptable levels of performance or competence. The steepness of the curve is determined by a number of factors, which relate to the individual and the circumstances in which the learning and the performance are taking place. These include, for the individual:

- ability, previous experience and knowledge;
- understanding of what is expected;
- assessment of own ability and levels of confidence;
- belief in being able to reach the desired level of performance;
- expected outcome and desirability/undesirability of outcome;
- motivation to learn.

The circumstances, such as the skill of the person carrying out the instruction or coaching, the conduciveness of the environment to learning, the pressure under which the individual is expected to learn, the amount and speed of change occurring, feedback from managers, colleagues and influential others, etc, also have a direct bearing on the steepness of the learning curve. These factors will be discussed in far greater depth when aids and inhibitors to learning are considered. A typical curve would appear shown in Fig. 3.1.

It is not usual for the learning curve to show what happens after the desired level of competence has been attained. There is an almost implicit assumption

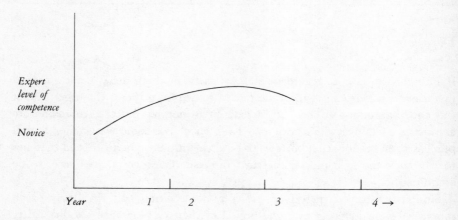

Figure 3.1 The learning curve

that it remains constant. This is not the case. Knowledge, skills and expertise decay unless they are maintained or refreshed.

To calculate the rate of depreciation, assets' useful lives are estimated and their capital cost (less any residual or scrap value) is depreciated over that time-period. This is done as an accountancy procedure on the balance sheet, with the depreciation charge being added to the operational overhead of the unit in which the asset is being used. Alternatively, it can be added to production costs. In both cases it forms part of revenue costs, to be recouped from sales, charges or fees. Other revenue costs such as maintenance, regular part replacements, and lubrication, can be incurred to extend the useful life of the asset. The comparative effectiveness of these can be calculated and choices made accordingly. For example, it is possible to work out whether regular maintenance will prolong an asset's useful life at a cost less than its estimated depreciation rate. Alternatively, it is possible to work out whether the risk of breakdown during the expected life of the item merits maintenance costs. It may be more cost effective to let it decay, rather than spend money to make the asset last longer.

Maintenance decisions

This accountancy technique can be adapted to apply to decisions regarding the development of staff. As with maintenance decisions (which should include actual expenditure and down-time) similar choices can be made about investing in the maintenance of a staff's level of competence. Decisions of this nature should be made following consideration of the consequences of each course of action available, including that of doing nothing.

Learning is a risky and sometimes painful business, and the chance of failure may seem high. The effort required to remain up-to-date, especially in some of the high-tech industries, can be considerable. It requires as much personal commitment as well as work-related effort and expenditure. (How many employers, for example, pay for their employees' individual membership of professional bodies, or buy their trade journals?) A critical question is whether the perceived rewards of maintaining professional knowledge and skills will be felt worth the effort on the part of the individual. In other words, an individual will want to know 'What's in it for me?' This need not be money, but the rewards (or consequences) must be desirable to the individual concerned in their own terms. Treating learning of new ways and experimenting as a normal part of the job can help reduce these natural fears. The pay-offs for both the individual and the organisation can justify the investment needed. Plant may eventually be scrapped and equipment written off, but the human resource has the capability to grow beyond predicted potential and increase in both self-worth and value to the organisation. Instead of being one-off events, development activities can become a form of routine maintenance.

There are certain external factors that can be damaging to morale. Rapid change and the consequent uncertainty, frequently, can result in a decline in morale. It is not very likely that demotivated, demoralised staff will be inclined to engage in an extensive development programme that will take them even further into uncharted, scary waters. Nor is it likely that someone will agree to attend evening classes to learn desk top publishing when the organisation has no computer equipment capable of running the software. Planned development focused towards goals that can be seen to address the difficulties that accompany change can reduce fear and help maintain morale, as well as providing the chance to acquire new skills.

Maintaining employee competence can have pay-offs that are greater than the cost incurred. Equally, the cost of doing nothing can be very great – failure to maintain levels of competence, through refreshment and renewal of skills, inevitably leads to a drop in performance from the levels previously attained and desired.

- drop in performance:
  —drop in quality of output;
  —customer dissatisfaction;
  —increased production costs through wastage of materials, time;
  —increased safety hazards;
  —ineffective working, misdirected effort.

- drop in morale and reduced commitment to work – by individuals and/or work group (this can become incremental):
  —increased staff turnover (wastage of previous training and expertise);
  —loss of potential and latent talents;
  —loss of loyal staff;
  —feeling of decline instilled in others.

The benefits of investing in employee maintenance can lead to a release of talents which is enriching for both the organisation and the individuals. Even though learning can be risky and stressful, stress (of the right type) is a necessary part of the human condition and is needed to stimulate brain and physical vitality. Absence of challenge and stimulation leads to boredom and lassitude. Sabotage can be a common outlet by means of which workers who are unstretched by their jobs, and left to plateau, find amusement, distraction and challenge. Development can provide the challenges needed to engage interest and provide opportunities to test ideas and alternatives in settings where the risk can be more controlled.

Staff who are engaged in areas of work which benefit from development, tend to stay with the organisation as they feel there is something to be achieved; they do not stay as passengers. Their contribution remains positive, as their skills develop in tune and in line with the organisation. Their knowledge of the organisation, its customers and environment remain available to the organisation, and the constant renewal of skills helps to keep knowledge fresh rather than historic. Staff working on maintenance and procedural tasks in stable environments need not be excluded from development. Even if in the long run it is better to leave systems as they are, they should be evaluated regularly and compared to others being used elsewhere. It is also worth while to check to see if thinking and applications have been advanced by other organisations. Monitoring and reappraisal in this way is a means of providing development opportunities for staff, without threatening them unduly.

The staff who stay but are not part of the organisation's development tend to become guardians of the past, living with fond memories of some Golden Age. They are the 'mind guard' of the culture, tellers of stories and practitioners of the rituals. Important in some ways, they can inhibit change, stultify growth and demotivate their peers. The depreciation of people of this nature is invidious and can have negative incremental impact on the work of their group and the wider organisation. Anyone who has worked with a 'wet blanket' will know how difficult it can be to remain buoyant, enthusiastic and optimistic.

The opposite impact can result from taking action to slow down the decrease in the levels of competence. It is possible for the depreciation to be reversed and the organisation's collected talents and skill base to grow and expand. The virtuous cycle can be contagious. Just as demotivated staff can infect the enthusiastic, so developing, forward-looking individuals can encourage and help the growth of their less adventurous colleagues.

Example 3.7

A teaching department decided to increase its research activity over its planning period of five years. Research was regarded by existing staff as an extra chore for which no time had been allowed; recognition was not given, nor were facilities made available. To change this view, young staff with only first degrees were recruited as posts became vacant. They were encouraged to study for higher degrees and appropriate support was given. Within a four-year timespan, 25 per cent of all staff were following courses of study which required them to undertake research. A target of 30 per cent involvement in research was thought to be needed to build a critical mass to influence other staff and lead to research being seen as a normal, everyday activity.

Of course, making decisions to invest in the maintenance of existing staff resource involves some risk. There is the risk of their leaving to work for a competitor. But likewise, there is the risk of their staying and, despite efforts to keep them fresh, suffering the effects of 'professional stagnation'. The chances of this happening are greater than if action is taken to maintain and increase skills. Staff appreciate attention, especially when it means they are treated as unique, respected individuals. They tend to react accordingly, repaying their employer with the same treatment.

WHO PAYS?

There is a recurrent debate regarding the best ways of ensuring that the organisation funding an individual's development retains the benefit of the investment. This is a direct consequence of staff being seen as an organisational asset. Having made a considerable investment to enhance and extend skills, release latent and potential talent and establish a distinctive competence, it should be no surprise that an organisation wishes to protect its resource base and ensure it does not give its advantage to competitors.

One of the reasons for setting up the Industrial Training Boards in the 1960s was to equalise the investment being made in training across companies in the same industrial sector. The grant/levy scheme was devised to penalise those companies that did not train their staff but relied on being able to obtain skills from companies that did. Some changes have occurred in thinking since then, but training and development can still be seen as a competitive weapon. It also involves the individual obtaining a benefit. In some quarters it is believed that when an individual receives training at the expense of one organisation, there is a tendency for that person to cash in on the benefit by obtaining a higher-paid job with another company. Consequently proposals have been made about ways in which staff can be 'tied' to the funding employer, or required to pay back the cost of their training expenditure in the event of their leaving. Consideration has also been given to how charges can be made to the new employer as a way of recouping the training costs. This poses the question under consideration here – how can the true cost of training and, especially, development be calculated?

DO NOTHING

A final way to look at the investment decision is to explore the 'do nothing' option more fully. Superficially, doing nothing may appear to have no cost. It does, however, have consequences which may incur costs or lost opportunities.

How often are the risks and consequences of *not* developing an organisation's staff considered? Training and development have come back to the fore as indicators of a well-run organisation. Not many now would admit to not investing in people. However, those providing basic training only, without engaging fully in developmental activities, do not create the opportunities for development and learning to happen, nor do they encourage staff to take advantage of them. The ones that do so shine through, providing beacons to an alternative way of managing staff. They do not do this entirely for altruistic reasons; they have a sound business justification. Some, for example, Ford and Rover, are in highly cost-conscious, competitive industrial sectors. They must believe that funding learning and development will pay dividends.

When faced with a static, ageing workforce, a rapidly changing environment, a shrinking market-place, increased competition and a deskilled labour pool, there are few other options available to ensure that staff stay abreast of change and remain able to perform to the standards required by staying at the peak of the learning curve. The 'do nothing' approach can have a negative impact on organisational performance, but how often is this quantified? Total quality management provides examples which show that quality control systems, monitoring of performance and correcting mistakes can incur far more expenditure than 'getting it right first time'. Similarly, having to deal with the consequences of stagnating, unskilled, unmotivated, bored, inflexible staff can take more managerial time and effort than setting in motion mechanisms and systems that will enable them to learn and establishing a climate in which to develop their skills and benefit from the challenges of change.

Example 3.8

The travelling representative was a sullen but hard working, individual. As a result of organisational restructuring, mobile staff were no longer required. The only individual left was redeployed into a large service department. Despite counselling and offers of support, the member of staff's performance dropped to a barely acceptable level and the sullenness developed such intensity that the chill could be detected from outside the building. No one quite knew what to do and it was implicitly decided to leave the person 'to stew'.

Later, for other reasons, it became necessary to move the individual again, this time into a specialist department. Because of the nature of the work, training in different areas was needed. As no external training was available, coaching was the only solution. The individual took immediately to the new role, and blossomed. The sullenness was replaced by hesitant signs of happiness; occasionally, traces of a smile were seen. The level of performance increased dramatically and from being a problem, the individual quickly began to make a valuable contribution.

Getting the right people in the right place, investing in their development, aiding their learning and giving them appropriate attention can have unforeseen pluses for everyone.

SUMMARY

This chapter has shown how the cost of development can be seen as an investment for its future well-being, rather than as a drain on scarce resources. By focusing on the price tag of training and development, an organisation can overlook the way its human resources add value to its output. Some approaches have been taken from accountancy to demonstrate how different ways of treating human resources can alter the way in which decisions to invest in people's development and job satisfaction can be influenced.

It is possible to treat the human resource as an asset. Most commonly, employment expenditure is shown as a cost on the organisation's balance sheet. Other techniques can be used that demonstrate the value of staff's efforts and the worth of the investment in their development. The usefulness and utility of development can be calculated to help argue for resources to invest and to evaluate the effectiveness of the decision. This evaluation can be linked to an assessment of skills and performance, to aid the identification of areas for future action.

As financial and other resources are audited, human skills can be identified so that the total value of the organisation's skill bank can be assessed. Again, this approval can be used for development planning and can help other human resource decisions such as work planning. An audit can also inform strategic planning by contributing to a SWOT analysis. As well as identifying which skills need to be developed, the organisation can see which it has to obtain or do without in order to implement its strategic plans.

Knowledge of the organisation's total skill resource helps achieve recognition of its own distinctive competence. Often one's own staff are devalued when viewed in comparison to those of other organisations — that is, until replacement staff are being sought! Treating staff as long-term capital assets changes the way in which recruitment, selection and development decisions are taken and seen. The need for initial training is well-known and frequently acted upon to ensure that staff progress up the slope of the learning curve as rapidly as is effectively possible. But once staff have reached the top of the learning curve, they do not stay there without other action being taken to keep them at the peak. The decline in skills can be paralleled to the depreciation of capital plant. Decisions are made to engage in maintenance as a way of slowing down this decay. Alternatively, a do-nothing decision can be made. The same happens with staff's development. Without investment to maintain levels of performance, staff's motivation and skill levels decline. With maintenance, their skills can continue to increase, and as untapped potential is realised, they may actually outstrip predicted levels of performance.

The question of who pays for development is a recurring theme. There are arguments for the individual paying, or the employer. In sectors where the workforce is highly mobile, a valid case can be made for an employing organisation to, somehow, share the costs of developing skills which will be used eventually in several organisations. Alternatively the investment can be treated as a loan to the individual, who is required to repay the employer on resignation. These arguments tend to get in the way, inhibiting development activities. The distraction is partly irrelevant when the skills level of the whole country is in decline.

The do-nothing option may be attractive when time and money are in short supply. But this decision, while having short-term benefits, is a recipe for long-term failure. Too many factors are diminishing the level of available skills, and the continued failure to act to reverse the trend will affect more than the country's financial well-being.

This chapter has attempted to equip those who are committed to development and learning with some techniques taken from accountants and financial experts. If the arguments can be presented in the terms of the powerful and the decision-makers, there may be an improved chance of success. A search of the literature has not revealed many other sources of help in human resource accounting. Those which are available tend to focus on costs rather than investment decisions, so this is an area that may benefit from further development.

4
Learning and development

INTRODUCTION

In this chapter the process of how learning takes place will be outlined. Any manager wishing to help and encourage skill development and learning needs a basic understanding of what happens to individuals as they go through the process. It is easy to say that this process is concerned with the psychology of the individual and that, as this is an advanced science, it is beyond the ordinary manager. This is not so. True, there are some very complex ideas and theories about the learning process, but there are also some simple, straightforward principles. These will be discussed with a view to helping to understand what the individual learner may be experiencing. Thus informed, managers should be better able to reduce inhibitors and enhance the positive aspects of learning.

WHAT IS DEVELOPMENT?

Education	→ Teach	→ Knowledge
Training	→ Show	→ Skills
Development	→ Learn	→ Person

The terms were defined in more detail in Chapter 1. Education is involved with transmitting concepts and ideas. The process normally happens formally in a specially designated place and is generally controlled by a person who possesses knowledge of the concepts and ideas being taught. The 'teacher' sets the agenda and then guides and aids the understanding of the person who is receiving the education. Training, on the other hand, can and often does take place in everyday settings. The process tends to be more concerned with doing a job and applying understanding and knowledge to the performance of a task. Often the desired outcome of training is the acquisition or improvement of skills. The process is controlled by a person who has expertise in the relevant skill area or who is expert at helping people develop their skills through structured learning experiences.

Development is different:

Development puts the person – or the organisation – at the centre as an emerging being with a developmental history and a future potential. Unlike training we can apply the developmental idea and process to individuals, groups, organisations or societies. The impulse to develop comes from within but in response to the person's or organisation's environment.

Compared with training, development . . .
1. involves self-motivation and people thinking for themselves;
2. is more holistic, takes the whole situation into account;
3. deals more with the long-term;
4. deals with 'no right answer' situations.

[Boydell 1992]

The above implies that development, in this sense, builds upon existing knowledge, skills and experience; it need not be focused in the same way as training or education. Because it is more concerned with the release of potential, it is a voyage into the unknown. One marvellous human ability is the capacity to continue to learn and develop skills and abilities well into old age. (The numbers of mature students involved in Open University programmes and the University of the Third Age demonstrate this.)

However, the needs and requirements of older learners are different from those of people who are following education or training programmes. Instead of learning from new, they are building, extending, transforming, adapting what already exists. It is therefore worth spending a little time considering how these learning processes differs from the processes of those learning for the first time. There is a vast body of knowledge, based on extensive research covering the development and learning of children. While this does have some relevancy here, the learning of adults is somewhat different. The body of knowledge in this branch of developmental psychology is not nearly so extensive.

THE LEARNING PROCESS

The human brain's ability to learn new material is infinite – there is no known limit to its capacity. There are some opinions regarding cognitive ability or levels of intelligence, but these are not conclusive; nor is there any definitive explanation of how the brain functions. Various psychologists have come forward with suggestions regarding the way in which the cognitive processes operate and the nature of intelligence. However, although it is accepted that it is possible to 'teach old dogs new tricks', old brains have different needs from young ones – if only because they have more in them.

How the mind works

The working of the mind is known as the cognitive process. Notwithstanding the complexity of this process, it is possible to draw a simplistic model based on the conclusions of many researchers. Basically, the mind takes in information through a number of receptors. These inputs are subjected to a selection process, during which the mind decides whether it wants to receive the information. (You may have heard your colleague speak, but do you recall what was said?) The information is edited so that only the selected part of the information is received. It is then compared to information previously received by the brain and framed to fit into the existing view of the world and attitudes held by the individual. A possible response to the information is formed, tested and given. The action and reactions that occur are stored in the memory for future use. As the mind receives more information and engages in more tests, so the memory store becomes 'fuller'. The 'data base' grows and takes longer to search. Also, the information stored becomes more complex, which increases the propensity for distortion, and attitudes becomes more firmly established. It is known that people search for evidence to confirm their existing frames of

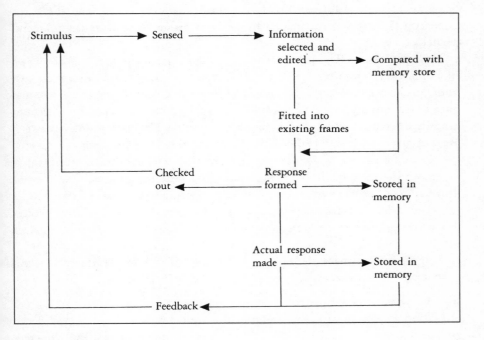

Figure 4.1   How the mind works

reference and that, during the process of selecting information, they discount evidence that suggests alternative versions. Thus older learners have a rich bank of experience complemented by reinforced attitudes. If learning new ideas challenges the existing frames of reference, some initial work will be needed to help the individual deal with the 'threat' to their existing concepts.

The early learning process

The cognitive process in children is far less complex than that of adults. Their experience and knowledge base is not as extensive, so information is not subjected to the same degree of selection and comparison. Attitudes have not been reinforced to the same extent, and they are not as deeply held. New information does not present the same type of challenge to the child's mind-set.

The most widely quoted authority on child development is Piaget (1953). He describes how the development of the cognitive processes is not a result of maturation, nor the influence of the environment, but an interaction of the two. Thus an organism adapts itself to the environment by action, and 'Intelligence extends this creation by constructing mental structures which can be applied to those [structures] of the environment.' Later, Piaget describes how, as the organism develops, its cognitive structures move through three 'levels'. The learning occurring during this developmental process is not 'the thing the organism takes in but the process by which it makes sense of its environment' (Inhelder, 1962).

Piaget's three levels – sensory-motor, pre-operational and operational – chart the progression from birth to the age of about 16. At this age, Piaget claims, individuals become less egocentric and develop coherent cognitive schemas which are initially sequences of action. Later, they can take into account interdependent variables and intangible concepts. He distinguishes between development and learning. The latter he describes as the acquisition of a specific piece of information, while the former is the ability to use this information; in other words, learning is the content, development the process. The biggest limitation of Piaget's work is that it stops at 'maturation'. That, he assumed, is when an individual stops developing. What happens once the cognitive process has become operative can only be speculated upon, as Piaget does not consider adult learning.

Piaget's notions have some value and are not dissimilar to Bloom's (1956) taxonomy of learning, which identifies six hierarchical stages:

1. Knowledge of simple facts, terms, theories.
2. Comprehension of the meaning of this knowledge.
3. Application of this knowledge and comprehension in new and concrete situations.

4. Analysis of the material to break it down into its constituent parts and to see the relationship between them.
5. Synthesis of the parts into a new meaningful relationship, thus forming a new whole.
6. Evaluation and judgement of the value of the material using explicit and coherent criteria, either of one's own devising or derived from the work of others.

Unlike Piaget's theory, Bloom's definition of the learning process allows learning to be repeated many times during an individual's life as new situations are encountered. Consequently his work is more applicable to the learning of adults. For children, each new experience is an opportunity for more and different learning; for adults, experiences are framed and conditioned by previous learning.

Learnt attitudes and behaviour

The initial learning occurring during an individual's early years makes a significant contribution to their attitudes. Personal construct theory was developed by Kelly (1980) to describe how each person establishes a view of the world which is used to explain what is happening. The constructs help the individual to prepare responses to situations and other people. Personal constructs form the basis of the individual's attitudes and underlying value systems and are formed over a long period as a result of education received formally and from influential others, experience, social conditioning and, some would argue, hereditary factors. Personal constructs are deeply ingrained and can become enmeshed as part of the individual's personality.

Constructs are used to help individuals to create their own personal framework within which to operate. For most of the time, the constructs are general principles used by the majority of the population – the shared values and basic assumptions of the society in which the individual lives. Some major parts of the construct system are unique to the individual. They are that person's mind-set. The mind-set takes the individual through the routine of daily life. It allows pre-conceptions to be made so that appropriate preparations can be made for predicted chains of events which enable the individual to assess how a person or situation is likely to be presented; regardless of whether that person or situation has been encountered before.

Example 4.1

What happens during selection interviews is common knowledge. Most people have attended one.

> The chairman of the company's board is likely to be white, middle-aged and male. He will shake your hand on introduction. You wait to be asked before you sit down.
>
> The new head of the local primary school will be female, middle aged and plump.
>
> The constable who responds to your report of a lost wallet will be younger than you, tall, in uniform, white and male.

The mind-set also predetermines behaviour patterns. Physical responses to situations and people are learnt in a way which is similar to the development of the cognitive processes. Skinner (1971) wrote about 'behaviourism', arguing that it is outside factors which affect the behaviour of the individual. Rewards reinforce and punishment discourages certain behaviour patterns. Learning which behaviour patterns lead to rewards and which do not starts early in life and ranges from the obvious: 'If you do that again I will slap you/stop your spending money/keep you in', etc, to the covert: 'She smiles at me so I will make sure she gets a bigger helping of pudding', 'He asks awkward questions so I will give him all the dirty jobs'.

Another way in which behaviour patterns are learnt is through rehearsal and practice. An individual uses information already in the cognitive store and acquires more if needed to prepare for a situation. It is almost as if the individual were preparing to act a part in a play. One thinks oneself into the situation and prepares appropriate responses to predicted stimuli. Things go very wrong when the wrong script is prepared. The person who has arrived at a friend's formal dinner party expecting a casual evening will know how it feels.

Learnt behaviour can become as set as thought patterns. Once these patterns and mind-sets have been learnt, it is not easy to change them. A simple illustration of this is the folding of one's arms: can you remember when you first learnt how to? How do you do it? Does the right go over the top, or the left? Try folding your arms as normal, and then doing it the opposite way. Does it feel uncomfortable?

How behaviour is learnt

Behaviour is acquired in four steps:

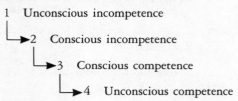

1 Unconscious incompetence
→ 2 Conscious incompetence
→ 3 Conscious competence
→ 4 Unconscious competence

The first step is when the individual does not know that the skill or knowledge is lacking. Someone starting to drive a car might not know the difference between the accelerator and the brake, nor might they have the skill to use both feet at the same time as using their hands and turning their head.

The second step is when the individual becomes aware of what is not known and realises what they cannot do. Faced with a chess set and a grand master, one would very quickly realise that the pieces do different things and that the game has rules and tactics.

The third step is when the beginnings of competence are displayed. The person is able to do things, but needs to think about their actions, or to refer to rules and check-lists to guide performance. Filling in a form for the first time requires careful following of notes and instructions. These should not be needed for the twentieth time.

The final step is when performance of the skill or use of the knowledge becomes an integral part of normal behaviour and need not be thought about. The individual finds it difficult to understand how someone else cannot do or does not know. Eventually it is possible that the skilled individual does not know they know it or how they do it. Try thinking, very carefully, about how you walk up stairs.

Example 4.2

A skilled plasterer was once asked how he plastered a ceiling. He nearly fell off his scaffold thinking about it and trying to explain. He gave up and tried to demonstrate his technique, managing to make a mess. Bringing his unconscious competence back into the forefront of his mind very nearly took him back to being incompetent.

Unconscious competence can be compared to the cognitive routine called 'tramline thinking'. This occurs when a mental routine or pattern of behaviour is so normal that the individual does not think about what they are doing and goes on to 'automatic pilot'. That is how you find yourself driving down a road, unable to remember whether the last set of traffic lights were at red or green: your mind was occupied thinking about the report that has to be written for tomorrow. Tramline thinking can also be the cause of such mental errors as putting the milk bottle in the oven rather than in the refrigerator. As the thought processes are not scrutinised or checked, they are free to run on. This can result in simple mistakes or serious accidents.

Reason (1990) describes how difficult it is to detect errors of this nature. Relevance bias leads to an individual drawing boundaries around information according to preconceived ideas. This can prevent consideration of another, totally different solution to a given problem, or assimilation of a piece of information which could be equally valid. Similarly, the definition of a situation, albeit partial, may appear to be good enough if the constructs so far developed seem to fit. The overlap between the individual's view of the world and reality may appear to contain enough common material to enable the individual to decide whether their interpretation is correct; the truth may be totally different. The true version of reality may include information that totally changes the meaning of the part that overlaps with the individual's interpretation. These blind spots can inhibit an individual from learning alternative approaches, simply because they do not see there is a need to do things differently.

Example 4.3

Public libraries have, throughout their history, maintained information about their neighbourhoods. This may have been in the form of information files, cuttings taken from local papers, biographies of local people and information about local companies.

During the 1960s and 70s the terms 'community librarianship' and 'community information' became more widely used. Many library staff could not understand what the difference was between these new ideas and the services they had always provided. The subtlety of the differences in type of information to be provided, the changed definition of 'community' from geographic area to social group and the means of delivery of the service were not easy ideas to understand in theory. However, the nature of the service given to the user in practice was very different to that provided by the traditional library service.

An understanding of the learning processes is helpful, as it gives some insight into what needs to be done by managers and concerned others to help adults acquire and develop knowledge and skills. The saying 'You can't teach an old dog new tricks' is wrong. But it *is* impossible for a closed mind to learn. Adults inevitably approach any situation with preconceived ideas, no matter how open-minded they may try to be. Steps need to be taken to unfreeze their thinking and prepare their minds for alternatives and the new. Before considering how to help individuals unfreeze their mind-sets, question their constructs and alter their behaviour patterns, it will be useful to look at mental blocks in a little more depth.

Mental blocks

'Mental blocks' are those features that inhibit the cognitive process, rather than preventing learning. Obviously some do both, especially those concerning the individual's motivation to learn. Blocks to the cognitive process limit the mind's ability to function to capacity, prevent it from interrogating the memory store fully, and do not allow it to record experiences properly.

Stress

Stress is a main block to effective cognitive functioning. A certain amount of stress is needed to stimulate the production of adrenalin, which in turn stimulates creative imagination and provides the drive for action. Too much stress, however, leads to panic or incites fight or flight reactions. Excess stress comes in the form of too much (quantity) or at too a high a level (quality). Both lead to overload, burn-out or physical and/or mental collapse. The diagram of the mental process given at the beginning of this chapter illustrates how the mind can function at a surface level. When subjected to excessive stress, the deeper levels are not properly accessed. As a consequence, previous experiences are not drawn upon, or they are remembered incorrectly or are distorted. This leads to the sort of error referred to by Reason (1990), and to poor decisions or action. Sometimes the inability to access the memory store and limited processing capacity can result in prevarication or inaction.

Preoccupation

This is another block. If an individual is having to deal with a major issue which is taking up a significant amount of brain space, it is difficult for attention to be paid to other matters. Even if these other matters may be relatively more important, it can be difficult to forget the issue preoccupying the mind. For example, if the board meeting which will consider your expansion plans is to be held on Friday, the one-day course on Thursday to improve your media skills cannot be expected to have much impact. It is likely that your mind will be preparing for the meeting, rather than processing the contents of the course.

Time pressure

In similar ways, time pressure limits the mind's ability to function to full capacity. While the proximity of a deadline, like execution, can focus the mind wonderfully, it can also force it into panic. Panic is different from the 'fight/ flight' reaction. The latter happens when the body prepares to defend itself from attack by producing adrenalin. This enables the muscles to make extra effort so that the individual can either run away from the danger or can stand and fight.

Blood is taken from the organs that do not need it so that those that do can have extra supplies. Thus an individual can experience an extraordinary clarity of thought and detailed memories of a threatening experience, or their mind can be a blank. Panic, however, clouds the thinking and muddles the cognitive process. Memories get juggled and the thought processes get confused.

Overload

Too much stimulus can lead to overload. This is evident during times of rapid change. While it may seem to be a wonderful opportunity for learning and growth, the amount of learning required and the radical nature of the new can mean that individuals are unable to cope. This does not necessarily reflect on their abilities to cope – it can be more to do with the unmanaged, uncontrolled nature of the changes affecting them and their organisation.

Example 4.4

The head of the local comprehensive school was completing a four-year part-time MBA course. Exams would be held before Christmas and a dissertation, requiring some research, would have to be finished by the following Easter.

During the third year of her studies her school had been given responsibility for managing its own budget as a result of national policy changes. The school governors and head were to become responsible for appointing staff for the first time. The head was thankful for her studies as she would have the chance to apply some of the theoretical learning. During the first year of the changes no staff had left, but two had indicated that they would probably leave the following year. Budget management had been difficult.

During the summer, the Department of Education announced that parents would be able to decide whether to opt out of local authority control. In practice this would require extensive consultations between groups of parents and governors. The staff would also need to be kept informed of what was happening, as the area was well-known for the strength of the grapevine.

The staff were also edgy as the local education authority had agreed to pilot the trials being held prior to the introduction of new examination and assessment methods. These changes would shift the emphasis to the assessment of skills rather than knowledge, and would require learning profiles to be constructed for every student in their final two years at school. This was expected to be very different from the traditional methods currently in use and would require all those involved to undertake a major rethinking of both teaching and assessment methods.

Because of skill shortages, the head had had to go back to teaching in her original subject, technology, two years previously. As the subject is affected by rapid progress, the taught syllabus changes virtually every year. The head expected that some major revisions would need to be incorporated into the teaching programme.

Was it any wonder she approached the start of the new school year with some trepidation? Another 'golden' learning opportunity?

Emotion

Emotion is another influence on the way stimuli are processed, sometimes leading to the choice of an appropriate response. Judgement can be impaired by the influence of unrelated factors such as mood or preference. The expression 'the heart ruling the head' is sometimes used to describe this influence. Sometimes, though, gut reactions can be as good as carefully thought-out solutions, especially when some of the other influencing factors come into play (such as time).

Intuition

Intuition is different from emotion. Intuition is a sense-experience, knowledge and judgement combined with feeling. It can be difficult to distinguish all the factors which contribute to knowing that one course of action is right and another wrong. Because of the difficulty in identifying these factors, intuition is discredited when compared to logic and rational approaches. This may be unfair. The inability to separate causal factors may simply be due to the fact that the brain is functioning at deeper, subconscious levels, rather than in the conscious.

Tiredness

The demands of modern organisational life take their toll of physical as well as mental well being. It has been shown that learning is inhibited if the mind cannot function fully. If the body is under undue pressure, is exhausted and run-down, it is likely that the brain will be too. The mind needs time for reflection and to enable reframing to take place, the body also needs time to rest or simply to do other things. One of the (false) assumptions often made about the current model of effective managers is their ability to continue without sleep, rest or relaxation. In some organisations even being ill is taken as a sign of weakness. Managers are put under pressure to work through colds and flu, by themselves as much as by others, and are expected to continue to be effective. It is not possible for someone to learn new skills effectively with a temperature of 102°.

Intelligence

Intelligence is generally seen as a single dimension – something you either have or do not have. The ability to think, the capacity to learn and the detail kept in the memory, commonly are used as measures of intelligence. In fact these three abilities should be seen as different dimensions which are separate cognitive processes. The processes also operate differently in different individuals.

Memory and the retention of detail is a skill that can be learnt. Many of the techniques that are taught to improve recall are designed to help the individual remember by association. However, being able to recall detail from the cognitive store depends, as do all the other cognitive processes, on the mind's ability to operate effectively. If the cognitive process is jammed, memory aids alone cannot unjam it.

Gender difference, learning style and recall all demonstrate how individuals function cognitively in various ways. It is more important to recognise, however, that there are difference *forms* of intelligence. Sternberg (1988) identifies seven different cognitive abilities:

1. *Verbal abilities* – the ability to use and understand speech, (including the use and understanding of metaphors and the defining features of words).

2. *Quantitative abilities* – computation such as adding, incrementing and interacting between numbers.

3. *Problem-solving* – the ability to represent problem and to identify solutions.

4. *Learning abilities* – to remember through repetition and rehearsal.

5. *Inductive reasoning* – the ability to perceive relationships between related items and concepts.

6. *Deductive reasoning* – the ability to draw conclusions from information provided about a problem.

7. *Spatial abilities* – forming and identifying visual representations.

Different forms of intelligence are needed to carry out the full range of tasks required in a modern complex society. Just because they are different does not mean than one form is intrinsically better than another, but society places greater value on some forms of intelligence than others. If this leads to the lesser-valued forms of intelligence being neglected or ignored when considering how people learn, there is a danger of discounting a number of necessary cognitive skills. The brain surgeon could not get from home to hospital to perform the life-saving operation without the efforts of the car mechanic and road builder.

Gender differences

As well as differences in forms of intelligence, there are some differences due to gender. The debate which has surrounded gender difference seems, for the time being, to have concluded that, in general, women are better than men at verbal ability tests, while men are more able mathematically and in the manipulation of spatial relationships. As most formal, organisational decision-making processes use mathematical methods, it would follow that this style of working suits more men than women. Alternatively, situations that require the use of verbal communications suit more women. (These, of course, are sweeping generalisations, as research has found that the differences *within* each sex are as great as those between the sexes.)

Learning styles

Some interesting work has been done on learning styles. Four styles of learning have been identified. The ways in which people learn can differ so significantly as to affect whether or not an individual is able to absorb a certain lesson. None of the styles is better — they are just different, but a person designing a learning event should appreciate that these differences are likely to be present in the target population.

The different forms of intelligence and the other factors that influence the cognitive processes are described here in a very simple form. Having some insight into how people's thinking patterns operate can help to guide the manager who wants to help others learn. Adult learning, by its very definition, requires a person to change something. This may mean doing the same job in a different way, or doing a different job. Both require that the current skills, knowledge or attitudes are questioned and, if need be, changed. For children, learning is part of the ageing process, but, as Piaget described, once a certain level of maturity is reached, the pace of learning slows down. In some cases, it can cease or go into reverse. To continue learning through adulthood requires consideration to be given to the factors that can impede questioning and attention given to the steps that can be taken to minimise any negative influences.

LEARNING TO LEARN

Learning is a skill, which some would argue is conditioned out of the child by the formal education process. The key to learning in adults is the ability to question. Children do it all the time, but a certain stage is reached when the maturing adult is expected to accept the world as representing reality. Acquiring or retaining the ability to challenge a version of reality and the assumptions it contains is not easy. The person asking awkward questions tends to make life difficult for those who do not know the answers. The questioner is a trouble-maker, a maverick, a rebel, and is treated as such. We use our construct system all the time to help to make sense of what would otherwise be a chaotic world. To do this, constructs must have some stability and reliability. Constantly challenging them would destabilise individuals to such an extent as to make them ineffective. There are situations, however when constructs need to be re-examined, if only to check that they remain valid and current.

Questioning assumptions

The ability to ask questions is not as simple as it might seem. Throughout formal education and initial training the learner is taught the right way, 'the way we do it here', and is encouraged to accept what is being shown. Questioning is rude, unnecessary, even insubordinate. However, there is seldom only one way of doing a job. Sometimes, because of economy or safety, there is a *best* way under particular circumstances, but this need not be the only way. When dealing with people, the chances of there being only one way to treat, manage or develop them is remote. But the result of the conditioning is to discourage the learner from asking awkward questions. When one has been told repeatedly that a certain fact or approach is true or the only way, it can be quite difficult to know that it need not be so and that challenging it is possible.

Example 4.5

Fred bought a holiday retreat in Picardy. It was a small cottage in a village in the midst of beautiful rolling limestone countryside. The cottage was in need of modernisation, particularly the sanitary facilities. The cottage had come complete with a 'thunderbox' at the bottom of the garden. The waste soaked directly into the earth. This, to Fred's twentieth century way of thinking, was barbaric, unhygienic and environmentally unfriendly.

Discussing his concerns with his neighbours, he was advised to have a cesspit dug by the owner of the local chateau. This, he was assured, would deal with the waste hygienically and efficiently. Bacteria would break down the effluent, leaving a harmless liquid that would naturally disperse. Right, thought Fred, and arranged with the local builder to draw up plans. It would only cost £2000 all in − a fifth of the price of the property.

Two months later, on his next visit, he mulled over his 'investment'. It seemed to be a lot of money for a loo. As he sipped his wine one evening, he mentioned his dilemma to the café owner and butcher. The latter, being somewhat direct in his manner, laughed and told the Englishman that the whole village thought him 'fou'.

Firstly, the cesspit pit would not work. Fred and his family did not spend long enough in the cottage to produce enough 'food' to keep the bacteria active.

Secondly, the present arrangement was perfectly hygienic. The limestone broke down the waste in a similar way to the bacteria in the proposed cesspit pit. In any case, the size of the local population was hardly big enough to pollute the countryside.

Thirdly, the owner of the chateau was well known as a know-all who knew nothing.

Poor Fred nearly spent £2000 unnecessarily because he had ascribed knowledge and authority without good cause and had no reason to question what had been said.

Similar false assumptions can be encountered as one moves from one organisation to another. Practices at first thought to be normal can subsequently appear bizarre in the light of later experience. Retaining and acquiring the ability to question can therefore be important.

Lewin (1968) studied group processes found in decision-making and the ways collective attitudes may be influenced. He found that if people are persuaded to express an attitude publicly that is different from their privately held views, they are more likely to change their private views in line with their public statement. This process is known as 'reducing cognitive dissonance'. Thus if an individual can be persuaded to comply with a group consensus, it is likely that the individual will later continue to behave in a consistent manner. Lewin identified three stages needed to change someone's attitudes:

1. Unfreezing – when the mind-sets are relaxed and constructs examined.

2. Changing – when new alternatives are explored and considered.

3. Refreezing – when the new attitudes or behaviour patterns are established.

To unfreeze deeply held views and relearn well-practised behaviour patterns, help and guidance may be required:

1. The existing views or patterns of behaviour need to be made explicit and overt. Often attitudes are routinised – they are believed because they always have been and behaviours are habits. Giving feedback and reflecting

an individual's expressions are ways of opening up the current practices to scrutiny.

2. Alternatives have to be considered to see if they are acceptable and can possibly be acted upon.

3. The new attitude or behaviour has to be learnt.

4. The learning has to be put into operation and practised and the surrounding factors that affect implementation must be made to be conducive so that inhibitors are reduced.

5. The desired reward needs to be attained, to avoid reversion to the original patterns or attitudes. (External pressure and the power of social groups can force the individual back into old ways, unless some guarding mechanism is established)

Questioning one's existing beliefs and behaviour patterns is an important part of any change or development programme, but building a vision of an alternative is essential. Without a view, even if initially it is vague, one would travel randomly. Once there is a sense of what is to be achieved, it is possible to analyse what has to be done to get there. Understanding one's own mind-sets and constructs is a critical first step to working out what action is most appropriate.

Example 4.6

For some people, giving up smoking is easy. For others it can be the hardest thing they have ever done. Not only is nicotine an addictive drug, but whole patterns of behaviour and social routines are built around the process of lighting and smoking a cigarette. One inhibitor for smokers that prevents them from kicking the habit successfully is an inability to 'see' themselves not smoking.

There are some techniques that can help in building a vision of an alternative. For example, the repertory grid technique, described earlier, was developed primarily to elict personal constructs, and can be used in a manual form or using one of several computer programmes. The work of Andrew and Valerie Stewart (1982) will be helpful for any one wishing to pursue this in more depth.

A more accessible technique for a manager is one that is loosely called 'reframing'. Whether in a mentor role as a line manager, or as a colleague, helping someone challenge and re-present their attitudes and patterns of behaviour can be an extremely beneficial way of helping them learn. It is not so easy to reframe one's own mind-set alone, but it is possible with concentrated mental effort. The technique works by asking questions like the following:

- 'What do you think about X', or, 'How do you do Y?'

- 'What made you think [or do] that in the first place?'

- 'How does thinking that [or doing that] affect your work now?'
  'Does it help, or does it get in the way?'
  'In what ways?'

- 'If there are any alternative ways of thinking or doing that, what are they?'

- 'Are any of these possible alternatives? If not, why not?'

- 'Which of the possible options do you prefer, and why?'

- 'What do you need to do to adopt one of the options?'

- 'Which is most feasible and why?'

- 'Which are you going to select, and what are you going to do to take up the favoured option?'

Example 4.7

In a large multi-professional organisation, it was normal practice for the training manager to sign the travel expense forms of staff attending business meetings of their professional bodies. The meetings were in no way connected to training or development. The staff's membership of committees and sub-groups enabled them to exercise their broader job responsibilities – influencing professional policies, enhancing the reputation of the organisation, developing contacts, etc. As the expenses were paid from the budget head set aside for travel and other business expenses, the training manager had no authority to challenge or refuse payment. Yet because the form had a box for the training manager's signature, the finance department refused to pay unless the document was duly signed. Attendance at such meetings was regular, and frequently involved around ten journeys per week. Simply reading and checking the forms consumed about an hour of the training manager's time. Sometimes sorting out discrepancies and inaccuracies could take a lot longer. Because it had always been done that way, it continued to be so done.

Challenging mind-sets by asking probing questions, unless done carefully, can be threatening to the individual. After all, the very roots of value systems are being disturbed, and assumptions are being made explicit. It is likely that some of the beliefs and behaviour patterns may seem to be illogical and even embarrassing to the person being scrutinised. In the example given above, the training manager may be reluctant to relinquish signing the forms as, even though there is no real authority vested in the procedure, there is some referred authority. Account also needs to be taken of the blocks mentioned above. In-depth questioning requires skilful execution, time and patience. Questioning of this nature cannot be rushed. Probing one's memory for the origins of some of the practices may require time and peace. A stressful examination, even if it is self-induced, is not conducive to unfreezing. More likely it will lead to paralysis as a result of frenzied over-analysis, resistance, or *post hoc* rationalisation to preserve the individual's self-esteem. Consequently the person helping in the reframing process should be aware of the need:

- to slow things down;

- to reduce the quantity of items being subjected to cognitive processing;

- to limit the complexity of the item by focusing and maintaining attention on the particular aspect of behaviour and attitude;

- to be prepared to deal with (and ideally discharge) the emotion that may be generated.

With care, this approach can bring about a major shift. A deeper understanding can be achieved by a process of examination, unfreezing, exploration of suitable alternatives and learning alternative ways of seeing or doing.

Since the questioning of attitudes is being discussed, it is fitting to ask *why* anyone should want to explore alternatives to what may be deeply held beliefs, or should want to consider changing patterns of behaviour that have been followed for the bulk of an individual's life. The answer is that the world in which we live is changing at an unprecedented rate. One aspect of this is the chaos being created in the environment. Another aspect is that the very technology designed to help the human race in some ways is mitigating against that aim. One can see why, twenty years ago, the explosion of information caused major data-handling problems. One solution was the development of computerised data bases to store and aid retrieval. Another use of computer technology has served to speed up the flow and quality of information. The consequence of these separate technological advances had been an even bigger explosion of information.

SUMMARY

It is known that unless learning is equal to or greater than the rate of change, the organism will become extinct. As with the speed of information transmission, the process of extinction, too, is getting faster. The changes in the skill requirements of a modern industrial society demonstrate this. The learning process cannot rely on evolution alone. As a consequence, both individual and organisational learning is a pre-requisite for survival. The alternative to this, if the learning cannot be speeded up, is that the rate of change must be slowed down. This requires some control over the environment and the organisation in context. This will be considered in the final chapter.

This chapter has explored how the individual learning process takes place and what can inhibit it. There is no definitive truth about how the mind works or how learning happens. Several theories have been drawn upon to illustrate how the process is thought to operate and to develop a simple model. In this model, the mind functions at several levels. For effective learning to take place, the cognitive process needs to be operating fully. Some of the blocks that prevent this effective operation have been discussed.

One of the most commonly experienced blocks found at work is that of stress. The pace and degree of organisational change put pressure on everyone in different ways. This includes the pressure to learn and develop skills. There is also an expectation that managers will deal effectively with a number of different things at once; the mind is flexible, but not infinitely so. There is a limit to the number of complex thoughts that can be processed at any one time. There is also a time requirement. Understanding and reflection need both brain space and time space. Sometimes the deadlines imposed do not take account of this need.

There is also a failure to take account of the different forms of intelligence. The use of centrally determined standards of educational achievement force assessment to be made according to easily administered systems and measures. These fail to take account of different styles of learning and different forms of intelligence. The full range of intelligence is needed by society to enable the whole range of tasks to be performed. However, some are ignored or devalued. Failure to take account of these when constructing developmental activities can inhibit the learning of others.

Ways of removing some of these blocks have been described. Most require managers to reflect on what it is they are trying to achieve and then to learn a number of ways of getting there. Fundamental to this are the skills of learning and asking questions. These two tend to be discouraged and so a key task for managers is their reacquisition and helping and helping others to relearn or retain them.

To counter unrealistic expectations, some changes are needed in organisational cultures and managers' behaviour. These, too, are areas in which skill development and learning can help. For if learning fails to occur and an unrealistic set of assumptions are left unchallenged, not only will the rate of change overtake the organisation's ability to respond and adapt, but all its managers and staff will be burnt out. How organisational learning can be achieved will be explored in the final chapter; the next chapter will examine some of the other blocks to individuals learning and what action can be taken by managers to minimise them.

5

Blocks to learning

INTRODUCTION

This chapter develops some of the ideas discussed previously. The cognitive process of learning has been outlined, and some of the factors preventing its effective operation discussed. This chapter moves on to look at the inhibitors that relate to individuals personally, and those outside the direct control of the individuals concerned.

Those inhibitors which pertain to individuals are different to cognitive blocks. Individuals may not be aware that their mental processes are not being as effective as they might be. Some of the blocks, especially those caused by excessive stress, may be accompanied by a belief that everything is working as well as it might in the prevailing circumstances. This is tantamount to self-delusion. The individual may be aware of some of the other blocks to be discussed. Motivation and levels of commitment are examples.

Influences external to the individual concern working conditions, both physical and atmospheric, and the behaviour of others. Factors in the wider environment may also have an impact on the learning abilities of an individual or group. These can have a direct impact on the opportunities available for learning and the ways in which the learning acquired may or may not be transferred to work. For example, the way in which the computer software producers frequently modify or replace programs in an effort to maintain market edge hardly encourages people to learn how to use a particular product thoroughly.

INTERNAL BLOCKS

Motivation

Handy (1985), in attempting to define motivation, says: 'We use the word ambiguously. Does this mean we are unsure of what we really mean by it?' He goes on to argue that if the process of motivation were better understood, it would be easier to understand what motivates others. Motivation is peculiar to the individual in a particular situation at a given time. It is the force that drives someone to act or not to act, to apply effort or withhold it, to seek a specified outcome or eschew it. Consequently, what motivates one person to do something or not to do it is different from what motivates the next.

The driving factors that influence an individual's willingness to learn are central. Video Art's *You'll soon get the hang of it* comments on behaviours such as: 'He's trying to win'; 'She keeps coming back'; 'It looks as if she is enjoying it'; 'Oh dear, he's given up'; 'Perhaps he didn't think he was getting anywhere'.

Much attention is given to the potency of money as a motivator, but it isn't the only one. Although Hertzberg's ideas (1966) have been criticised by other academics and may look outmoded in our cash-driven society, many of his findings remain valid. An easy test to find out is to ask colleagues what encourages them to do more and what causes them dissatisfaction at work. The chances are that their replies will not be too dissimilar to the findings obtained by Hertzberg:

Motivators

- The work itself.
- Responsibility.
- Advancement.
- Growth.
- Achievement.
- Recognition.

Hygiene factors

Unless the individual perceives them as being satisfactory, these factors serve only to demotivate:

- Quality of interpersonal relations among peers, with supervisors, with reports.
- Job security.
- Working conditions.
- Salary.

Sources of motivation

Accepting that there are grounds for criticism and that flaws existed in Hertzberg's methods, some pointers to motivation can be found. For example, being engaged in challenging tasks that require new ways of working to be learnt and applied directly, provides the learner with real reasons for making the effort to learn. On the other hand, a person who is expected to engage in a protracted period of development because it *might* be good for their career, can hardly be expected to be brimming over with enthusiasm.

One critical question that must be satisfactorily answered, for an individual to be motivated to learn is: 'What's in it for me?' This is not a selfish question. Rather, it is the individual's search for reasons why energy, effort, enthusiasm and expectation should be committed in one direction rather than another.

Work itself, as one of the main sources of motivation, can become even more important as a vehicle for development. Development just for the sake of it is not an end in itself. Growth without a purpose is the ideology of the cancer cell. Individuals have aspirations for their careers, a wish for more interesting work, a desire to perform better, to get the job done easier in less time, and so forth. The organisation's motivation for investing in the development of its staff is to obtain increased productivity, effectiveness and improvements to working practices, and the job must get done. The way in which that job is defined makes the differences between a job that is boring and unchallenging, and one which provides satisfaction and the opportunities for improvement.

The work of Hackman and Oldham (1975) complements that of Hertzberg and shows that a 'satisfying' job comprises areas of work that provide for:

- Skill variety (being able to use a range of talents).

- Task identity (being able to be have some ownership in the task).

- Task significance (knowing the task has some meaningful purpose).

- Autonomy (being responsible for one's own work).

- Feedback (gaining information regarding the outcome of the work).

The sense of achievement and the need for recognition encompassed in the above 'satisfiers' are very similar to those identified by Hertzberg and are common sources of motivation. Quality supervision is essential for jobs to meet Hackman and Oldham's conditions of being well-designed. The quality of the relationship with the supervisor is given by Hertzberg as a main reason for demotivation.

The main criticism levelled against Hertzberg is that his work has not been updated to take account of the changes in the world of work, and he assumes that everyone is driven by the same motivation. The decline in job security and the increased emphasis given to money as a motivator have altered people's perceptions of their jobs. There has always been a hidden agenda behind individuals' drive to develop their skills or expend additional effort. The thoughts, 'Will I get more money; will I be promoted; will it help my career; if

I learn x?', have always been present. Ask a typical group of managers studying for an MBA, and many will say that these considerations had an impact on their decisions to commit themselves to three years' part-time study. But there will be others who have different motives, for example, interest, the desire to do a better job, a sense of being able to achieve more, or a feeling of being under-stretched. There are certainly those who are driven by desire for money and career enhancement, but there are also others, who are driven by different factors. It is wrong to focus on one group to the exclusion of others. The danger of doing so is that the demotivators will be addressed, while the motivating factors are ignored. Hertzberg claimed that hygiene factors, if they are right, are accepted as normal and so cease to affect levels of performance and satisfaction. It is only the motivators that continue to spur individuals on to do more and take new risks.

Unmotivated learner

There are those who cannot see what is in it for them. They do not share the belief in the value of making the necessary investment in learning. Any investment contains elements of risk, and to some people the risk factor is too high. These people cannot see the potential pay-off available as a result of investing effort in learning and development. They cannot see the point and are not swayed by argument. They are simply not motivated, and until the right reason for them is given, or the point is made in a way that makes sense to them, they will be content to stay with the status quo.

Commitment

Motivation is the drive that gets the learners going; commitment keeps them at it. So often, it is easy to take the first steps, but maintaining the momentum takes something more. This is where the support and encouragement of others matter.

Exercise 5.1

Sally decided to apply for an Open University post-experience course. One reason for doing so was the outcome of her recent appraisal. Her manager had told Sally that she had high potential but needed to develop her theoretical understanding if she was to make further progress. However, things were not good for the organisation – trading had been very bad during the previous 12 months and the outlook was bleak. The general feeling among the staff was that they were lucky not be facing redundancy.

A correspondence course starting in January seemed to be the answer. It would not take time out of work and would allow Sally to pace herself in line with other job and home demands. Fortunately a suitable programme was available and Sally's manager agreed to pay the course fees. All looked fine until pressures mounted around 10 December.

Sally's partner's parents were due to stay for the Christmas holiday. Shopping had still to be done. The spare bedroom had acted all year as Sally's study. This needed to be cleared and cleaned before the holiday guests arrived. Work was hectic and an assignment was due on 15 December.

Sally's commitment was tested to its full. In the circumstances it would have been easy to give in. After all what would happen? Nothing, in the short term; in fact life would be a lot easier. It would be Sally's longer-term development that would suffer, and her career would develop less than it would have if she had withstood the crisis. The support of the manager and her partner in these sorts of cases is critical. The manager especially, as an instigator and in the managerial role, has a responsibility for helping with work allocation and sustaining her through the difficult patch.

Situations such as these should not be regarded as the learner's problem alone. Firstly it is not necessarily a problem; rather, it is another learning opportunity. Secondly, learning, even outside the direct working environment, if it is connected to the job, is a work task. Thirdly, work tasks are the responsibility of the individual, but their manager's key responsibility is to help them carry out those tasks effectively. Anyone facing difficulties requires and deserves the help and support of the manager. They do not deserve the blame that goes along with 'It's your problem.'

Managers who are really committed to learning and development are not those who cannot be bothered or who are disinterested. They are prepared to put in and maintain the effort needed for learning. It is a tiring, difficult process especially for the learner. It takes their effort and energy. Time and space are not available for other activities. Thinking is hard work. Learners are people who can see into the future – not clairvoyant, but people with a vision and a feel for what is going on and how that will impact on their own and their organisation's future. They are able to see the wider purpose of doing something and are able and willing to make the effort needed to follow through on longer-term decisions. Complacency on the part of the manager and/or learner is the enemy of commitment.

Resistance

Resistance is a positive form of complacency. The latter is a state of contentment and satisfaction – it does not demand thought, beyond checking that the comfort level is adequate. Resistance takes energy, as it is deliberate opposition. The manager who resists change can do so openly or covertly. Open resistance – refusal to agree or to alter ways – is ultimately a question of discipline. Covert resistance is more difficult to deal with.

Covert resistance can itself take two forms. The term 'dumb insolence' used to be used to describe the person who said nothing but made it quite plain that the course of action chosen was not to their liking. The other form of covert resistance is sabotage. The individual may publicly agree with the changes proposed while privately taking steps to undermine the plans. Unless an actual deliberate act of sabotage is discovered, this type of individual can be very difficult to deal with. Trainers know them all too well. They are the people who are *sent* on courses. They spend their time not disagreeing with the learning points, but questioning the point's relevance to their situation. They introduce red herrings or argue on behalf of other people.

Resistant workers are those who do not want to change. They are happy as they are and believe that the current systems work well enough. They may not say so, complaining along with the rest of the workforce. However, the current system may bring them their rewards and so it would be against their best interests if new approaches were introduced.

> It should be borne in mind that there is nothing more difficult to arrange, more doubtful of success, and more dangerous to carry through than initiating changes in a state's constitution. The innovator makes enemies of all those who prospered under the old order, and only lukewarm support is forthcoming from those who would prosper under the new. Their support is lukewarm partly from fear of their adversaries, who have the existing laws on their side, and partly because men are generally incredulous, never really trusting new things unless they have tested them by experience. In consequence, whenever those who oppose the changes can do so, they attack vigorously, and the defence made by the others is only lukewarm.
>
> Machiavelli's *The Prince*

Resisters also include those people who do not want to know. They close their minds for a number of reasons. One common reason, not often expressed, concerns the (rightful) fear of the unknown. This fear can be greater than the dangers contained in the actual change. The vacuum created by the lack of knowledge can give the person's imagination scope to run riot.

Another reason for resistance is the fear of hard work. This should not be taken to imply that the individual is lazy. Learning requires mental energy and concentration. It is well known in educational circles that the normal span of concentration is around 20 minutes. Hence typical lesson lengths are 30–40 minutes. This allows time to settle down, do other things and close at the end of the lesson. This figure is, however, for practised learners. Mintzberg (1973) says that, on average, chief executives of large organisations engage in 22 activities per day. The majority of these last for less than 11 minutes. As a consequence, senior managers are not used to concentrating, so learning new ideas or development skills may first require that the skills of concentration need to be relearnt. The thought of learning may present the learner with a situation which contains a lot of risks, unknowns, and the possibility of hard mental effort. It is no surprise that short-cuts or ways of avoiding the task are found by those who are not highly motivated by the learning in the first place.

Sometimes resistance is based on rational rather than affective reasons. It may be that the individual has thought carefully about the changes and has come to a conclusion based on experience and knowledge. That conclusion may be founded on sound logical arguments which have led the individual to believe that the course of action being proposed is flawed or wrong. Simply dismissing these people as Luddites is dangerous. Their thought processes may have led them to consider aspects of the proposal that the enthusiasts have overlooked or ignored. As part of the development of the system of personal constructs, an individual looks for confirming evidence of perceptions and dismisses disproving evidence. Listening to the doubters is a way of ensuring that both the pros and cons of a proposal are given full consideration.

One must distinguish between those with genuine grounds for resistance, and those who like to find fault with everything, simply because it is new. The true Luddites wish to conserve their past ways and are opposed to change, without regard to any merits the change may offer. It is rare to hear it said openly, but the reason for resistance is often found to be: 'I don't like it.'

Attitude

Luddites do not just resist change. Their attitudes are constructed in such a way that gives them a conservative mind-set. Their experiences have shown them that most changes are for change's sake and that the old ways on the whole are the best. These methods are tried and tested. There is no good reason, so they believe, why they should not continue to work well in the future. Moreover, these new-fangled ideas are unknown. There is no guarantee that they will work. Just the opposite is likely; they could make matters worse. Things have been allowed to get slack. What is really needed is a return to the well-known ways.

This pattern of thinking can be very difficult to challenge. As shown by the quote from Machiavelli, such doubters need examples – not trials, but fully working demonstrations. Sadly, it is common for any new idea to have teething problems during the early stages of implementation as those involved learn how the systems, methods and procedures work. Time, practice and experience are needed to get over early difficulties and progress up the learning curve, but these initial problems confirm the Luddites' predictions of matters being made worse.

Open opposition and closed minds are easier to confront than those who do not express their views. They may keep their opinions private and appear to go along with proposals, but their resistance creates barriers to learning. Their opposition may be subconscious, based on constructs, attitudes and concerns that the individual is unable to articulate. They may not even be aware of their own opposition, as they just feel uneasy about what is happening. They will approach the new idea or task with trepidation and be very cautious about engaging in activities. If they do start they may be very easily discouraged by early difficulties and will be quick to find reasons why they should give up.

Exercise 5.2

Irandhir was very enthusiastic about the installation of the electronic mail system. She agreed that it would solve many of the internal communication problems. All internal memos would be abolished, and the over-pressed typing staff would be able to concentrate on improving the quality of the external mail. The distribution system, which had never worked well, would be simplified and used only when it was essential for documents to be exchanged between staff.

No one could doubt Irandhir's commitment, until the hardware was due to be installed and all managers were expected to attend a two-day training session. Irandhir had not understood that she would have to learn how to use the mail package (albeit a user-friendly one) and a word processor, as she would have to type in her own messages.

She arrived with her colleagues at the training centre on the first morning, but during the coffee break she made an 'urgent' telephone call to her secretary. On her return she told the trainer that a crisis had occurred and she was obliged to return to her office.

Ability

Mental ability can prove to be a block. Everyone has a limit to their mental competence, as well as having different forms of intellect. Some research has been conducted by Brunel University to ascertain levels of mental competency. Based on the work of Elliott Jacques, the researchers argue that individuals' intellectual abilities are delineated by the time span over which they are able to operate and the amount of discretion they are able to exercise over a task. Thus those who can only perform effectively on comparatively quick tasks with tight supervision, they claim, do not have as great an intellectual capacity as those who are able to perform effectively on tasks that last a long time without supervision.

An alternative view is offered by Sternberg, whose work was referenced earlier. He suggests that there are different forms of intelligence, employing different mental abilities. For example, spatial abilities are different from numeracy, and different again from deductive reasoning. Sometimes the reason why people fail to understand or to learn is that the message has been framed in the wrong way for their mind-set. This has nothing to do with an assessment of levels of mental ability and is more to do with the fact that people understand in different ways. The failure of communication may be due to the transmitter's inability to send a clear message. If communication is to be effective, it needs to be transmitted in terms the receiver can understand, rather than in the way the sender wants to send it.

In Example 5.2, the manager responsible for making the proposal to install electronic mail may have believed that everyone realised that they would have to use a keyboard and input their own message. He would not have known that Irandhir had been taught to play the piano by a teacher who rapped her fingers with a ruler every time she made a mistake, and that since then Irandhir had had a horror of any form of keyboard. This has nothing to do with her level of intelligence, nor its form. Her attitudes have been formed by her experience. She may not be conscious of her horror or its cause; nevertheless, it serves to disable her learning.

To expect someone whose ability to understand drawings is undeveloped to be able to follow a flow diagram of a new system is unfair. Similarly, not everyone is equally able to perform complex calculations or prepare detailed balance sheets. If they could, there would be no need for accountants.

LEARNING STYLE

Kolb's learning cycle (1974) underpins much current thinking about adult learning and the development of skills. It also provides a working guide for the construction of learning activities. The cycle consists of four parts (Fig. 5.1). The cycle demonstrates how a learner must pass through each stage to ensure that the learning is thoroughly acquired. Honey and Mumford (1982) have developed on the cycle and also Anglicised it. They have developed the idea to show how individuals can make the best use of their learning strengths, and how to minimise weaknesses. While everyone has their own preferred mode of learning, the aim is to become a balanced all-rounder; until that is achieved, however, strengths and weaknesses can get in the way of effective learning.

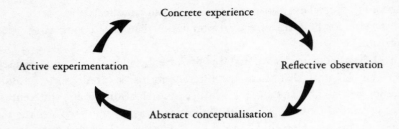

Figure 5.1 Kolb's learning cycle

Similarly, managers can inhibit the learning of others by playing to their own strengths only.

- An *activist* will not find it easy to concentrate on the article being circulated in readiness for discussion at the next staff meeting.

- A *reflector* would prefer to gather information from external sources and produce a report on the findings, rather than make exploratory visits.

- A *theorist* would prefer to debate principles, rather than share experiences with colleagues.

- An *experimenter*, however, will find it easier than a reflector to try out different scenarios before interviewing a difficult member of staff.

LEARNING ABILITIES

Learning requires practice. As with concentration, learning also requires skill and hard work. If they are not used, the skills becomes rusty and eventually lost. The Open University produces a 'Preparing to Study' guide for adults returning to study. This and similar texts are concerned mainly with the skills needed for academic learning, but they can also have some value for managers who want to freshen up their learning abilities. Reference to such a text, using information sources and libraries, can open up a totally new world of ideas. There are also, for instance, techniques that help to speed up reading.

Note-taking, if done in a purposeful fashion, can help memory and speed up the assimilation of ideas. Learning to write in a way that is both concise and precise is another useful skill. The Plain English Campaign has produced some useful guides and training materials to help managers simplify their messages so that communication and understanding by others is eased.

A technique which helps to structure thoughts and concepts is that of mind

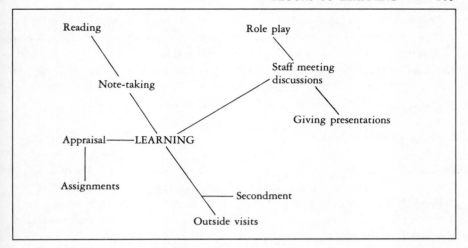

Figure 5.2 Mind mapping

mapping. Developed by Buzan (1973), it provides a way of linking ideas and showing the relationship between concepts (see Fig. 5.2).

DEALING WITH BLOCKS

Self-confidence

Lack of self-confidence and, more importantly, a low sense of personal efficacy are major blocks for adult learners. Unlike children, adults have a great deal to lose when engaging in learning new ways or ideas. Existing skills will have been acquired, practised and refined over many years. A certain level of competence will have been achieved, and the individual will derive a sense of achievement and satisfaction by using those skills. Learning means going back to the beginning. The level of competence returns to that of a novice and the result, initially, is more mistakes than successes. The learner feels a fool, and probably looks one at first.

Fear of failure is often high. Questions like 'What will happen if I can't?', 'What will happen if I fail?' flood through the learner's mind. Sometimes, too, the question, 'What happens if I achieve?' can also be a block. If the learner has no visions of what it would be like, for example, to conduct a staff meeting in a totally different way, their ability to learn alternatives can be inhibited.

Sometimes the learner is unable to express these blocks. Fears tend to be deep-seated and it may be difficult for the learner to articulate what it is that is obstructing them. This is when a patient sponsoring manager, prepared to give time, can help the learner identify the block(s) and bring into the open any fears that may be inhibiting learning. Asking questions such as, 'What will happen if . . .?', 'What will the consequences be if you do or don't do . . .?' will help the fears to be addressed and then hopefully laid to rest.

Disengagement

This block is difficult to identify and can be very difficult to deal with. Individuals do not recognise the need for learning. They are blind to the changes that are occurring around them and, lemming-like, continue in exactly the same way as before. They will resist proposals, not on the ground of opposition to the ideas, but because they are against change itself. They believe that change for change's sake is a drug to which some managers are addicted. Their resistance makes them deaf to argument, and the depth of their belief enables them to withstand forces such as peer group pressure.

Their resistance to change stems from their failure to identify with the organisation, its goals and their work-group. They also have no sense of the changes taking place in the world around them. Resistance of this nature can be a result of tram-line thinking which has become so deeply entrenched that the individual concerned does not even realise that they are in a tram-line. In some cases, the individual may have been taught not to think or question, for instance in organisations where the way to progress is to 'keep your head down', 'do the job as it has always been done' and 'don't rock the boat'. This is not the approach of a learning organisation. Anyone challenging the status quo is more likely to be punished than rewarded for doing do. To help an individual who is trained in this ethos to change their thinking patterns and their total acceptance of current practices is, in itself, a developmental task.

Some people are unable to loosen up their thinking, or else they do not want to. In some cases, ignorance can be bliss. The refusal to learn, and total resistance to change, however, need not result in catastrophe immediately. Some organisations have been able to live on for a considerable period, carried forward by momentum. But eventually they collapse. The same can be true of individuals. Some are able to carry on, beavering away in their own manner, and it is possible that they will be left to do so by their organisations. This may be a deliberate choice made by a manager who has decided that the 'cost' of trying to change the particular individual is too great. Alternatively, the manager may have avoided the issue. Some individuals are not allowed to continue in their blissful ignorance. If theirs is an area of work which is critical to organisational achievement, it may not be desirable to leave them. Their inability to learn then becomes a different issue that requires another managerial response.

OTHER PEOPLE

Other people can erect blocks that inhibit an individual's learning; sometimes deliberately and sometimes inadvertently. The interactions between the individuals in a work group are extremely complex. Some features of group life are known only to a group's members and are carefully kept away from outsiders (especially the manager). Other features are only apparent outsiders. Detailing all these features is beyond the scope of this book, except insofar as they can affect the learning of the group and its individual members. Anyone wishing to explore group dynamics in more detail is referred to Handy (1985).

Groupthink

One of the most important phenomena of group behaviour was identified by Janis (1972). During the early 1960s, President Kennedy assembled a group to advise him on the Cuban missile crisis which was then developing between Russia and the USA. Disaster in the Bay of Pigs was only just averted. In studying the fiasco, Janis identified five features common to this and other critical situations. These concerned the way in which groups develop a

> mode of thinking that people engage in when they are deeply involved in a cohesive in-group, when the members' strivings for unanimity override their motivation to realistically appraise alternative courses of action.

In other words, the existence and well-being of the group becomes more important than the purpose of the group. The features of what Janis termed 'Groupthink' are set out below.

Antecedent conditions needed for Groupthink

- High cohesiveness of the group members.

- Insulation of the group from other people.

- Lack of methodical procedures for search and appraisal – the judgement and expertise of group members is considered sufficient and superior.

- Directive leadership – decisions are made to suit the leader's (perceived) wishes, rather than on sound, reasoned arguments.

- The group operates under conditions of high stress, with little hope of finding a better solution than the one favoured by the leader or other influential people.

Symptoms of Groupthink

- An illusion of invulnerability – very optimistic and able to take extraordinary risks because no one voices dissent.

- Collective rationalization – contrary evidence is easily explained away.

- Belief in inherent morality of the group – there is no possibility of the group's decisions being considered unethical.

- Stereotypes of out-groups – the group believes that if others do not agree, they are enemies.

- Direct pressure on dissenters – the group acts collectively to subdue rebels.

- Self-censorship – doubts or dissatisfactions are not expressed to outsiders.

- Illusion of unanimity – cabinet responsibility is tightly enforced.

- Self-appointed mind-guards – the 'rightness' of the group is enforced by collective agreement.

Symptoms of defective decision-making

- Incomplete survey of options – alternative options are rarely considered.

- Incomplete survey of objectives – they are neither fully nor clearly specified.

- Failure to examine risks of preferred choice – the consequences of the chosen course of action are not worked through fully, if at all.

- Poor information search – because the decision is 'right', there is no real need to check the information base.

- Selective bias in processing obtained information – even if checks are made, any contradictory evidence is discounted.

- Failure to reappraise alternatives – during implementation there is little, if any, consideration of other options as a means of validating the chosen course of action.

- Failure to work out contingency plans – there is no need, as the possibility of failure is unthinkable.

Janis identified Groupthink in high-powered political decision-making groups, but similar features can be found in any group that establishes a strong identity for itself. Another term used to describe such groups is a clique. Cliques are 'fat and happy', self-satisfied with their own state of being and resistant to any questioning about their operation, constitution or membership. Such groups oppose change, whether it is initiated by members or outsiders, unless it is clear that the proposed change proves no threat to the group's culture. Action is taken to insulate the group from outsiders, or they are ignored, unless they have more power than the group. Insiders are subjected to a range of group forces to ensure conformity. If they do not conform, they risk being ejected.

The Hawthorne studies

The Hawthorne studies are a classical account of the effect of group pressure. The studies were conducted at the Western Electric Company of Chicago during the 1920s. During their investigations the researchers found some very clear patterns of group behaviour that still hold good today. The studies' overriding conclusions were that membership of a group is important to many people, and that the norms and objectives of the group are influential in setting the norms and objectives for its individual members.

Two separate groups were observed. From the first group, it was found that productivity increased and was maintained as a result of the attention being paid to the group by the observers. Group members were able to establish good working relationships between themselves and their supervisor, as they had freedom to establish their own pace and to divide the work among themselves. The level of social contact made work more pleasant.

The second group produced different findings. This group established norms for rates of production which were regarded as fair and proper. Anyone going above or below the set rate was either a 'rate-buster' or a 'chiseller'. Both were seen as deviants and were subjected to rebuke, mockery or social pressure to conform. If deviants did not get back into line, the end result was likely to be ostracism. The group norms were given more importance than company norms, in order to protect the group. The group norm was to provide individuals with a variety of work and to build up slack resources to balance for days when production was down. Acceptable patterns of behaviour were set for the supervisors by the group. They were not to act officiously or take advantage of their positions – if they did so, the group combined against the supervisor by playing tricks, exerting pressure on and excluding the individual from social interactions. The differences between the two groups may have been due to the fact that the first group comprised all women and the second all men. Regardless the findings from both illustrate how group pressure on individuals is exercised to ensure conformity and prevent changes being imposed on group practices.

Learning, in the environment established by the second group, would be contrary to the established and accepted norms and would be treated as deviant behaviour. Any individual trying to develop new skills, even with organisational approval, would be excluded or subjected to social pressure. Pressure of this sort took the form of ridicule, or even damage to work, to make the deviant abandon new, threatening ideas. Even if the person trying to effect change had the authority to do so (eg the supervisor), the reaction could still be the same. Action would be taken to prevent the changes from taking place and to preserve the status quo. The concept of dynamic conservation is useful to help understand how a group or even a whole organisation can actively strive to stay the same.

Group culture

There are other aspects of group behaviour that affect individual learning. These are the elements of a particular group's culture. First described by Roger Harrison and further developed by Handy (1985), organisational culture is a very rich concept. The term's popularisation, sadly, has diminished its richness and, as a result, the idea of culture change is made to seem easy. This is not so, for the culture of a group contains features that are embedded firmly into that group's way of being and thinking. These features are not easy to alter and it may take years for the effect of learning and action to be seen.

A group's culture develops over time and is a product of its history. The initial purpose of the group – its reason for being – combines with the aspirations of the founding members. These set down the foundations of the group's uniqueness. During the group's formative stages, collective norms are established and accepted by group members. If the norms are not accepted, they are either changed or the dissident(s) leave the group. From these norms, standards are developed to which, it is assumed, existing members and new members will adhere. The standards and assumptions underpin the behaviour patterns that become 'the way we do things here'. Group pressure, as in the Hawthorne studies, is used to ensure conformity.

The culture, thus, is a product of a group's history. It is also a product of its technology. Woodward (1965) carried out some interesting work into the structures and operations of companies in different sectors. She showed that the effectiveness of an organisation depends on its ability to devise a structure that is right for its technology. In some cases this means having an organisational form that is able to maintain some consistency; in others, structures and means of production need to be adaptable. In both types of organisation the ability to learn is important for continued survival. Making enquiries into alternative approaches, (failure to do so is one of the dangers of Groupthink) is a means

BLOCKS TO LEARNING • 111

of checking that poor decisions are not being made. Monitoring the organisation in its environment, assessing the effectiveness of the group, and checking operating practices, are ways of mitigating against imagined invulnerability. In some cases these checking processes are simply termed 'market research' and could be customer/staff surveys, or comparisons with others in similar areas of business. Checking ensures that existing systems retain their effectiveness. But, unless the group's culture sees learning, including the challenging, confronting and questioning that is inherent to it, as a normal feature of organisational life, checking will not happen.

Size, too, is a determinant of culture. Small groups begin to divide into sub-groups when the initial group increases beyond eight people. The dynamics of groups alter as they increase in size. The tendency for this becomes marked when an organisation has more than 200 staff. One main change can be found in the richness and complexity of the culture.

Example 5.3

A new manager was brought in to make some radical changes to an administrative team. This was no criticism of the abilities of the team members, but the systems they were using were generally regarded as being out of date. They had been efficient in the past and had done the job needed to provide the control mechanisms required at the time. However, the organisation was moving to a devolved management structure and now required systems that enabled local decision-making by managers, rather than them absolving them from responsibility.

The staff gave the new manager every hope of success. They appeared to be willing and keen to introduce change. They complained about the amount of hassle the existing systems had caused, its rigidity had provided line managers ample ground for complaint. However, as each part of the system was examined, the manager was told by staff how vital it was, or that another part of the system depended on the first part, or that the particular operation was required by an external organisation, or that it was the best and only way that a particular job could be done.

As time passed only limited changes were being made, and this gave rise to more criticism. It was decided that the staff were not knowledgeable enough so, as the opportunities arose, better qualified staff were recruited. The manager found, however, that despite their enthusiasm, professionalism and early levels of confidence, the new ideas they brought very quickly were forgotten as they were inculcated into the established patterns.

The manager tried to identify the 'mind-guards', those who set the agenda and limited the group's choice, but found that a social leader could not be easily spotted. It seemed that the authority in the group moved around and sometimes was even lodged with one of the new staff.

It almost seemed that the ways of being and doing were deeply rooted in the fabric of both the people and the systems. One possible way to achieve the radical degree of change needed was to discard all the manual systems and introduce a computer-based application. Another was to move a significant number of staff and bring in yet more new recruits. A third was to devolve the administrative system totally and retain only the essential parts in the centre.

What should the manager's response have been to this high degree of resistance to learning?

THE MANAGER

The behaviour of the manager can create blocks to learning very effectively. The Hawthorne studies, the work of Hertzberg and the phenomenon of Groupthink all demonstrate the key role played by the person with the influence in the group, be it the manager, supervisor or leader.

Relationship

It is not only the manager's role in the group that can contribute to or damage learning; the relationship between individuals and the manager's personal style are also important. The Hawthorne studies demonstrated that if the manager misused the authority vested in the role, the relationship with the group became unproductive. The relationships between the manager and individuals can enhance or damage those individuals' motivation and commitment to development.

Much has been made recently of the line manager acting as a mentor. This suggests a special relationship with one or two individuals – for one person cannot effectively mentor many. Accepted wisdom in some quarters is that a manager should be required to appraise no more than eight staff. Yet most managers have responsibility for more staff. A key managerial skill is the ability to treat all staff equitably as individuals in their own right. It simply would not be possible (nor even desirable) to act as mentor for all staff. To ensure that all staff receive equity of treatment and attention, the manager needs the ability to judge the needs of individuals and develop response appropriate to them, the situation and the manager's own preferred style.

The relationship needed to foster learning is no different to that required for effective working. Built on a basis of trust and mutual respect, the working relationship should be positive for the individuals and the employing organisation. Without these conditions, neither party will be disposed to take the risks which are part of learning and development. An individual is unlikely to invest in learning without the support and encouragement of the immediate manager, unless it is a case of 'in spite of rather than because of'. A manager will probably be reluctant to expose what could be seen as weaknesses to a recalcitrant report by admitting to personal development needs. Nor will the manager be likely to be open to feedback from someone who is thought to be unfairly critical. Effective learning needs partnership.

The work of Honey and Mumford (1992) describes how a manager's learning style, if it is unbalanced, can switch off the learner. An over-enthusiastic activist will not be very helpful to someone whose dominant style is that of a reflector. Likewise, the manager who adopts the tell-and-sell approach to decision-making will be unlikely to delegate a new project to an assistant.

Situation

There is another dimension to be considered – the situation of the individual, manager or work group. This plays a part in helping or inhibiting the learning of any of the parties. The theories of leadership that emphasise the interrelationship of the task and group also take account of the situation. If the individual is new to a task or a situation, there is a greater need for close supervision and direction. A worker who is confident and competent will require less attention. Similarly, in a learning situation, a learner who is skilled in learning will be more able to cope with the uncertainties presented by the opportunities than someone exposed to the experience for the first time.

A work group that is used to making changes in a positive way will be able to learn almost as a matter of course. The members will be familiar with the process, if not the content. But a group that has been used to stable conditions and sees the future in negative terms will need more careful treatment. This need not be directive supervision, but attention should be given to the 'condition' of the individuals so that support will be ready if anyone requires assistance.

A manager who has to manage this sort of process will also require support and the opportunity to reflect on the experiences. Without it, the manager could easily feel cast adrift in the situation and unable to make the most of the learning opportunity.

Organisation

The organisation's culture can dominate any preferences in style of individuals or managers. It is the organisation that creates the situations in which individuals learn or do not learn. The culture either fosters learning (there will be a lot more said about this notion later), or it can actively discourage it. Even if an organisation claims to be committed to the development of its staff, embracing change in a positive way, its actual behaviour can be just the opposite. Many organisations are rightfully criticised for being heavy on rhetoric and light on action.

The company brochures may talk of its commitment to the delegation of responsibility to the lowest feasible level of decision-making. The managing director may be active in the local Training and Enterprise Council and heard to speak publicly about the importance of equality of opportunity. But what is the reality of the staff's experience?

The McKinsey Organisation '7S' analysis is used in Example 5.4 as a vehicle to look at one instance of organisational reality in comparison to organisational records.

Example 5.4

Structures The number of management levels denies first ine managers decision-making opportunities. The degree of centralisation removes responsibilities from line managers, allowing them to divert challenging or difficult tasks to central staff.

Style The predominant managerial style is *laissez-faire*, which in practice means that training and development activities are *ad hoc* and resources are allocated in unfocused response to individual requests. The application of learning is more accidental than planned. The organisation is in the communications business, yet internally relies on the 'grapevine' to keep staff informed.

Shared Values The organisation's stated policy is to promote and reward on the basis of achievement. The reality is that those who drink after work with the MD are the ones to get the plum jobs. The organisation says that it puts customers first, but it is not unusual for staff to be called off the customer care training course by their managers, to attend to more urgent matters.

Systems The systems are old-fashioned and laborious. They are self-perpetuating, having in-built opportunities for errors and requiring duplicate records to be maintained. They do not provide the information needed for managerial decision-making, thus requiring the creation of supplementary systems.

Staff The social leaders in the organisation do not subscribe to its goals. They are prepared to be time servers but not to change, thereby laying dead hands on the aspirations of more committed staff.

Strategy The written strategy consists of generalised statements of intent. No resource implications or contingency plans have been considered.

Skills The computer staff's skills are out of date for more modern equipment. Updating them would require intensive training. The strategy proposes to take the organisation into applications which will require skills which are not available among the existing workforce.

An organisation with a culture similar to that given above is not likely to encourage individual members of staff. One could not expect them to be motivated to learn or to develop their skills. The culture does not welcome questioning or challenging of existing modes. Many organisations transmit this sort of message, without intending to. The practices of influential people, policy implementation or lack of action, and the operations and procedures used, paint a truer picture of an organisation's ethos than do the platform speeches of the MD to the local TEC or Chamber of Commerce. The desire for change may exist, but making it real is another matter. While the organisation is learning how to learn, it may block, demotivate or lose many good potential learners.

SUMMARY

This chapter has looked at ways in which development and learning can be inhibited. Some of these blocks may be intentionally constructed; most, however, are created unwittingly. An individual may, intellectually, be able to recognise and agree with the need for change, but because of some deep-seated past event or fear of failure or the unknown, be unable to make the first step needed to change. This is like the potential channel swimmer shivering at the edge of the swimming pool.

Learners need to believe that there is some good reason for them to expend the energy and effort to make the start and, perhaps more importantly, to carry on. Learning is hard work and requires continued effort. It also requires support. Managers are well placed to provide the help and encouragement. They are also the people who have to deal with the individuals who resist change.

Resistance comes in several forms, some of which take the shape of open opposition. But in other cases the reasons for resistance are not obvious – not even to the resister. If resistance is preventing learning and change, it is up to the manager to find ways of addressing and reducing it in suitable ways. Even if the source of opposition lies in the attitudes of the individuals concerned, the manager can find appropriate ways of opening up mind-sets, encouraging exploration of existing attitudes, and facilitating the consideration of alternatives. This need not be a punitive process; rather, it should form part of an organisation's learning culture.

Individuals' abilities to learn are different. Just as there are different forms of intelligence, so there are different learning styles. While the overall aim is to become a rounded learner, each individual tends to have a preferred style which conditions individual learning and the way in which the learning of others is perceived. This can either help or hinder development.

Learning is not easy. It is a skill in its own right and needs to be practised for the learner to remain competent. The recency of a member of staff's exposure to learning needs to be taken into account when development plans are being considered. It may be that the individual learner does not want to admit to being out of practice and to needing to learn how to learn again. For adults, the learning experience may bring back unpleasant memories of childhood, punishment and failure. In adulthood, the risk of failure can be greater and so consideration and understanding needs to be given by the manager to the degree of risk the individual is facing. Some people, despite the consideration of their managers, are simply disengaged from the organisation and its need to learn and develop. They are the people who oppose learning, and because they have been taught to keep their heads down and to preserve the status quo, are unable to appreciate that the world around them may be changing quickly.

The dynamics of work groups are complex and difficult to read. The interplay of relationships, history and the need to preserve a group's identity, can build very strong barriers to learning. Alternatively they can foster a healthy, questioning environment, in which change is welcomed enthusiastically but with moderation. The worst dynamic is that of Groupthink. This phenomenon creates an illusion of invincibility and superiority which is counter to learning and positively works against the development of skills. The strength of group pressure can control an individual to such an extent that the willing learner is squashed and obliged to conform to preserving the status quo.

The manager is not a passive actor on the stage. A manager's behaviour can be exemplary, encouraging risk, helping staff through difficult patches, fostering a sense of enquiry and learning; or it can kill the motivation to develop. However, the dynamics of the group constrain the manager's ability to influence change. Interpersonal relationships between group members and their managers are critical in the creation of a developmental climate. But the situation in which they all find themselves also plays a part. The overall environment has some impact but, more directly, the culture of the organisation determines the limits of an individual manager's ability to act, and to influence the culture within the work group.

This chapter has been concerned with the blocks to learning and the negative aspects of organisations, work groups and individuals. The next chapter will move on to look at more ways in which development activities can be constructed to overcome some of these blocks and facilitate learning.

6
Opportunities for development

INTRODUCTION

This chapter will explore the many everyday work occasions that arise as opportunities for the assessment and development of skills. Assessment has already been considered, so brief reference only will be made here to this aspect of development. Far more attention will be given to the occasions in everyday employment that can be developed for the individual, the manager and the organisation.

It is important not to lose sight of the fact that, while personal growth and development are very important, work-related development has to be the prime consideration for an employer. However, in organisations that have previously operated in stable conditions and have valued static working practices, encouraging any act of learning may be beneficial for both the individual and the organisation, as it will be a means of freeing up thinking to prepare for and stimulate change. And even when the needs of the job and organisation take preference, personal growth may be a very welcome and desirable second objective.

This chapter will follow the employee's life cycle with an organisation so that each opportunity, as it presents itself, will be considered. Some – for example, disciplinary hearings – may seem strange development opportunities, when their whole connotation focuses on the negative aspects of performance. But, true to the ethos proposed earlier in the book, such opportunities can be reframed to be seen in a way that enables their positive features to be abstracted for all concerned.

APPOINTMENT

An individual's term of employment with an organisation does not begin on the first day of work. The interactions that occur during every stage of the recruitment and selection process all have an impact on the eventual success or failure of the appointment. The image and aspirations created in the mind of the employee, and the expectations of the employer, are initiated during these early stages. These can have lasting effect. Herriot (1987) has done some useful work on the ways selection processes impact on candidates, and the effect they have on the long-term success of the post-holder. The promises and opportunities used to attract candidates remain in the memory of the person eventually appointed. The long-term (and perhaps uncommunicated) goals set with the ideal candidate in the mind of the manager remain as measures of performance. The more that can be done during the recruitment and selection process to share these different views of the role, the greater the chances are of the appointment being a success for both parties.

Recruitment

The most common method for attracting external candidates to vacant posts is the use of public advertisements, either through job agencies or the press. However, the actual process of recruitment begins (or should begin) before the advertisement is written. A description of the job and outline of the role should precede any other part of the process.

Job description

Any good personnel management textbook will contain advice on how to prepare a job description. There are different schools of thought regarding the amount of detail that should be given. Some argue for a very precise listing of all the major tasks to be carried out by the post-holder; others say that a broad indication only of the general areas of activity needs to be provided. A lot depends on the level of the post and the amount of flexibility that will be required in the future.

In their extreme forms, there are major problems with both these approaches. One is the problem created by a description that is too detailed. This results in a very long list of duties, setting the scene for future arguments about what should or should not be done, because 'It's not in my job description'. On the other hand a job description that is too general can lead the job-holder to flounder or go off in another direction to that expected. Perhaps the worst job description is one which expects the job-holders to turn their hands to everything and use every one of the full range of human skills. The right approach, obviously, lies somewhere in the middle and should reflect the needs, practices and context of the employing organisation.

Person specification

The job description provides the framework for the person specification. Again, several different techniques are given in the personnel management texts. And, again regardless of technique, the specification should be used to create a profile of the skills, abilities and attributes being sought. This profile becomes the measure against which candidates are assessed. It is fairly common practice to send a description of the job to prospective candidates, but there are mixed views regarding sending out the specification.

Advertisement

The advertisement should explain the purpose of the job, giving an indication of its main areas of responsibility. It should also tell candidates what skills and attributes are being sought. This helps candidates decide for themselves whether they meet the requirements. The ideal advertisement is one which does not attract those who do not meet the criteria. They should be able to screen themselves out from the information provided.

Recruitment packs

Some organisations distribute recruitment packs giving background information about themselves and the job. The cost and effectiveness of packs of this nature are issues for each organisation to assess. They can add considerably to the cost of the recruitment process, without necessarily helping prospective candidates assess their own suitability. Packs, regardless of the standard of production and gloss, do not necessarily help candidates decide whether to apply or not if they contain irrelevant information. Nor do they contribute greatly to the organisation's overall publicity effort. Candidates tend to be discerning and can quickly see through gloss. A good pack, however, can help to begin the induction process of the person eventually appointed, enabling the post to be located in the context of the whole organisation. Particular images about the organisation will be created and candidates, inevitably, will begin to get a feel of the culture.

The advertisement, job description, person specification and information packs, as well as the organisation's existing reputation, all contribute to building an image in the minds of applicants and the potentially successful candidate. This image will comprise expectations the individual will hold about their future in the job and about what will be expected of them. The culture of the organisation will be portrayed in what it says about itself, which will begin to allow the individual to get a feel for what it is like to work there.

Some organisations, because of difficulties in attracting suitable candidates, build misleading pictures of the job, overselling themselves and their future. Sometimes, an erroneous picture is created without intent. Organisations can also show themselves in a worse light than is true, reflecting a poor image held by staff preparing the recruitment literature.

Selection

The selection interview is the point at which candidates meet the organisation and its representatives in the flesh. Many messages are given to the future employee(s) about what is expected of them and the 'real' nature of the organisation. Candidates may meet potential future colleagues – both those they are intended to meet and those they are not. Each contact they have with the organisation contributes to the total picture. This picture will inform decisions the individuals make about the job and the part they might play in the organisation if their application is successful.

If an unrealistic picture is built up, it may be that the candidate is appointed to do a job that is different from the one wanted by the organisation. Alternatively, the appointee may have expectations that the organisation cannot meet. This difference of understanding may not become evident for some time. The selection process should be designed to ensure that the candidates receive the message intended, to enable them to make their decisions on an informed basis and so they start their new job with an accurate initial picture of the organisation and what is expected of them. Someone who leaves a post quickly is perhaps the most frequently given example of an appointment failure. The biggest failure, however, can be when the post-holder is unable to leave the organisation.

Example 6.1

The advertisement was for someone to head up the District Health Authority's training and development service. It said that someone was required to change the service from one which was reactive and ran courses, to one which was 'strategic and geared towards enabling staff to acquire the skills needed for the achievement of future plans'. The grapevine said that it was a good opportunity, the personnel director was far-sighted, and the openings for achievement were many. The recruitment literature was full of the right words, and the strategic plan was ambitious.

The interviews were held in the training centre. This was a slightly shabby staff residence, but was due to be replaced in the near future by purpose-built accommodation. The selection technique was modern and well-run and comprised a presentation to a panel and three sequential, one-to-one interviews. The job seemed challenging and do-able, the people pleasant and professional. It appeared to be an attractive and acceptable position.

The reality, however, was very different. The office accommodation (not seen during the interviews) was sub-standard. The internal politics of the organisation were extremely unpleasant and external constraints meant that many of the plans were unachievable. The staff were demotivated, cynical and very suspicious of change. The administrative procedures were laborious and the sort of service demanded by the majority of the managers and their staff was for basic, job-related skills training. Ideas of strategic and future orientated development were revolutionary and unconnected to reality.

Fortunately for everyone, the newly appointed training manager found another job within the year.

The recruitment and selection process is crucial in ensuring that the post-holder's views of the job and the organisations are realistic. If they are not, the consequences can be damaging for everyone. They should provide a firm base for future development which enables the individual to grow within the organisation; this base must be built during recruitment. If it is built on poor foundations, digging it up for reconstruction can be very difficult, expensive and time-consuming – assuming, of course, that it is even possible.

If there is a shared, realistic conception of the job and its future, the appointment process can be used to construct realistic development plans. The appointment process focuses on the individual's skills and attributes, and so any weaknesses and gaps will have been identified. These can be used during the early stages of drawing up a development plan. Thus activities will be tailored to the individual and their job from the very start of the appointment.

INDUCTION

The recruitment and selection process does not stop when the offer of appointment has been made, and training does not start on the first day. Both processes are linked by *induction*, which serves two purposes. It includes the individual within the organisation, by sharing the cultural norms and assumptions. Sometimes this is carried out formally, in a structured induction programme. More often, however, it is done informally. Everyone the newly appointed person comes into contact with contributes something to the organisation's jigsaw. Induction also helps the person to see their role in the context of the organisation.

A developmental approach to induction sets the stall out for the future. New staff receive the information they need so they can see themselves and their role in the context of the organisation as it is now and how it is to become in the future. This is done by sharing the future plans, in detail, with the individuals and discussing the factors that will influence the achievement of those plans. This requires more than an address by the chief executive to the one-day induction course organised by the personnel department. The line manager of the new appointee should spend time talking through the meaning of the words and the plans. The line manager has to be well-informed and needs to understand both the plans and the organisation, to discuss the implications of the plans with the post-holder in the context of their individual job, in terms of what it means for the role and what will be required of the individual person. This requires the manager to have a grasp of the issues. Early induction of this nature will prepare the individual to grow in and with the organisation. In this way, their initial constructs will be based on good quality information and their aspirations will be realistic and in context.

TRAINING

Training (as opposed to development) can also be developmental. The normal approach to job-focused training is to concentrate on the narrow skills or knowledge to be learnt so that the job itself can be performed effectively. This is particularly so in the case of external short courses. But, even when in-company training courses are part of an overall plan, each course tends to be limited to a few precise, mutually exclusive objectives – rightly so. It is possible, though, to widen the focus so that each course has a longer-term contribution, like bricks in a house. The linking mortar is the development plan. Development plans will be discussed later in much more detail. Even very specific training can be constructed in a way that contributes to the individual's growth and to that of the organisation by being orientated to the future as well as to the present. The following examples compare two different approaches that can be taken to achieve similar objectives.

Example 6.2

Health and safety update for managers
Objectives:

1.   To inform managers of the changes to the HASAW legislation,

2. To consider recent judgments and the ways in which they affect working practice,

3. To examine the ways in which 'Sick Building Syndrome' may affect staff absence.

Programme:

9.30	Introduction and welcome
9.45	Legislation update by Rt. Hon. Sir Fred McNulty JP
11.00	Coffee
11.15	Case Law and Practice by Geoffrey Newman, Chief Inspector, HASAW Commission
12.30	Lunch
1.30	Sick Building Syndrome by Dr Christopher Blanchard, Chief MSO (Occupational Health) at St Pancras Hospital
2.45	Tea
3.00	Managing Staff Absence by Iain North, Director of Personnel, British Sugar plc
4.30	Close

Example 6.3

Health and safety update for managers
Objectives:

1. To bring participants up to date with changes caused by recent legislation and case law.

2. To consider the impact of these changes on working practice.

3. To examine the nature of 'Sick Building Syndrome' and to consider how it may affect staff health.

Programme:

9.30	Welcome and introductions
9.45	Group discussions of previously circulated summaries of case law and legislation
10.30	Overview by Rt Hon Sir Fred McNulty JP
10.45	Coffee
11.00	Case study to help participants focus on the ways in which the changes may effect them and their organisations
12.15	Summary by Geoffrey Newman, Chief Inspector, HASAW Commission
12.30	Lunch

1.30 Sick Building Syndrome – cause and effect by Dr Christopher Blanchard, Chief MSO (Occupational Health) at St Pancras Hospital

2.00 One organisation's experience, by Iain North, Director of Personnel, British Sugar plc

2.30 Group discussions about British Sugar's experience and consideration of alternative approaches that could have been adopted

3.45 Tea

4.00 Preparation of individual work plans

4.30 Close

The two programmes are extremely similar in objectives and content, but the approaches taken are very different. The first requires participants to listen and think. The second is designed to encourage thinking through questioning and sharing experiences with others, including the experts. Some sessions allow the managers to consider alternatives and question actual events, test out ideas and subject their own experiences to peer appraisal. The final session focuses on what the participants could do as a result of their learning during the day. Different from the usual 'action planning' session, it would emphasise jobs to be done.

When a manager is sent to be trained, good practice recommends that some preparatory work is done before the course. This should take the form of working out the reasons for attendance and what is intended to be gained from the training. After attendance, the actual experience should be compared with the intent, the training evaluated and ways in which the learning can be applied should be considered. Sadly, all too often, training sessions are taken in isolation. The pre- and post-briefing sessions should not be regarded as being separate events, but as integral parts. The final consideration of ways in which the training can be applied, allows the real value of the training to be put to the test. Some training may not be immediately applicable, but this should not prevent consideration being given to the sorts of situations where the ideas may be used.

Performance management

Performance management is a term increasingly being used to cover a number of personnel techniques. It is a process which has been derived from American personnel practice and is designed to marry organisational objectives to personal expectations, and vice versa. It draws short-term needs into the parameters of the long-term whole. Bevan and Thompson (1991) say that, while it is a widely accepted concept, a clear definition of the process is somewhat elusive. From a literature review and survey, they conclude that the concept is made up of two thrusts: reward-driven integration and development-driven integration. Both aim to link the work of individuals closely to the organisation's goals. Regardless of which thrust the process is following, managing performance comprises:

• sharing organisational objectives;

• setting individual objectives;

• allocating work;

• monitoring progress;

• reviewing performance;

• identifying development needs;

• rewarding achievement;

• evaluating process.

This process may seem to be highly structured and systematic. This can be built in the way in which the approach is adopted, if so desired, and in some organisations this will be the most effective way of using the technique. It can provide a mechanism for planning and harnessing human resources as part of the implementation of the organisation's strategic plans. Alternatively, it can be used to provide a high degree of flexibility. The provision of structures to allocate work in a way that links individual objectives to the organisation's and reviews progress allows unforeseen developments to be accommodated quickly. Staff are able to change the direction in which they are expending their efforts and quickly acquire the skills they need to do so. These feedback loops, rather than restricting a manager's scope for action, can actually help to remove the need for control mechanisms and thus facilitate decentralisation.

The way in which an organisation chooses to use this approach is for its managers to determine. Before making this decision, consideration should be given to the organisation's culture and the desired management style in conjunction with the needs of the individuals within it. It is also possible to decide which thrust (ie reward-driven or development-driven) should be followed. In a culture which uses mechanisms such as performance-related pay and accelerated promotion to recognise achievement, the reward-driven thrust will obviously be more appropriate. However, in a culture in which personal growth and devolved responsibility are valued more than pay, it is possible that a developmental approach will be better. It is always possible to build a performance management systems that employs both thrusts, as and when appropriate. Care is needed to ensure that the system is a congruent whole, that allows options to be combined and built upon. Otherwise, staff may receive mixed messages and may then accuse the organisation of shifting the goal posts.

Example 6.4

Hamburgers are out. Vegetarianism, healthy eating and cheap pizzas have killed the market. These were the conclusions the management of Burgabars, a chain of hamburger restaurants operating in the Midlands, came to when they found their takings had dropped rapidly. The accountant's prediction for the year end results was very gloomy and the market research forecast indicated a marked downturn in sales. The management team had no choice but to take stock.

There seemed to be three options available to them:

• do nothing;

• close down;

• change direction.

The team decided on the latter. Instead of seeing the changes in the market-place as threats, the team reframed them into opportunities. Instead of bucking the trends, the team decided to go along with them. Burgabars would become Earth Foods.

Earth Foods would be a provider of meatless take-aways and eat-in meals. It was decided to aim at the health conscious adult rather than children, teenagers and their parents; but on the advice of market researchers, the management team chose to avoid the keep-fit fanatics and health food cranks. This dramatic change in market would require the managers of the outlets and their staff to take a new approach to their work. To help this change occur smoothly, the management team decided to adopt a process that would both manage the company's and its managers' performance.

Using performance management, the management team prepared a plan of action lasting two years. The first year would be devoted to setting the objectives and standards required and skilling up all the workforce to achieve the desired outcomes. The second year would consist of reviews of performance, recognition of achievement to emphasise the desired standards, distribution of rewards, as well as any needed remedial action and highlighting areas for further development.

The management team started the process by developing a concise set of

---

objectives aimed directly at the overall goals of the business. These were to stay in business and to change market image within two years. Once the subordinate objectives had been agreed, they were shared with the outlet managers. The managers were encouraged to test them out by considering what would help and what would hinder their achievement, and how they would know whether they were attaining the objectives. The managers and their line managers on the management team identified what each needed to do or stop doing in their own outlet, and what action would be needed for that particular staff group.

Each manager was required to go back to their own outlet and conduct the same process with their staff. On the basis of these consultations, work and development plans were established for each outlet and each member of staff. The management team had decided that each plan should contain indicators of success. Obviously trading figures were the main measure of this, but, because some of the changes were qualitative, other indicators were also needed. Changing from a fast food joint into one which appealed to a different market segment required the creation of a totally different image and patterns of behaviour. It was deemed essential that all the staff should be involved in identifying for themselves what these should be. This was to ensure ownership and commitment to the changes from the start of the programme. It was also decided that staff should be involved in monitoring progress against the agreed indicators which had been developed.

An interesting example of the approach's success occurred in the Balsall-in-Arden outlet. As this outlet was located in the town's main shopping street, the plan was to close for a week to allow for refurbishment. The manager and staff decided that the week would be used for retraining and publicity. The closure was timed for the local school's half-term holiday, and agreement was reached with the head teacher that Earth Foods could use the school's kitchen. For the first part of the week the staff learnt how to prepare the new dishes and rehearsed a different approach to serving their customers (each other). By the Thursday, they felt ready for the dress rehearsal. Every Friday the school hall was used by the local retired community. The members of the Friday Club had agreed to be guinea-pigs. Press coverage was arranged and good photographs of the staff appeared on the front page of the Saturday edition. The outlet reopened the following Monday.

These arrangements had all been made by the local manager. Planning the training and the negotiations with the school head to obtain the facilities in the school had been new ventures. A member of staff who had done some temporary work with the local paper some years previously had suggested the photograph and so had been charged with the task of getting maximum publicity. The training had involved every member of staff and they had all given feedback to each other on the dishes and standard of service.

The public's response to the outlet's reopening was very good. Initial trading outstripped expectations and remained high even after the time when it was predicted to dip. All the staff had been involved and so were justly able to feel pleased with their success.

This opportunity had allowed the manager to find ways of developing the staff's talents in a way that was directly linked to business needs. The short-term pay-offs were obvious; the long-term ones less so. Nevertheless, benefits would have been accrued that would be realised. For example, the sense of joint achievement would improve team working, motivation and job satisfaction. Viewing the service from the customers' view would enhance service quality. Managing the performance of the parts enables the synthesis necessary for the effective management of the whole to take place.

Performance management provides a means of communicating what is happening within the organisation and the direction in which it is going in a way that has immediate meaning to the individual members of staff.

One question is raised by everybody at the receiving end of change: 'What does it mean to me?' Performance management, if followed through to its conclusion, gives a framework that will help individuals answer that question.

Career management

The idea of career management can cause problems and apparent contradictions for organisations implementing equal opportunities policies. How can promotion be open to equal competition when individuals are following planned career paths? How can the opportunities for progress be equally available to all when some are on fast tracks?

These questions can place an organisation on the horns of a dilemma. It is not appropriate to debate the issue fully here, but many of the texts that should address the issues do not do so. Equal opportunities practices are, of course, good employment practices. If these are encompassed within the design of career management programmes, progression achieved on the basis of job-related abilities and access to the starting point is open, the principles of equality of opportunity should be satisfied.

Career management also may imply that the control of individuals' futures is taken out of their hands. They no longer have control over their own destiny or freedom to choose. This need not be the case. In fact, planning a career can give individuals a wider range of options, opening up career avenues which previously might have seemed closed. This can be the case particularly in organisations that have several career ladders separated by professional divides. A well-constructed career planning system will provide links between these ladders, allowing individuals to cross and recross. The career plan need not be a sort of snakes and ladders game governed by throws of dice, but it should contain recognisable routes up down and across the structures, enabling individuals to progress and find their level as their skills and circumstances permit, in a way that does not label individuals as successes or failures.

As with any aspect of human resource management, career management is about enabling individuals to perform to their best abilities in a job that provides them with the rewards and satisfactions they seek. As with any technique it is not a cure-all; it should be part of an overall approach to managing and developing an organisation. Career management allows a way forward for individuals to be planned on a longer-term basis, while providing for the organisation's future skill needs. It is a matching process which links an individual's current ability and potential with the demands of the job now and the strategic needs of the organisation in the future.

The key to ensuring equality of opportunity is to ensure that the criteria used to diagnose organisational need and to assess individual ability and potential are based on factors that are bias free. This means that effort has to be put into the analysis of the job requirements and definition of the skills criteria, and that stereotypical assumptions of skills and behaviour patterns are challenged. Using succession plans as part of a career management approach means that the career advancement process is made explicit, so that people know what they have to do to get ahead. The criteria are not secret and the crowned prince can no longer sit unassailable on the throne.

Mayo (1992) gives a model of how the succession planning process may be put into practice. This is set out in Table 6.1. In addition to these opportunities, Mayo indicates how the matching process may be take place. Following good recruitment and selection practice, the key is the use of a well-defined person specification. It is normal practice to use one when a post is vacant, but there is no reason why a general person specification cannot be constructed for groups or levels of staff. Once built, this can be used as a development profile against which a staff's skills can be assessed.

Example 6.5

The senior partners form the management group of a large architectural practice. The nature of their business was changing and a series of near misses had made them realise that the organisation's middle managers, who were heads of professional groups, did not possess the skills needed to carry the organisation through the troubles it was facing. The middle managers were professionally qualified individuals, who in the past had been promoted for their technical abilities. Some had received some management training, some were skilled almost by accident of birth, others were not. In the unprecedented conditions being faced, the management team, at the outset, were aware only of the shortfall in performance. They knew that the old approaches and ways of working were no longer working, but they did not know exactly what they and their middle managers were missing.

With the help of an outsider, the management team reframed the definition of the practice's business. From an organisation structured on professional divides providing a jobbing service, the management team decided that they were or should be an organisation that provided an integrated project management service organised by client type. This would require the previous professional heads to become project managers leading teams which would cross professional boundaries.

As part of the redefinition, the management team was encouraged to think through the sorts of behaviours they thought would lead to success or failure of these teams. Groups of middle managers, drawn from across the whole practice, were invited to do the same. From these deliberations a composite profile of skills and behaviours was constructed. The middle managers were then asked to appraise themselves, one colleague, and their senior partner, and be appraised by their staff against the profile. The resulting appraisals were accumulated and a feedback report prepared for each middle manager. This provided two pieces of data. It gave the manager a picture of the sorts of behaviour that would be expected in the future by the whole organisation, and a full assessment of their current abilities to carry out those behaviours.

From this picture the individuals were able to prepare their own personal development plan with an appropriate senior partner. Some were able to decide that they did not want to go in the direction chosen by the organisation. Others decided to return to their professional origins rather than become managers. A third group who became the project managers were able to construct personal work plans. These work or business plans specified the targets needed to get each project group working effectively in the agreed timescale. The plans were different for each group and took into account the business priorities and the make up of the particular team. Each of the project managers also prepared a personal development plan designed to equip them with the skills they would need individually and collectively.

Some practice-wide development activities were organised, and in addition individuals worked on their personal needs, with periodic reviews as they implemented the reorganisation. Six months into the change programme a comprehensive review was carried out. Using the redefined statement of purpose as an indicator of success, the total organisation performance was assessed by accumulating the assessment of individuals against the profile. Other wider business measures were used to ensure that overall performance was seen as the sum of the parts plus.

On the basis of this total assessment, action areas were identified to help the weaker groups attain the levels of the stronger groups and to help the stronger continue to develop and make progress. At the start of the change programme, it had not been possible to distinguish between the levels of achievement and performance of the different project managers, and they had all been paid at the same level. The profile allowed bench-marks to be identified, to enable a meaningful remuneration structure to be developed. It also provided an independent means of assessing performance. The profile thus established the foundations for an evaluation of the jobs and a way of allocating rewards on criteria that could be seen to be fair.

Table 6.1 Mayo's succession planning model

Individual career planning processes	*Joint career planning processes*	*Organisational processes*
• Occupational choice, assessment, counselling • Career planning workshops • Self-development plans, activities • Pre-retirement courses • Career resource centres • Career seminars • Use of career planning computer programs • Writing CVs and personal growth profile	• Appraisal and development reviews • Potential assessment centres • Career guidance, development centres • Mentoring • Career counselling, career planning • Outplacement, sabbaticals, secondments • Career breaks, alternative methods of employment	• Appointment processes • Career structures • High flier, career development schemes • Organisational, grading structures • Succession planning • Creating opportunities for experience • Personnel resource planning • Defining person specifications for jobs

No matter how good a career management scheme is, or how fair recruitment and selection processes are, there will always be some disappointments. It may be that a particular individual who has worked hard for the organisation for a number of years and has had a rewarding career, comes to their own decision that the pressures the organisation is facing and the changes it has chosen to make, no longer fit with their aspirations or meet their needs. It may be that the individual wants to develop a particular set of skills or work on certain projects that do not fit into the organisation's portfolio. There may be nothing wrong with their level of performance, but the individual may not have the attributes being sought for further career advancement. Being passed over may leave this person with a bitter taste, but an open career management scheme allows the individual to see what is happening, so personal decisions regarding future career plans are made on the basis of information rather than impressions.

PROMOTION

A post available for internal promotion by competition can provides another opportunity for development. It is not uncommon for promotional posts to be offered for competition, either between staff within an organisation or between them and outsiders. This may lead to a stressful occasion for everyone involved:

- The manager is concerned to get the right person in post, treat the existing staff fairly and maintain productivity during and after the process.

- Internal candidates want the opportunity to demonstrate their ability and longer-term ambitions. They also want the 'best' person to get the job. If they do not get the job themselves, they want someone whom they respect to get it.

- Those watching from the sidelines want the process to be dealt with properly, creating not too much unrest and distress, a chance to influence the final decision (perhaps), and someone to be appointed with whom they can work and respect.

Job definition

The opportunity for development exists for all the actors at every stage of the process. As described earlier, the starting point is for the job to be clearly defined. This requires the manager concerned to be precise in thinking about the requirements from the job holder. This may provide an opportunity for the manager to adopt a new way of thinking; it may also require some previously held assumptions to be challenged. The sensitive nature of promotions may provide the reason for introducing new selection methods that are regarded as being better predictors of performance than other methods which may have been used. This is also an opportunity for learning. (Dale and Iles (1991) describe in greater detail how this can happen.) Good practice dictates that feedback should be given to candidates after the selection decision has been made. This should be made available to successful and unsuccessful candidates alike at appropriate stages of the process. Giving feedback requires the use of sophisticated skills, especially if the individuals concerned have cause to be particularly sensitive. It is reasonable to assume that some of the candidates who have been rejected will require feedback to help them deal with the sense of rejection and the disappointment of not being promoted, while seeing what needs to be done to develop their skills. Giving quality feedback can also prepare the unsuccessful individuals to accept the person who has been successful.

Applying for promotion

Applying for a promotion within the employing organisation in some ways is more difficult than applying for a job outside. Being known means that making an application requires the individuals to be accurate about their track records and achievements. It is not so easy to be selective about one's past as it is when applying to another organisation. It is also necessary to draw attention to potential and hidden talents. Going through this process can actually help an individual appreciate their own skills more clearly. Some people find it very difficult to make an assessment of their own abilities, tending to sell themselves short.

Self-assessment and feedback

Comparison with other candidates can help self-assessment and indicate other areas where developments can be made. A good selection process should stretch and challenge candidates, without threatening or playing games with them. It should assess, in realistic and relevant ways, their current and potential abilities. The experience should provide an individual with some material to think about and some ideas of what to do next, whether successful in the particular application or not. This opportunity is enriched if there is feedback. Giving feedback needs skill; receiving it requires a willingness to act on the contents. The process of giving and receiving feedback is a very important developmental event, which can so easily go wrong.

The successful candidate should not rest on their laurels. The processes of self-assessment and selector examination are likely to have revealed some weaknesses, gaps in skills, or areas where additional (or new) development could be made. It is unlikely that someone appointed to a new job will be skilled in all its operational areas; some skill development will be required. If the promotion process has been constructed to be job-related and relevant, the candidate should have obtained information regarding shortfalls in likely performance. A thorough debriefing and exchange of perceptions after the decision has been taken to promote can be used to inform the beginnings of a development plan.

DISCIPLINE AND PERFORMANCE PROBLEMS

The word 'discipline' is used in common parlance to mean the correction of bad or wrong behaviour. It contains suggestions of requiring an individual to do things against their will. In a climate of development, improvement and growth, discipline need not have these punitive connotations. It can be used to convey a sense of shared, mutually agreed and accepted standards – standards to be met because people want to meet them; standards that can be stretched, not because people want to break or bend the rules, but because they know they can do better and want to extend themselves and their organisation.

This is the philosophical position, theoretical and somewhat idealistic. The reality is that people do not meet standards, not do they work for the achievement of organisational goals. Some of the reasons for this may lie with the individual, some with their circumstances and the situation. In other cases, third parties are responsible for an individual's poor performance. Stewart and Stewart (1982) describe many of the common causes of performance problems and ways of managing them. Problems with an individual's or a group's performance can also provide a very rich opportunity for development of skills and learning.

The individual concerned, the manager and the whole organisation, can all learn from the experience. Zoll (1974) has written an action maze for use as a management training exercise called 'Joe Bailey', which portrays a typical problem. As with every management situation, there are no right or wrong answers, only best or worst solutions. Joe is experiencing difficulties. Before transferring to his current work-site he was generally regarded as one of the company's best workers. Shortly after his move, for no apparent reason, he started to go absent. Depending on the action taken by the manager, the situation gets worse or better. Typical of a maze and real life, the story contains twists, unexpected happenings, undisclosed information, emotions and other people. The point of the exercise is to draw attention to the key actions needed to resolve the situation satisfactorily. The situation concerns not just Joe's problem, but the decisions available to the manager.

Turning a performance problem into a learning experience requires perhaps more patience and tolerance than invoking the formal disciplinary procedure, but the pay offs can outweigh the initial investment. In addition to patience and tolerance, a developmental approach requires:

- Investigation of why the standards are not being met. (This will mean listening to the individual(s) concerned and gathering data.)

- Discussion(s) with the individual(s) concerned to hear their perception of performance standards.

- Identification of the discrepancies in current levels of performance and those required.

- Deciding if the shortfall in performance really matters. (It may be that, on consideration, the discrepancy is unimportant in the long run, if, for example, the area of work is to be changed or the member of staff is due to leave.)

- Identification of ways of dealing with the discrepancy. (In some circumstances, formal disciplinary measures are the correct solution, for example in cases of wilful breach of rules, deliberate misconduct, etc).

- Agreement on the course of action to be followed *by all parties concerned.*

- Allocation of resources needed.

- Agreement on monitoring and review processes.

- The self-discipline to stick to the agreements.

It is not unknown for such agreements to be broken by the manager, because there was insufficient time or because something more important turned up. Cynical staff can be found in most organisations who have had the 'treatment' from several managers. Some will have been reprimanded for not complying with standards or achieving agreed objectives. Both parties may have started on the implementation of the development plan, but within a short space of time the resources are not available, the manager is too busy, the objectives change and the member of staff concerned becomes a disaffected poor performer. Or staff will have been accused of not changing to the new ways fast enough to suit a newly appointed manager, who hands out reprimands more often than bouquets. After this has happened several times, the reprimands have no meaning, and as it is a reasonably safe bet that the manager will move on, the members of staff can afford to sit it out. After all, who wants a bouquet of faded roses?

Example 6.6

The six gardeners had worked in the park for most of their working lives, which spanned 10 to 30 years. In their time they have seen supervisors and area managers come and go. Each had their own way of doing things — some more hair-brained and faddish than others, some sensible and some just stupid. The oldest gardener had been apprenticed just after the war by a man who became the head gardener at Kew. So the staff knew who was right. They also knew that each supervisor and manager would move on more quickly than they. All they had to do was to keep their heads down and get on with their jobs.

Admittedly, some of the supervisors could make life a bit unpleasant, but being philosophical people, more concerned with growing beautiful plants than reacting to temper, the gardeners felt they could weather their supervisors' tantrums. In any case, what could the supervisors do? They all needed the gardeners' skills, which would not be that easy to replace. One thing had been true of all of the transient managers — though they had been very good at finding fault, very few of them had been able to tell the really excellent work from the good. The truth came out when the oldest gardener retired. At his celebration, the top boss presented him with a pot plant grown in his own hot house.

REWARD ALLOCATION

Rewards have to be given in a currency of value to the recipient if they are to have any worth. The use of performance-related pay has sparked off interest again in motivational factors.

Pay

Most research shows that pay is a demotivator if it is wrong, but as a motivator, it has only a limited value. To have any great impact, the performance-linked element of pay has to be a significant proportion of the basic salary, and the individual must have significant degree of personal control over achievement. Someone who is very dependent on the efforts of others to be able to meet the desired targets, and for whom only 2.75 per cent of take-home pay is performance-linked, is not going to be as motivated by money as the person who works alone and whose pay is, say, 80 per cent linked to performance. However, regardless of the proportion of pay that is linked to performance, a critical factor in the acceptability of any scheme is the way in which it is operated. The way in which the mechanisms operate will have an impact on an individual's inclination to be open and honest about development needs.

Quality of work

On the other hand, research into motivational factors also indicates that interesting, challenging work and feedback are most likely to stimulate an individual and to have positive effects on the inclination to work. Encouraging and helping individuals to develop their skills, and ensuring that the work can be related to the organisation's purpose, can help to create a sense of the future. A framework which defines what is expected from individuals and which rewards accordingly can be constructed, in a way that will accommodate the shifting sands of uncertainty and create a purpose with tangible rewards. These rewards, if related to the development of an individual's capabilities, should in this way have currency to the person concerned. The Rover and Ford Motor Companies resource development programmes in any subject area, because they recognise that an individual who is committed to developing their own abilities is more likely to be committed to developing their work-related skills. Such investments in learning will be mutually beneficial and rewarding.

Similarly, managers who are interested in the development of their staff's abilities is likely to be concerned about their general well-being. It is also likely that such a manager will ensure that staff are properly informed and appropriately involved in decision-making. Research, as noted above, shows that the quality of the relationship between managers and their staff is another key to motivational levels, the quality of the working environment and the work being done.

A part of this relationship is the giving of quality feedback. Ways of doing this will be considered later in greater detail. Quality feedback is that which relates to actual performance and is based on evidence, not to be used against but to inform the manager and individual and to provide some guidance on areas which could be improved. Working with the individual, the manager can help to unpick the factors that contributed to a success just as much as examining a mistake or weakness. Feedback provides an opportunity for the very best reward — genuine recognition of achievement.

Being faced with a task that is hard because it is new presents both a challenge and a risk. The risk is double-edged. On one side there lies failure; on the other lies the chance of success. The sense of achievement and the glow of attainment are the obvious outcomes of success, but success brings its own dangers. It can change an individual's self-perception and take them into realms previously not countenanced. Being good in previously unrecognised areas can take the individual into a different world. Failure, however, may confirm a poor self-image or it may bring disappointment. It may prove that the assessment of one's own abilities was correct. But there should be no reason for not trying.

The opportunity to learn how to do a new task and to develop the needed skills, if a balance can be found between the fear of failure, the desire to fail, (to confirm the existing poor self-image), the fear of success and the wish to succeed, provides a major source of motivation and the chance of great rewards. One of the best rewards for an individual is the sense of achievement obtained from a job well done.

STRATEGIC PLANNING

Strategic planning tends to come in and out of fashion depending on the management textbooks and writers currently in vogue. The term can describe a highly centralised technique, or a participative, devolved exercise. In its latter form, the technique can create the opportunity for the development of skills of staff at all levels of an organisation.

The way to begin a strategic plan is to conduct an analysis of the organisation in its situation. This usually requires a definition of the organisation's primary purpose and an assessment of the threats and opportunities in its environment. To distinguish the two, a realistic comparison between the organisation's environment and its ability to respond needs to be made. Johnson and Scholes (1989) provide a useful outline of the process. The most frequently used technique for conducting this comparison is a SWOT analysis. Typically, this focuses on strategic resources such as buildings, assets, image, products, cost structures, etc. However, perhaps the most important strength and/or weakness, and the most difficult to assess is staff's ability.

Changes in the labour market, the cost of labour, skills shortages and economic fluctuations require that more attention be given to the skills base of organisations. The human resource is now being valued and so as with any asset needs to be audited. Assigning a monetary value to the staff resources is a partial improvement. To make full use of skill recognition, the audit should be used to create a skill bank − a data base of each individual's abilities and talents. This takes time to collect and effort to maintain, just like financial records.

Example 6.7

The company was a leading provider of squash equipment. The British market, however, was declining. The people who had taken up squash with the enthusiasm of their teens were now approaching middle age. It was well known that this market segment replaced their equipment only when needed and their taste tended to be conservative. They did not respond to fads of fashion as younger people. Most money was to be made in fashion sports gear for the young. Sadly for the company, squash was not appealing to the young and was not likely to do so in the foreseeable future.

The company was faced with two alternatives – to diversify, or to find new markets. Its research suggested that there was a possible, but diffuse market in Europe. There, interest in the sport was greater and more young people were entering and staying in clubs. The opportunities to diversify were severely limited because of the existing intensity of competition in the other possible markets. The company chose Europe.

When planning the strategy, the company's major weakness was seen as its inability to do business in any European language. The marketing director had been told firmly that, if the company wanted to penetrate, it must be able to converse with the customer, on their terms and in their own tongue.

The company decided against employing specialist staff to strengthen the existing sales staff. This would simply take too long. Instead, it conducted a language skills audit of all its staff. To everyone's relief, this showed that the total language skills present in the company were far greater than had been initially thought. Rather than training from scratch, the development need that emerged was for refreshment and updating in all major European languages and changing from conversational to business vocabularies. This proved to be much quicker and cheaper. It also drew attention to the previously hidden talents among staff such as secretaries, junior clerks, and even one of the production supervisors.

It did not take the company long to break into the European market. One of its major advantages was its ability to trade in all of the European countries because of its superior language skills. This strategic ability gave it a distinctive competency and a competitive edge over its rivals. Within two years a gloomy future had changed dramatically into one of expansion.

JOB DESIGN AND CHANGE

Jobs can be defined, as can organisational structures. Neither processes occur as often as they should, however. Too often collections of tasks and groups of jobs are lumped together in an *ad hoc* manner, and then surprise is expressed when things do not work smoothly or in the way intended. Operations designed to be simple become complex and self-serving over time. A common reason for these flaws is that the job or tasks are set up in ways that make them not do-able by human beings – the skills required may be contradictory rather than complementary; or the various elements of the task may require such different approaches. The people trying to work effectively become confused or the skills required are simply too wide ranging. Another common reason for dysfunction is poor recruitment, for example the appointment of staff who are too able for the level of the job.

Example 6.8

It had been company policy to appoint school-leavers, with qualifications in English, maths and at least one other subject. The company had an excellent reputation for being a good employer and had never had any problems in recruiting staff. Because of increased youth unemployment the personnel officer decided to recruit the 'best' candidates. To her, these were the people with the most experience.

After a year of this informal policy, the managing director demanded an enquiry. There had been increased levels of unrest amongst the junior staff. Turnover was low, due to a general decline in vacancies in the region, but requests for internal transfers had rocketed. During appraisal meetings staff had been *demanding* training courses and, complaints were being made for the first time ever about the standard of management. The enquiry uncovered the personnel manager's policy and the conclusion reached was that the new recruits were unstretched by their jobs and were looking, unconsciously, for other outlets for their mental abilities.

This is a classic case of poor recruitment. Development activities would provide a way of channelling the new staff's excessive zeal until more productive places could be found for them. But, of course, the best answer is to define the level of the job to be done and to match the 'best' candidate against job-related criteria. It is always better to group tasks so that similar ones are integrated, and there is also some variety built in.

Other incidents of bad design may not be so easily recognised or cured. In the case of poor organisational design, the consequences may take so long to emerge that their origins are difficult to trace. Because of the nature of organisational life now, the classical models of organisational type are no longer holding true. The purpose of organisations and hence their form need to be able to change quickly.

Example 6.9

The advertising company restructured to form a new division to respond to an emerging market. The new division would be responsible to the Head of Public Relations and carry out some operations that were previously regarded as administrative work. It would process all its own accounts and invoices so that it could be close to its suppliers and customers in all aspects of work. The Head of the central accounts department saw this as the first nail in the coffin. While the central staff reacted to requests, they were not very co-operative in setting up new systems.

After six months, the Head of the new division asked to see the Managing Director with bad news. Customers were lodging complaints about being sent two bills for the same piece of work, and were being harried for non-payment when payment had been made. Two of the most important clients were threatening to take their business elsewhere, and a major supplier had just called to say the contract was not worth the financial hassle.

What was happening, it appeared on examination, was that the finance department were refusing to let go of their systems 'because of the requirements of the auditor' and were refusing to accept payment on invoices other than those issued by themselves, for the same reason. Meanwhile the staff in the new division were refusing to follow audit procedures because they were seen to be too inflexible. The time that should have been spent sorting out the customers' and suppliers' queries was being spent arguing about who was to blame for the mistakes.

The design of jobs is fundamental to performance. Most of the personnel textbooks encourage a reductionist approach: the job is analysed into its component parts, reduced to its basic elements (Example 6.10 below). An alternative way is to look at the job as a whole (Example 6.11). This is done by asking 'What is its purpose?', and 'What will a successful performer be doing?' The inbuilt error in the first approach is that tasks can get put back together without having any underlying logic. The weakness of the second is that key functions may not be specified clearly enough for the job-holder to know what they are meant to be doing.

The ideal position is a combination, so that a picture of the whole job is built which includes indications of standards and results expected. It is essential that the areas which are the responsibility of the post-holder alone are clearly specified.

Example 6.10 – Defined by analysis

Job purpose:
To be responsible for the effective and efficient provision of the customer liaison service.

Tasks:

1. To ensure that customer records are adequately maintained;

2. To arrange for personal, telephone and written enquiries to be answered within the specified timescale;

3. To carry out investigations into complaints and make recommendations regarding remedies;

4. To manage the staff of the section, providing adequate facilities for their productive work and ongoing development.

Example 6.11 – Defined by outputs

Job purpose:
To be responsible for ensuring that the agreed quality of customer service is attained, maintained and improved.

Areas of responsibility:

1. To establish and maintain administrative systems;

2. To provide a customer enquiry service;

3. To respond to customer complaints.

4. To manage and develop the section's staff.

A well-designed job should encompass certain factors. These have been drawn from the work done into motivation and job satisfaction. They also take account of certain philosophical beliefs about people at work. For example, it is assumed that most people want to do a fair day's work for a fair day's pay, that most people are honest and want to treat others and be treated by others with respect.

When designing a job, managers should be mindful of:

- the variety of tasks to be performed (not too many, but enough to maintain interest, stimulation and changes to the levels of physical and mental activity);

- the degree of repetition (work study, ergonomics and occupational psychology have found evidence of physical and mental damage being caused by highly routinised tasks);

- the level of responsibility for discretion of work and decision-making (this should be congruent across the range of the job and appropriate for its level in the organisation);

- the degree of control and self-determination in the choice of activity, the way the job is done, quality of output and achievement of overall objectives;

- the existence of overall goals and availability of feedback;

- the perceived value and meaningfulness of the job (ie that the tasks have a real purpose or function);

- the opportunities for social contact and the development of working relationships;

- the opportunities to make use of existing skills and to develop others.

ORGANISATIONAL CHANGE

Times of change, especially if they affect the whole of an organisation, can be traumatic for all concerned. If handled and managed well, however, they can provide many opportunities for growth and development.

Even the negative aspects of change can prove to have a silver lining. Redundancy or redeployment are perhaps the worst consequences of change. Other bad elements include downgrading, being required to carry out undesirable duties, or being under-employed. There is no wish here to diminish the pain that these circumstances can cause; there can be no denial of the scars carried by some people as a result of badly handled change. However, it need not always be like this. Steps can be taken to ensure that people are treated with respect and dignity. Even if the pain and trauma cannot be reduced, action can be taken to make sure that people suffering are given sensitive consideration.

On the positive side, change can be exciting, stretching and rewarding. This, too, can be painful, but usually in these cases the rewards outweigh the pain. Plant (1985) describes how positive change can be achieved. One fundamental way of making change positive is communication. This means more than simply telling people what is happening. Of course this is important, but they need also to be told about the implications of the changes and how the people involved will be affected. The question on everyone's mind will be 'What does this mean to me?'

There are examples of assessment centres being used as vehicles to communicate changes in role to managers. The centre technique can convey the meaning and practice of some of the words. The criteria can be developed to elicit the skills that will be required to respond to and deal with the new conditions. The activities can be designed to demonstrate the sort of incidents that could realistically happen in the near future. (See Dale and Iles (1991) for fuller details.) There have also been some occasions where a centre has been used to help managers decide whether to accept redundancy or enter into retraining (Cane and Powell, 1989).

When changes result in an individual leaving an organisation, this need not mean the termination of a career or working life. Some organisations have provided their staff with outplacement counselling and retraining opportunities. This may seem extravagant at a time when the organisation is likely to be short of money, but staff deserve help, support and reward, even on the termination of their employment contract. Some of the departing members of staff will need and welcome help in thinking through their options and career futures. If the line managers are skilled already, because they have adopted a developmental approach to staff management, opportunities for reflection, skill assessments and feedback can be provided at no great cost. If there is a wish to extract as much good out of a poor situation, usually it is possible for some benefit to be achieved. On the other hand, if everything is seen in shades of black and staff are simply handed their P45s and final cheques, it will be hard to see the good.

On a lesser scale, changes to an organisation, even if only a small part of a section is to be involved, can be approached in a developmental way. Incidents such as the following can be explored:

- Slack times can be used to invest for the future; the need to investigate alternative approaches will require the search for information and reflection;

- Questioning of existing methods and comparison can ensure that the best practice is being followed;

- Stopping particular routines or patterns of behaviour gives space to learn other or new skills.

Example 6.12

The new computer package being installed in the accounts department had its own word processor. This meant that standard letters could be produced immediately by the accounts clerks, rather than handwritten drafts being sent to the typing pool. The typists, thus, would have some slack capacity.

The marketing department was exploring the cost of producing publicity fliers, but the graphic design costs at first glance appeared to be prohibitive. One of the typists had been doing an RSA typing course at night school and had seen a demonstration of a desk top publishing package. She was keen to use the package but could not see how she could do so at work.

A coffee-break discussion of the dangers of the reduced workload in the typing pool between the marketing assistant and typist brought together the two wishes to produce good-quality fliers and use a desk-top publishing system. The answer to both ambitions was possible. The change in the accounts department, the threat to the typing pool and the needs of the marketing department had created a development opportunity.

EVERYDAY WORK

Finally the seemingly prosaic occasions must be examined. It has been said that everyday work occurrences can become learning and development opportunities. But how can the routine (boring?) jobs that have to be done to enable the organisation to function be made interesting, stretching and rewarding? Perhaps they cannot, and it would be misleading to pretend otherwise. Nevertheless, many tasks and jobs can be improved to provide experiences from which skill development can occur.

The way to make this improvement happen largely concerns the approach taken to planning and allocating the work. It is all too easy, when under pressure, to ask the member of staff who is known to be able to do the job to get on with it, or to do the job oneself. This way, no one learns, but the risk of failing to complete the job to the standard required in the set time-scale is reduced. Asking someone whose skill level is unknown to do the job does involve a greater chance of failure, and the likelihood of the job taking longer to complete.

Management should involve taking some control over one's environment, forecasting of peaks and troughs, and planning of workloads; it should be possible to spot the tasks that will provide development opportunities for staff before they become urgent. Having carried out appraisals and audits of staff's existing skills, development needs and aspirations, it should be possible to identify which members of staff will benefit most from a particular experience.

To make the most of these opportunities, the manager must play an active role. Delegation should not be a synonym for abdication. The manager must remain in touch and aware, so that interest, support, remedial action, encouragement, reward and praise are available when needed. The sort of delegation decision made by the manager ought to be determined by the characteristics of the individual report. Some people need close supervision. The experience and skill levels of members of staff also influence how work should be allocated to different individuals. The skill of a manager is evidenced in the use of judgement to identify the appropriate level of involvement and at which stage an intervention can usefully be made. Thus delegation can vary from: 'There's an investigation to be done into the suitability of a new computer package. Would you have a go at it please?', to 'We need to investigate the suitability of a new computer pack. We will meet tomorrow to plan how to carry out the investigation, decide who will do what and work out what help you might need.'

There are several distinct stages to taking a developmental approach to work allocation.

- *Planning*
  — Working out what the job will entail.
  — Identifying which job would be 'best' done (in a developmental sense) by whom.

- *Monitoring*
  — Keeping a watching brief over progress.
  — Opening doors to enable the person doing the work to do it, but not doing the job for them.

- *Challenging*
  — Questioning chosen approaches, without threatening or undermining confidence.
  — Checking that the person doing the job has examined alternatives fully and understands the reasons and implications of their choice.

- *Highlighting*
  — Drawing attention to learning points.
  — Helping the reflection processes.
  — Focusing on achievements, especially if the going is getting tough.

- *Rewarding*
  — Giving due praise and acknowledgement.
  — Telling others about the achievements.

- *Using learning*
  — Finding opportunities to use the newly acquired or developed skills, so that they are practised and further developed.

- *Moving on*
  — Once an experience has been gained, life does not stop there.

It may for some people. There is the example of the individual who had one particular experience twenty times. There is no real reason for this to be the case. Learning and development is a way of life. Therefore planning the next phases of development should overlap with each job and task, as and before it is completed. In fact, development should be a continuous, seamless, whole way of working.

SUMMARY

This chapter has explored the occasions that occur as part of normal life within an organisation. These occasions start before the actual appointment of a post-holder is made. The definition of the job and specification of the requirements needed for its successful performance are the first components of building a developmental job. The way in which the recruitment process is designed and managed also conveys messages to candidates about what would be expected of them if they were to be appointed and what they can expect to receive in return. The information gathered by the candidates is both that intended to be transmitted, and that which is not.

Training provides an obvious opportunity for development, but it must be remembered that attendance at courses is no proof of learning. Some courses can deal with the here and now, others can be more long-term. Some can be designed to train the participants in very specific skills, and others can be designed to help the individual learn processes and techniques that can be transferred to other situations.

Performance management is a topical, popular term which integrates eight stages used to ensure that individual energies are harnessed towards the achievement of organisational objectives, while ensuring that the people obtain the rewards they want and deserve for their efforts. The way in which the process is implemented could make it developmental or it could be mechanistic.

Career management provides future career paths for individuals and future competent workers for the organisation. Some may see this technique as removing choice from individuals; others as a way of opening up access to areas of work which might otherwise have been closed. Again a lot depends on the way in which the technique is designed and implemented.

Disciplinary occasions and performance problems are normally seen in a negative light. They can be distasteful and unpleasant, and they tend not to go away. However, they can provide opportunities for remedial action, and it is worth remembering that industrial tribunals look for evidence of developmental action being taken by employers when investigating claims of unfair dismissal. The aim of disciplinary action should not be simply to get rid of an unsatisfactory employee. The process should aim to improve on unsatisfactory performance.

The way in which rewards are allocated sends out very clear messages to staff about the criteria being used in practice to judge achievement and failure. Most of the research that has been conducted has shown that job satisfaction is obtained from the nature of the work and that while pay levels, if wrong, can demotivate, if right they do not greatly motivate staff to expend more energies on their work. The forces that do increase motivation have been shown to be achievement, good relations with supervisors, and challenging, interesting work.

The processes used to create strategic plans can help staff to develop their skills and widen their view and understanding of their organisation. Perhaps they would not normally be involved in a particular level of work, but the compilation and review of plans create opportunities for participation, discussion, investigation and skill assessment. If included in the organisational assessment of strengths and weaknesses, skills can provide additional resources and possibly strategic advantage.

Jobs can be constructed either to build in development, or exclude it. Jobs can be a collection of tasks, or they can have a rationale and underlying purpose, linking complementary skills together into a job that provides variety, feedback and the opportunity to grow within it.

To many, change is threatening; to some it is there to be grasped with excitement. Regardless of the way in which change is embraced by individuals, it is now a normal feature of modern working life. The unknown contains unknown opportunities for learning, growth and development, but only if the individual wants to take them. There are (fortunately only few) occasions when it is impossible to make someone learn if they are totally resistant to learning. But if their job has been well built, the changes occurring round them should not be so threatening, but more a reality of life to be treated as just another part of the job. Developing staff will be more likely to see change and learning new skills as nothing special. The process of learning will be integral to understanding and coming to terms with the new. This will not be a rejection of the past, just moving on and progressing.

Finally, the chapter examined everyday work allocation. They are all concerned with the approach used by the manager responsible for staff. Most managers are involved in appointments, appraisals, performance and career management, etc, to a greater or lesser extent. They are certainly involved in delegating and planning their reports' work. The way in which this is done is at their discretion. The other processes may be confined by organisational practice and culture, but how managers deal directly with their own staff is within their control. This can be ordinary or it can be developmental.

The next chapter will look at some of the techniques at the disposal of managers to help them adopt this approach. But, as with all management techniques, they can be applied either well or badly (or not at all). How to do so is up to each individual to decide, based on their own skill levels and the culture of their own organisation. The different techniques are suitable for use in different situations, which will also be described and whilst the manager is occupying different roles. The differences in roles will be outlined later. Meanwhile, the message to take forward from this chapter is that if managers see the everyday as providing opportunities for their own learning, they are more likely to translate them into learning and developmental opportunities for their staff.

7

Development methods

INTRODUCTION

This chapter will describe the action any manager can take to contribute to their own development and that of the people around them. So far, most attention has been given to what steps a manager can take to aid the development of others. These include direct assistants and other staff, colleagues, and the manager's manager. Managers should not ignore their own development. Much of what has been about others applies equally to managers. To aid the learning of others, managers need to continue their own development and learning. The only assumptions that will be made about the ability to act will concern resources and commitment. It will be assumed that all resources, particularly money and time, are in short supply, but that commitment is not. The saying, 'Where there is a will, there is a way', holds more than a grain of truth.

The methods used in direct training will not be covered in any great detail, except when they can be directly transferred from the training room into the workplace. These methods and their use are covered more than adequately in other sources, for example Dale and Iles (1991), Harrison (1989), Blanksby (1988) and Eitington (1989). (The latter is a comprehensive guide to simple activities that can be used by managers to develop individuals and groups. Giving explanations and ideas on the use of techniques and instruments, it provides the novice with some starting points.)

This chapter will outline actions a manager can take without having to rely on the provision of other resources, or even permission. Training activities have their place in development, and are an extremely valuable way of acquiring and improving skills, but for learning to happen fully, those skills have to be put to use, so it is the development of skills on the job and the transfer of learning to the job that are a major concern here. It is also important to remember that training is task-specific, and development embraces the whole. Using the job itself and real work activities provides fertile ground for learning. They can cater for both immediate and long-term needs, broaden the individual's role, and contribute to the total development of the person and the organisation. The different methods that can be used to aid development will be considered and, as before, examples used to demonstrate their application. The emphasis will be on ease of use, so that it is possible for a manager to experiment without having to take too many risks.

A basic premise underpins this chapter. Kolb's learning cycle is taken to be an accurate representation of the process of adult learning. This belief has been used as a fundamental principle and has influenced the choice of methods. The methods will be both active – things to do, jobs to complete, goals which need to be translated into action steps, and passive – things to think about, reflect upon, and try out conceptually. The learning cycle moves from experience through reflection and conceptualisation, to experimentation and more experience, and demonstrates the need to integrate training with thinking and with work experience.

There is a problem with the way in which the cycle is usually illustrated. It is often shown as a closed loop, which can be taken to mean that one thing is learnt and then the next is started. Learning is not like that, it is a continuous, interactive, incremental process. Each experience is added to the individual's existing constructs. These are melded together to reinforce or help develop new concepts which are tried out and refined, based on the realities of experience. Similarly, patterns of behaviour are reinforced or new actions learnt, practised, abandoned or improved. A better representation of the learning cycle is as a three-dimensional spiral, as shown in Figure 7.1.

THE MANAGER

The manager's role in developing staff at work is of major importance. This will be discussed at length here, as the manager can transform an everyday event into an opportunity for learning. Alternatively, the manager can kill the richest occasion into a demotivating switch-off. So much depends on the attitude and commitment of the person who holds the purse strings (in terms of money and also other resources) and sets the climate. This climate-setting happens through example and demonstration of commitment. This requires action to be taken to help the learning of others and commitment by working on one's own learning. There are excellent texts which are designed to help managers with their own development. (For example Megginson and Pedlar (1992), Pedlar and Boydell (1985), Chambers, Coopey and McLean (1990), Whetton and Cameron (1991) and Pedlar, Burgoyne and Boydell (1986).)

They all begin from the belief that managers need to start with an

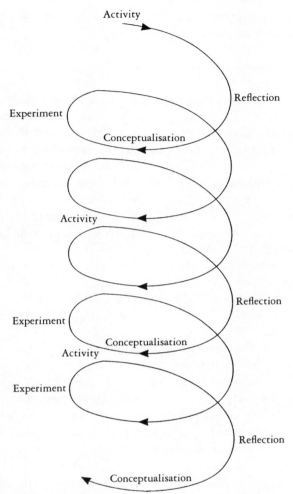

Figure 7.1 The learning cycle

understanding of their own performance development needs and learning processes as a preface to understanding and helping the development of other people. They also agree about responsibility – the individual is responsible for their own learning; no one else can be. You stand or fall by your own efforts, but you need not be alone. The managerial role confers extra responsibilities – not just for the learning of others, but for enabling it to happen. This is done by establishing a climate which fosters development, rather than one that kills learning. The nature of the learning organisation will be discussed later. While the ideal is to work in an organisation that is totally committed to learning, there are many which are not. Managers therefore have a responsibility to ensure that, even if the rest of the organisation is hostile to learning, they are not. Perhaps a difficult task, but not impossible.

Managing the work environment

The way in which the working environment is managed, and the attitude of the person in charge, set the scene. The human brain, like any other part of the body, requires exercise to keep fit and healthy. Mental exercise takes the form of challenge and stimulation. Work can be structured in a way that is stultifyingly boring, with the only challenge coming from devising ways of fiddling the expenses claims and the stimulation comes from working out who else is fiddling the most. Alternatively, work can be made interesting. The effort put into job enrichment, enlargement and rotation schemes in the 1960s demonstrates the commercial value of these approaches. Similarly, the investment being made by Ford and Rover in personal development programmes for all their staff show that there is worth and business reasons for encouraging people to keep their minds alert. The car makers are not concerned about which topic is being learnt; learning to learn is a process that can be transferred to work-related topics when needed. The acquisition of learning skills is important.

Admittedly the organisation's culture has an influence on the degree of commitment to learning that can be exercised by an individual manager. A bureaucratic, impersonal organisation can discourage efforts to develop skills, and some can positively punish those who dare suggest alternative ways of working. In this sort of organisation, everyday work is routine and boring, decline is depressing and demotivating and growth only results in overwork. This view may be the negative side of the coin, but to those working in this type of organisation an alternative view may seem patronising and slick. Nevertheless, routine work, decline and growth can contain learning opportunities, providing the manager manages the situation in an appropriate way.

Examples will be given below to show how these opportunities can be constructed. But before starting, the manager's existing attitude to this approach and the amount of basic knowledge is worthy of exploration. Some questions are given to enable you to test out your readiness:

- Name three recent books on management or organisations.

- Name three management magazines. -

- Where is the nearest library, and where does it keep its books on management?

- Name three management gurus. Why do they stand out from the rest?

- Where can you hire a management training video to show to your staff?
- When did you last:
  — Conduct a formal appraisal meeting with any of your direct reports?
  — Debate the effect the economic climate will have on your organisation with your colleagues, your manager, your assistants?
  — Invite your manager to talk to your staff about the organisation's priorities?
  — Discuss the achievement of your section's goals and standards with your assistants?
  — Give a member of staff an article to read?
  — Praise someone's work?
  — Think about your work in the abstract?
  — Spend time planning your own development?

These are not trick questions. They relate to some of the normal activities that a developing manager carries out *as a matter of course*. They are nothing special, they do not require vast resources, nor any specialist knowledge. They just reflect a frame of mind and an approach to managing oneself and others.

WHAT CAN BE DONE?

This section will explore some of the activities that occur during everyday work that can be exploited as opportunities for learning and skill development. Some may be painful and some embarrassing, but learning sometimes is an uncomfortable experience. Athletes use the phrase, 'there's no gain without pain'. This does not necessarily mean damage, but stretching the muscles leads them to protest, at first, to the extra work they are being expected to do. The brain complains in a similar fashion. Managers have been heard to say, during a period of rapid change, 'Stop the world until my brain stops hurting.' Learning new skills is worse in some ways than absorbing new knowledge or understanding the implications of change. Developing new skills requires them to be put into practice, usually in front of other people, often assistants. This means that the manager is vulnerable and at risk of failure – or possibly worse – looking foolish. But these are the reasons for not learning. On the other side is the risk of success and the danger of being praised.

Work allocation

It is normal for work to be planned, jobs defined and handed out and tasks allocated every day. The non-developmental ways of doing this include:

- not planning the whole job, doing it in bits;

- handing out jobs in a one-off, *ad hoc* fashion;

- giving the job to the person best able to do it;

- asking different people to do bits of the job;

- giving out separate parts of one job at different times to different people without explaining the whole;

- asking people to do a job without telling them why or the context in which they are working;

- not telling people or letting them see the results of their work;

- taking credit for other people's efforts;

- giving muddled instructions, no timescale and no indication of the standards expected;

- working on projects yourself in secret (your staff usually find out what you are doing).

The opposites of these constitute a developmental approach. Staff are not told; they are asked to do work. They are given the whole story and know the context in which they are working. (Mushroom management may produce a fine collection of fungi, but some can be deadly poisonous. Managing people in this way can have a similar effect.) The work is planned and the people who would gain the most as well as doing the 'best' job are involved. Each knows their part in the whole and what everyone else is doing, including their manager. They all know what the results of their work will be used for and are made aware of the consequences of their actions.

Example 7.1

The company produces an annual report for its shareholders, as required by the Company Acts. Traditionally the report has been a collection of legally required facts and figures, accompanied by the chief executive's highly conventional 'state of the nation' commentary on the company's performance. In previous years the company secretary (now retired) gathered the data with a great deal of secrecy from every section and department. She pretended to be doing anything but the annual report, believing that the figures would be inflated or deflated if people knew what she was really working on. In fact everyone did know and colluded occasionally to get one over on her. It was only her diligence that avoided some first class examples of tomfoolery being published.

The company, on the secretary's departure, created a number of new jobs, including that of head of corporate affairs. Faced with the annual chore, the new person in the post decided to put together a project team to produce a new-style report. The purpose of the report would be changed. As well as meeting legal requirements, in future, it would be used to publicise the company, internally and externally, to shareholders and other interested parties such as customers, suppliers and competitors. A new style was called for and a new way of presenting boring data was required.

The first meeting of the project group was designed to plan the whole project and decide how to work as a group. The second allocated different areas of work to the people who were interested and able to carry them out. The third decided how to monitor progress and to collate the work of the separate individuals. The fourth meeting was when the work began in earnest.

The end product was a highly professional, factual report that won critical praise. The staff involved had never worked together before, never on a project team basis, and had never been involved in the production of a legally required, prestige publication.

Delegation

Rather than being just an allocation of tasks, delegation is more to do with assigning responsibility for an area of work. One complaint often heard is that work is delegated, but the authority needed to carry it out is not. Delegating badly can be one of the most demotivating ways in which a manager can treat staff. Done well, however, it can involve the greatest possibility for development. Learning, it is agreed, is about taking risks. Being given the responsibility and authority for carrying out the whole of a new job on one's own can be challenging, stimulating and rewarding – delegation can contain so many learning pay-offs, if done in the right way. If done badly, however, it can almost inevitably lead to failure (or success in spite of the manager).

The golden rules for developmental delegation are:

- Be clear about the purpose of the work being delegated.

- Specify the boundaries of authority and responsibility.

- Provide the resources and support needed to carry out the whole job.

- Monitor progress, as agreed; do not check up.

- Be sure that the persons asked to do the work are able to do it their way, not your way.

- Believe they will do it to a better standard than you expect of them (and then wait to be proved right).

- Provide the support and open the doors when asked, but not until you are asked – do not interfere.

- Intervene only as a very last resort.

- Ensure that the person doing the job knows the result of their work.

- Make sure that acknowledgement and praise is awarded.

Example 7.2

The post of works co-ordinator was set up to link the work of the external service engineers and the internally based staff. The external engineers reported directly to the works manager and the internal engineers to the after-sales manager. The co-ordinator's role was to plan workloads, ensure stock levels were adequate, complete work dockets for invoicing purposes and to ensure the maintenance work on returned products was progressed speedily. This latter task meant allocating work to the external engineers to do when they did not have any call-outs to deal with.

This arrangement seemed fine when first suggested. In practice, however, because the co-ordinator had no authority over any of the engineers and there was no requirement for anyone to even tell him what they were doing when, he was unable to plan the work. In the end, the co-ordinator felt as though he had been set up. There was no way that work could be planned and he spent most of his time chasing up jobs or providing excuses to customers about the non-completion of their repairs. The engineers' workloads were uneven and they swayed between being bored and over-worked. This meant that some people got all the nasty jobs and others the easy ones. Eventually, everyone was fed up. A good idea had failed in practice because there had been no proper delegation of responsibility.

Projects

Special projects can present wonderful opportunities for the development of skills. They can be planned or opportunistic. Planned projects are those that arise as a result of deliberate decisions made to engage in particular areas of work. Because they are foreseen, they can be designed to allow the acquisition or development of specified skills.

Example 7.3

The organisation, a housing association, decided that it needed to change its image. It had been established in the 1970s to work alongside local authorities in the provision of specialist accommodation for people with disabilities. During its 20 years of existence, the association found that its role had altered. Local authority funding was drying up as a new emphasis was placed on private, individual ownership. People were buying council homes and building societies were becoming more prepared to lend to individuals with disabilities. Care in the community policies had led to an increase in interest from health authorities, both privately and publicly funded, and unexpectedly, a change in the size of damages awards made by the courts meant that some individuals had money to spend on their own homes.

The association realised it needed to change its approach, image and the type of service it was offering. To identify which of several options to chose, a project team was put together. The team consisted of the director of the association, the finance officer, two area managers, the administrator and the housing lawyer. None had marketing experience or project management skills. To start the project, the local university was asked to construct an intensive short course covering funding, marketing, public relations, an update on housing law and project management for the team. Following the week-long course, the team started work to plan the whole of their project and put their newly acquired learning to work.

The group's first task was to present to the management committee a menu of options, strategic plans for each, their resource implications and methods of implementation. After the committee's decision, the team's job would be to manage the implementation of the chosen strategy.

Opportunistic projects are those that occur as a result of events happening in the environment. These can be overlooked (deliberately or otherwise) or they can be exploited. It is not so easy to use them to meet pre-identified areas of need. Much of the learning unfolds as the project itself grows. These opportunities need to be grabbed, as they can be elusive. To make the most of such opportunities the managers should know the development needs of their assistants, be watchful for the opportunity and be ready to choose (ie make a deliberate decision) whether to grab it or let it go.

Example 7.4

A fire destroyed the corporate administration block over one weekend. No one was injured, but the computer system was burnt out. Even the back files kept in a 'fire-proof' safe had been damaged by the intense heat. The financial details of two of the subsidiary companies had been lost.

The director of one of the subsidiary companies immediately visited the bank and asked for extended overdraft facilities until the debtors and creditors identified themselves. For some months after the fire the company struggled to pay its way and found that it had lost considerable sums of money.

The second subsidiary set up a team of those 'who knew, those who cared and those who could' to reconstruct the lost knowledge. This action drew people together who had never worked collaboratively before. By pooling their individual information, the team managed to reconstruct most of the company's debts and outstanding accounts within a few days. They also identified ways of improving the security of the systems and found some significant areas which could be streamlined and simplified. Although the company lost some money as a result of double payments and bad debts, the improvements in operational efficiency produced long-term savings.

The key points for making a project developmental rather just another job of work are:

- Establish the purpose of the project and the desired outcome.

- Specify which skills are likely to be acquired or developed.

- Review the progress of the project and the development of the skills at regular intervals.

- Ensure that feedback loops are built in as the project unfolds.

- Question and critically appraise working practices.

- At the end, review achievement of the whole and its separate parts:
  — examine what went well – what contributed to and influenced success;
  — explore what did not go so well – why, could the weak points have been avoided or guarded against, what has hindsight brought, what could be improved for the future;
  — what were the failures – why did they happen, could they have been foreseen, how were they remedied (if at all), what needs to be done to prevent a recurrence.

- Identify what has been learnt from the project and what can be transferred to normal working.

By planning the project, even those that occur as unforeseen opportunities and which, at the time, may seem as crises, it is possible to abstract valuable experience and learning points which lead to the development of skills and working practices.

Example 7.5

Marie was indispensable. Her knowledge of the market was vast and even though she was a regional sales manager, her reputation with the company's customers was national. It was not uncommon for her to be asked for by name and to have her duties reassigned at short notice so she could do a 'special favour' for a valued client. As a result of her extensive experience on prestige projects, her skills became highly developed. The down-side of this was that the other sales managers were denied the opportunities to develop their skills in the same way. There was some jealousy but, as many of the projects involved a degree of personal inconvenience, they tended to let Marie get on with them.

The real consequences of this came on the day when Marie was rushed into hospital for emergency heart surgery. The training manager jumped with glee, not out of sadistic delight, but because he was pleased that the long-awaited opportunity had come. He had long warned the managing director of the folly of relying exclusively on Marie's personal willingness and talents. A development programme was quickly set in place for all regional sales managers so that the company was able to offer a continued level of support to its clients during Marie's absence.

When she was well enough, the training manager visited her and told her what was happening. Marie breathed a sigh of relief. She had been getting increasingly tired and less inclined to drop everything for special clients. She did not like to refuse, knowing that none of the others could take over, but could not see how she could carry on for much longer.

The managing director decided to continue and extend the development programme so that Marie could work herself back in gradually at the end of her sick leave, skilling up the other sales manager to improve the general level of support services to an increased number of clients. In the end, everyone benefited from the crisis caused by Marie's sickness, including Marie herself, who was able to develop her skills in a new role as a developer of others.

Deputising

Deputising, in the context of development, is the planned replacement of the manager by a report for the specific purposes of both covering a duty and for developing pre-determined skills.

Simply asking someone to step in or do a job is not deputising in this sense. A developmental approach requires that, before the event:

- the objectives of the exercise are to be agreed;
- the skills to be developed are identified;
- a means of reflecting and reviewing the experience is established.

Example 7.6

Colin was the financial systems manager, Leon the latest recruit with about a year's post graduate experience. Several other organisations used the same computer application and had set up a regional users' group. Colin normally attended their meetings, but he was aware the next was planned for when he was on holiday. Leon was beginning to show some skills in programming and Colin was keen for all his staff to develop an interest in this area of work.

He decided that he would ask Leon to attend the meeting and prepare a written report for Colin which could form a verbal presentation for the rest of the staff. Before his holiday, Colin briefed Leon about the background to and politics of the group. He went through the minutes of the previous three meetings and discussed with Leon the likely items for the next meeting's agenda. They agreed that Leon would develop his listening and political awareness skills, and the written report would enable him to practise concise report-writing (he tended to be verbose.) He would also be able to practise giving verbal presentations to a safe audience. He had not done any public speaking since leaving university and had said, during his first appraisal, that this was an area he knew needed some work.

Joint working

Some areas of work, specific tasks or projects present suitable occasions for joint working. The manager and assistant work together, sharing the responsibility and the glory. The manager employs coaching and mentoring techniques (to be described later) to share experience with the report, extend the skills of developing others and to help develop the skills of the report. This can be a very satisfying way of working for both parties. The questioning and search for understanding by the report can help managers challenge their existing assumptions, throwing new light on traditional practices.

Example 7.7

It was time to produce the annual digest of statistics. In the past, the production manager had done this alone, usually as near to the deadline as he dared. This year he decided he was not going to repeat the adrenalin fix and that the digest's compilation would be planned and shared.

Two months before the deadline, a team of three was set up, comprising the production manager, the operations supervisor and the clerk. The latter was to be responsible for the data collection, the supervisor would compile the various tables and the production manager would carry out the analysis of the statistics.

Explaining

Some reference is made above to the need to put jobs into context and to give full, clear instructions. Explaining requires more. As in the case of 'Martin' in example 7.8 below, this can be a deliberate attempt to ensure that staff not only know, but understand the context in which they are working and the reasons why things are the way they are. Time is needed to help staff work out for themselves the implications changes will have for them (see Bloom's taxonomy, mentioned in Chapter 4 (Bloom, 1956)).

The manager can do much to help this, by ensuring that the 'whys' and 'wherefores' are explained and that staff's questions are answered as fully as possible. This does take time and effort and can easily be seen as time-wasting, especially when there are tight deadlines to be met. Time spent at this point, though, can save so much that could be lost later. Misunderstandings, misdirected effort and disillusionment created by confusion and uncertainty waste far more time than it takes to explain the context, rationale and meaning of change properly at the outset.

Proper, clear explanations also provide reassurance. Uncertainty breeds confusion, lack of clarity feeds rumours. Sometimes it is important to repeat explanations so staff are reassured that the changes are consistent and that there is a direction for them to follow.

Coaching and mentoring

Coaching is described by Megginson and Boydell (1979) as:

a process in which a manager, through direct discussion and guided activity, helps a colleague to solve a problem or to do a task better than would otherwise have been the case.

While the coach need not be an expert in the problem area, it is normal to expect a certain level of expertise. A good coach does not do the job for the person being coached (demonstrations apart). Questions are asked, and suggestions made. These are intended to enable the coachee to copy, then practise and develop their own approach. In the words of a nursery rhyme:

I do it normal
I do it slow
I do it with you
Then off you go.

Mentoring is different. In some quarters, however, the term is used to refer to as an up-market version of coaching, which misses the subtle difference. Megginson and Pedler (1992) distinguish between the two by saying that, 'while coaching builds performance, mentoring is concerned with building a life's work'. To be successful in the role, the mentor needs to be able to establish a special relationship with the person being mentored. This is not such a precondition in coaching. As can be seen from sporting analogies, the coach and players can almost hate the sight of each other and still have a successful coaching relationship. The coach can stretch and challenge the players, who respond, perhaps for all the wrong reasons, but still develop their performance. In a mentoring relationship this would not work. Mentoring requires trust and respect, as the areas of concern in performance and development extend well beyond the boundaries of work into the whole life. A good coaching manager may be remembered; a mentor will not be forgotten.

Example 7.8

The new director of personnel was asked to describe the person who had the most effect on her development.

'It has to be Martin. He spent so much time talking to me.'

'What about?'

'Well, everything. His childhood, politics, the state of Europe and the economy, voting patterns, ways of working, types of contracts, union rights, power and abuse of power, managers, organisation design, marriage, music. You name it. We talked for hours, in work, after work. He trusted me. He would often say: "Just have a look at", by which he would mean "Do a full investigation and if you need any help come and ask." It was his readiness to listen and talk when I needed him that was good. He broadened my outlook and made me think about things I would never have considered otherwise in relation to work. It is now seven years since we separated. See, I'm talking as though we were partners. He was ever so upset when I handed in my notice. He did not talk to me during the six week notice period. But I still remember his examples and what he taught me. If any one person shaped me at work it was him.'

There are now some work-based training and development programmes that make use of coaching and mentoring. Perhaps the most notable is 'The First-

Line Manager' programme produced by Intek MacMillan. The learner, a first-line manager, works on job-related projects while following a structured programme. The programme explores particular areas of management via the projects, text and input meetings with an adviser and co-managers. The programme leads up to a final major project which should aim to address an aspect of work in need of change or improvement. A critical feature of the programme is that the projects are undertaken with the direct support and involvement of the first-line manager's own manager.

The differences between coaching and mentoring can be very fine, as the way in which the two techniques is put into practice are very dependent on the chosen style of the manager. Because of this, on the other hand, they can also be very different. It is important, therefore, to distinguish between the two and to be clear about their uses.

Learning from mistakes and successes

Saying we learn from our mistakes can be a truism. We may say 'I will never do that again, I will learn from that', but then promptly lose the real learning by doing just that. Learning, being the application of skills and knowledge, may require repeating the event and doing better a second time (in other words, practice). To make sure that skill development results, instead of adding the event into the memory store, a proper analysis is needed to obtain insight into the causes and effects of mistakes. This is not done to attribute blame. Often the reason for an activity not working is a combination of the actions of several individuals interacting in some dysfunctional way and a set of circumstances coming together at that particular time and place. Critical incident technique provides a way of analysing such events so that blaming and defensiveness can be avoided. This technique can be used to analyse successes in exactly the same way.

It is common that success is shrugged off as luck or as a result of fortuitous circumstances. But, as with failure, it is more likely to be a product of people and circumstances. By unpicking what worked, what proved difficult or what did not work, and why, useful models can be identified for future use.

Example 7.9

It worked! The first major sales campaign went a treat. After the celebrations and the congratulations were over, the sales manager brought the team together for the post-mortem. Some of the team members were a little puzzled, but the manager opened the meeting by explaining why he wanted to examine each stage of the campaign. The point of doing so was to identify what they had done right. Often when things had gone well, particular aspects tended to get lost in the overall buzz of success.

Using a flip chart, the manager asked the team to brain-storm each critical step. These were then listed in chronological order and the unique characteristics of each were identified. The team members were asked to rate the level of contribution each step had had to the overall success of the campaign. Finally, they were asked how they could ensure that the same or similar characteristics could be maintained or improved upon for the next campaign.

A typical page of the flip chart looked like this when they had finished:

Step	Characteristic	Rating 1–10
Publicity leaflets:		
• Audience	— carefully identified	10
	— market research checked	5
	— locations verified	7
• Design	— concept challenged	9
	— alternatives considered	3
	— final choice tested	4
• Copy	— brief drawn up by several people	6
	— copy-writer engaged	4
	— copy tested against design concept and audience profile	6
• Art work	— same people to give brief	6
	— checked against copy and concept and tested against audience profile	6
• Printing	— expensive process selected	2
	— good printer used	4
• Distribution	— coincided with media	6
• Timing	— advertising	4

The main points of the discussion were recorded and the main features noted in the work file so that they would be readily available for the next campaign.

Dealing with faults

A fault is different from a mistake. The latter is usually caused by an error. Faults can be systemic, or products of a system's dysfunction. *Systemic faults* are built-in traps which lead to failure. This type of fault can be found in procedures that have been in operation for a number of years and have not been adapted to meet new conditions. Alternatively, systems that have been adapted can be sources of systemic faults. The adaptations or modifications may have been made with the intention of improving the system, but, in fact, have distorted the underlying logic, so creating fracture points.

System dysfunctions means that the system works but achieves an unintended outcome. Another meaning of system dysfunction is the achievement of the desired outcome, but using inefficient processes. This may be caused by poor system design or by trying to do different, contradictory things at the same time.

Example 7.10

As part of a quality improvement programme, the company set up a customer queries and complaint point. The staff were recruited on the basis of their interest in and knowledge of consumer rights. Because this was a new venture, the company wanted to monitor its operation and so required information about the type of queries and complaints being received. Information was also wanted on how long it took to resolve a complaint and how much each cost. A systems analyst was seconded to set up systems and procedures designed to provide the information required by management.

A year after the section was set up, an evaluation was carried out. The quality controller was very disappointed to find that 60 per cent of the staff had left, and those remaining were disillusioned. Customer satisfaction rates had dropped and the number of unresolved complaints had soared.

After an investigation, it was concluded that the procedures the staff had been asked to follow to gather the data needed by management were complex and laborious. Complainants were angered by the detail they were required to give, and the staff believed that the forms and procedures directly prevented them from giving the sort of service they thought the company had wanted. The system was working, but against the company's overall interests. It was gathering the information it had been set up to collect, but in doing so, was preventing the intended job from being done.

Standing back from systems and questioning them can be truly developmental for the individuals and the organisation. How many of us, when asked why we do a particular job the way we do, would answer either, 'That's the way it has always been done', or 'That's the way we do it here'? To unpick systems and identify faults requires that the system's real purpose is ascertained. Only when this has been done, to everyone's satisfaction, can the faults be picked up. Techniques such as *faults analysis* can help to separate the different aspects of a system's weakness and work out what can be done to eliminate them.

Stages of fault analysis

- *Fault* – What is it?

- *Ascertained* – How does it show itself?

- *Caused* – What are its origins?

- *Effect* – How serious is it?

- What *damage* is it creating?

- *Responsibility* – Who has responsibility for it or the area of work; who owns the fault?

- *Action* – What can be done to remove or minimise its negative features?

- *Prevention* – What can be done to prevent this fault or similar ones from occurring again?

Staff meetings

Staff meetings are the most common formal channel of communication between a manager and the team. This is an area of normal activity which can provide perhaps the most readily available opportunity for development. Several references have already been made to ways in which team meetings can be used for different purposes. While most tend to be used to convey information and hold discussions about work matters, there is no reason why 'special' meetings cannot be held to consider broader, more futuristic matters. The team can be brought together to work on its business plan or strategy. This should open up discussions about the future of the team in the context of the organisation and its environment and highlight areas of work that are in need of improvement or development. Discussions about the state of business can broaden the horizon of some team members and bring into active consideration the strengths and weaknesses of the operations. Discussions of this nature can result in reflection and questioning and, in some cases, lead to quite dramatic reframing of basic assumptions.

Staff meetings can be used for training in two very different ways. The first way is not uncommon and occurs when particular areas of need are addressed as part of a regular meeting. An example would be the showing of a training video or discussion of an article of interest. The second way is to use the meetings to contribute to the development of the team as a whole. This approach can be different from the more normal approach to team-building. The activities include joint goal-setting, agreeing standards and approaches to group working, and exploring and improving the actual workings of the group and the interpersonal relationship within it. More sophisticated team-building can address decision-making processes, participation and problem-solving techniques. A way of extending this is to use staff meetings to continue the work started in an activity. The meetings are used to consider particular issues and to develop skills. Thus they build on 'away-days' by becoming 'teach-ins'. This use of meetings also helps the learning acquired during the 'time out' to be transferred back to the normal workplace.

Example 7.11

The team recognised that it was not very good at generating new ideas. Several areas of work were causing problems, but no one could come forward with ways of resolving them. There was a tendency for team members to make a lot of suggestions regarding possible solutions, but none ever really dealt with the real problem. Rather than going over the same ground time after time, the team agreed to use one of the most intractable problems as a means of learning more creative problem-solving techniques. A specialist in the area was invited to a team meeting to 'teach' two such techniques. The most contentious problem — car parking — was chosen as the example.

Using a rational approach to problem-solving (subjective expectancy utility) and a creative one (synectics), the specialist helped the team work through the problem. Having used two extremes to explore a difficult situation, the team felt more able to stand back from problems and chose a suitable way of dealing with them, rather than rushing in with solutions right at the beginning. Later, the team felt that it was not using its meeting time to best effect. Another 'specialist' was invited to a meeting to discuss the principles of running effective meetings and structuring agendas. This, too, was found to result in changes to behaviour and more productive learning.

Learning as a group had been found to be helpful. Peer group pressure could be applied to the backsliders. More importantly, learning together meant that more had been learnt. The collective memory is greater than its individual parts and so by more people being exposed to the experts, more of what had been said could be remembered. Thus learning could be reinforced and shared.

Job applications, selection and promotion

Applying for a job, be it internal or external, offers an opportunity for an individual's development to be considered. In many organisations, applying for other jobs is regarded as an activity to be kept secret. It is seen as a demonstration of disloyalty and betrayal. The manager will be in danger of losing a member of staff and will be faced with the inconvenience and risk of having to find a replacement. A competing employer will gain the benefit of the individual's experience and training obtained from the current employer and confidences may be divulged. The member of staff would not want their boss to know that they were thinking of moving. They might lose out on the next salary rise, and if they did not get the job, they would look incompetent and foolish.

Reframing the above scenario enables it to be seen as an opportunity for viewing one's staff through others' eyes and assessing their skills against different criteria. Questioning their state of readiness to progress into another role can result in a fuller appreciation of their strengths, or it may indicate areas where their talents are not currently being deployed to their best effect. This may be the cause of some dissatisfaction and the reason why the individual is considering a move. If it is possible to have an open and full discussion at the time the individual is deciding whether to submit an application for another job, the manager has a chance to take positive action to help with the application or, if the person is really irreplaceable, of finding ways to help them stay.

No person should be totally indispensable; on occasions, encouraging staff to leave the organisation may be the right thing to do for everyone. It must follow that if one is developing and progressing, one is also moving. Changing jobs, providing it is not too frequent, is a normal work activity. Treating it as such should also be the norm. The code of secrecy is anathema to development.

Completing an application for a job is an opportunity for individuals to review their career histories. Biography is a technique that can be used to help career planning. It requires the individual to identify critical phases or incidents in the past and explore how these have influenced the decisions that have led to the present. From this analysis the individual can gain a better understanding of where they are now and plan where they want to go to in the future. They will have given due recognition to decisions that were successful and gained insight from those that were not.

Being able to work through the process of applying for a job with a sympathetic manager can be more enlightening for both parties. If the individual does not leave, the relationship between the two will have been strengthened, rather than weakened, from the increased understanding both will have acquired. This insight and trust can be applied to the construction of a development plan for the individual which will extend them in their current job and perhaps increase their job satisfaction and skills. If the individual is successful in the application, the manager will know what has been lost, and what needs to be replaced, and should have gained a deeper understanding of why the individual left.

Appraisal

Sadly, appraisal is often treated as an administrative procedure rather than a technique. In the worst examples of its use it is used as a mechanistic system which focuses exclusively on the past. Examination of the past is useful; it contributes to the insight needed to make sense of the present. For developmental purposes, this understanding is gained to contribute to planning how to advance into the future. Good appraisal starts with a review of past performance to identify what needs to be started, stopped or done differently to move the individual, the job and the organisation forward in the desired direction. The best examples of developmental appraisal schemes are based on four very simple stages:

1. A joint review of past performance.

2. The establishment and agreeing upon of goals and objectives for the mid-term future.

3. The identification of development needs and work priorities, so that an agreed development plan may be drawn up.

4. The implementation of the plan.

Development plans

The origins of development plans can be found in some of the industrial training boards. The Local Government Training Board, for example, used them as a means of gathering information from which to plan training course provision and to help their registered trainers think through their individual needs. Their use also provided a vehicle for the discussion of progress between trainers and their line managers. However, because they were designed to serve the needs of an external training body, they were not so useful for planning and facilitating internal, job-related personal development. Now their use is geared more towards drawing attention to work activities rather than course attendance and personal needs in addition to job-related skills. Development plans can be used to broaden perspectives while focusing on priorities.

Example 7.12

Development plan

Objective: To increase political awareness (nous)

1. Attend board meetings with manager to observe the behaviour of others.

2. Discuss observations after the meeting.

3. Read Kakabadse A P and Parker C (1984) *Power, politics and organisations: a behavioural science view*, Wiley.

---

4. Discuss the concepts of organisational power in relation to the behaviour witnessed at the meeting.

5. Attend the next meeting to refine and check perceptions.

6. Discuss how the deployment of power and influence impacts on the work of the organisation and the individual's area of work.

7. Consider the negative and positive effects.

8. Discuss which need to be altered and how these changes may be best brought about in the context of the current power structures.

A fuller version of a development plan may contain several objectives aiming at the development of a broad skill area. It could contain many different types of activities, involving other people and have timescales attached. A development plan may be the product of an appraisal meeting, or may emerge from even more formal modes of assessment such as development centres or selection events. In some cases a plan may represent action which is required to be taken following a disciplinary hearing.

The main feature of such a plan is that intentions are made explicit in the form of behavioural objectives, the means of achieving them are specified, responsibilities are assigned, and resources are made available.

Learning contracts

Learning contracts are similar to development plans in some ways. The main differences are the involvement of a third party and the definitive nature of the agreement. The three parties involved are the learner, the learner's manager (or sponsor) and a provider. It is likely that the contract will be the product of some formal assessment, outlining course attendance, involvement in formal training of some sort, or the pursuit of a planned programme of learning.

It is possible for a learning contract to specify the desired outcome(s) and outline the responsibilities of each of the parties. The parties agree to fulfil the terms of the contract in the manner described.

Example 7.13

Learning contract between
(individual)   (manager) and   (tutor)
Start date: Completion date:

Goal
(What is this contract about, what is its title?)
Project planning and resource allocation

Objective
(What knowledge and/or skills are to be acquired?)

- Planning of major projects using computer-based techniques.

- Ways of planning details and allocating resources.

Activities
(How are the objectives going to be achieved?)

- Learn how to use computer-based modelling to help strategic choice.

- Learn how to draw up a critical path.

- Re-examine 'Planned Programming and Budget System' to see if it has any relevancy to modern conditions.

Resources
(What resources are needed, who may help? Who is responsible for providing and doing?)

- Attendance on an appropriate course in systems analysis (tutor).

- The use of computer facilities and a suitable software programme (manager).

- Discussions with the engineer about critical path (manager).

- Reading about PPBS and other systems for linking activity and cost (individual).

- Meetings with course tutor (tutor).

Assessment
(How will the knowledge/skill attainment be evidenced? What criteria will be used to assess competence?)

- Production of a project plan which contains timescales and resource needs.

- Demonstration of ability to use the approaches learnt to other projects by describing how process(es) would be applied.

- Discussion on comparative values and problems of PPBS and alternatives to modern conditions.

- Description of learning, problems encountered and the ways they were overcome.

Agreed   Individual

(Signed)   Manager

                                Tutor

Learning logs

Learning logs or diaries provide a mechanism for aiding reflection and conceptualisation of experience. They seem to be mainly used in programmes of study, especially those which aim to develop personal skills and qualities in ways which lead to assessment for the development of personal profiles. They do not seem to have been readily taken up in employment. Yet keeping a personal record can help an individual to chart and recall important learning. In some cases the log can jog the memory, letting the individual revisit the experience when the learning is in need of refreshment.

Forgetting is just as much a part of the normal cognitive process as learning, so it is not unusual that some lessons need to be relearnt or revitalised. This is especially true if the skills in question are not often used. The learning log can help store the memory of the skills in theory, if not their practice.

A learning log need be nothing more than a notebook kept in the bottom drawer of the desk. It may, on the other hand, be a formal document used in conjunction with a development plan. In the latter case, it is possible that the log will be seen by others, and therefore the personalised nature of the entries may be somewhat reduced. However, this does not necessarily reduce the power of a few simple, seemingly innocuous words to restore a memory.

The learning log may also contribute to the assessment of prior experience and learning. Some skills are difficult to evidence in the tangible form required for a portfolio, and insight is generally intangible. The log can provide concrete evidence of an experience and the reflections and understanding drawn from it.

Secondments and career breaks

The opportunity to have a break from work is most normally taken by women, to give birth to children and care for them during their early years. In most organisations, with the possible exception of universities, the chance of taking such a break for other reasons is rare. A few organisations permit career breaks to be made to enable an individual to conduct a specific piece of research or to complete some writing. These go under different names such as study leave, sabbaticals, unpaid leave, etc. Alternatively, similar development opportunities can be found in the form of secondments to other parts of the same organisation or to another with close links.

The major benefit of a break, from a development point of view, is the chance to stand back from the everyday and to take stock while engaged in other activities. Moreover, the other activities may facilitate the development of useful skills in their own right. Secondments provide the opportunity of seeing how different aspects of the same work can be done differently by different organisations. Within the same organisation, they enable the individual to see their own job from another perspective. If the organisation to which the individual is seconded is a supplier or customer, the secondee will be able to see other links in the chain. Through the development of corresponding skills and understanding, improvements can then be made to the process and the quality of the total interaction. They can also give entry into levels of management that would not normally be open.

The biggest problem with secondments and career concerns the re-entry back into the employing organisation and the return to the previous job. The transition needs to be handled with great care. The individual could feel as though they were stepping backwards, rather than continuing to develop. Indeed, for some people this experience can be so negative that any benefit gained during the secondment is eroded. Steps need to be taken to provide the individual with an optimistic sense of their future and development. Effort is also needed to ensure that the returning individual is reincorporated into the team and brought up-to-date with changes to working practice, thinking and the culture.

Example 7.14

Harry had been seconded to the company's major supplier to work on the development of production methods for the component that will be key in the company's new product, an advanced turbo motor. Harry was with the supplier for 18 very happy and productive months. He had worked well with the team there and had formed friendships with his new colleagues. They had been faced with some major technical problems and had produced some imaginative, economical and practical solutions. As a result of their work the development phase was finished sooner than anticipated and the team was broken up early.

Harry returned to his previous job as production controller with mixed feelings. He had enjoyed the excitement of leading edge work and had found the collaborative approach to problem-solving stimulating. He felt that he had gained much from the experience. His permanent job seemed far more mundane. Its main purpose was to ensure that continuous production ran smoothly.

Fortunately for Harry, his manager was also concerned about his return. On his first day he was called into the office for a debriefing and to discuss his future. He was asked to spend his first week refamiliarising himself with his staff and the state of the factory. He was forbidden to get involved in any routine business until at least the following week. At the end of the first week he was to discuss what he had noticed with his manager. At the end of that meeting he was asked to spend the following week working out how he could apply some of what he had learnt during the secondment to improve working methods in his own area. He was to submit a report to his manager on the following Friday. This report, he was told, was to include recommendations for developing new approaches of working and ways of resolving what may have seemed to be either intractable problems or areas of vague dissatisfaction, as well as the more obvious ones.

Harry was also asked to think about how he could continue his own development. How could he link his experience of project, developmental working to that of running an operation that relied on continuous steady state production? He was to produce a plan for discussion with his manager.

Briefing, debriefing and involvement in training/study courses

Preparing a member of staff to attend training courses should obviously be a part of ongoing development. The manager should go through the course's objectives, contents and method of delivery with the member of staff. The discussion should aim at reaching a decision about the suitability of the proposed course and its ability to satisfy the member of staff's needs, which it is likely to do only partially. The shortfall should be noted so that other ways of meeting them can be identified. The individual's and manager's expectations of the course were highlighted for use in evaluating the value of the event. Participants, it is believed, tend to get more from training courses if they have prepared and have thought through their expectations. Sometimes these expectations are very different from the course's reality. This is often because the preparatory work has not been done thoroughly, and the reasons for attending may have had nothing to do with the course's objectives and content.

After attending a course, the manager and member of staff should be prepared to discuss what happened and what was learnt. The experience of the course should be compared with the expectations and reasons for attendance. Again it is likely that there will be some areas of disappointment and unmet needs – no single course can fulfil all expectations. Recognising the gaps can help to identify areas that need additional attention. The debriefing has three purposes:

1. It should serve to aid the reflection/conceptualisation phase of the learning cycle.

2. It should focus on ways in which the learning can be applied to the job, and what action needs to be taken to help that happen.

3. The discussion should highlight the gaps and plan the next stage of the individual's development.

Involvement in a post-experience qualification course frequently requires some form of release from work to permit class attendance. A typical scenario is for a member of staff to disappear every Wednesday afternoon, be given homework and be expected to be successful by passing the assignments and examinations. Even though the class tutors may make efforts to relate the academic contents of the course to work, often the line managers do not reciprocate. Once the members of staff have achieved the qualification, the commitment to their training is ended. If the individual is not successful, they have failed. The manager's disinterest and lack of involvement may have been a contributing factor, but this is rarely taken into account.

An alternative and far more satisfactory approach is for the line manager to take an ongoing interest in what is being done during the course of study. This means:

- Discussing with the individual what they are studying.

- Asking, continually, if the content has any immediate application.

- Checking with the individual about progress.

- Asking if the next assignment needs anything from the line manager or the job.

By taking this sort of approach the line manager may find new ideas to think about or methods to develop. There may be fresh thinking to import or alternative ways of doing a particular job to try out. The individual may be struggling with an aspect of the course. Discussion with a manager may throw new light on the problem, or provide the chance for discussion with someone else in the organisation to resolve the difficulty. It may be that words of encouragement and support are all that are really needed.

The most beneficial way to exploit post-entry qualification courses is taking advantage of the ready availability of other forms of expertise in the shape of the course tutors and associated resources. Project work and assignments can form the access point. College tutors often encourage students to look for work-based projects so they can link theory to practice. The reverse is also possible. This integration approach to study and work can benefit the individuals directly involved and may also have spin-off benefits for other members of staff.

A work problem can be offered as a suitable area for study. Using the discipline of an academic project can allow totally new solutions or approaches to be considered.

Example 7.15

Mo and Marjory were discussing storage problems over lunch one day. Mo could not see how he would be able to accommodate the company's growing archives without taking over another filing room. This would not be very popular, as space in the head office was cramped. Releasing space for record storage would mean taking offices from staff in other sections.

One of Marjory's staff, Mark, was studying for an MBA at the local university and one of the subjects, she knew, concerned logistics. She suggested that perhaps Mark could help.

After discussions with the course tutor, a project was set up. Mark investigated the problem, discussed it with his tutors, carried out research, developed and discussed options with everyone who was likely to be affected and produced a set of recommendations. In effect Mark had carried out a consultancy exercise, at no direct cost and with specialist back-up. His proposals included some innovative suggestions that the company had never considered before. These were to transfer the paper-based records to a computer-readable format base and create a properly indexed archive storage system. The computer package, at first glance, seemed expensive. The capital outlay would be large. But Mark had done a cost benefit analysis which showed that the long-term saving in space costs and the benefits offered by other features of the package would mean that it would be cost effective over a period of three years.

The project was well-received by the University and Mark obtained a good assessment. Mo submitted the proposal to the director of finance who was suitably impressed and, in giving the go-ahead, opened the door to a new mode of thinking in the company. Other people started to consider how the latest developments in information technology could help solve problems that at first glance seemed beyond more traditional solutions.

Experiential risk

A fundamental reason behind the use of the outdoors in development training is the nature of the 'risk' presented by the experience to the participants. They are put into situations of which they have had no previous experience and therefore cannot rely on existing knowledge or skills. This exposure is to enable the participants to question their reactions, to develop the skills needed to cope with new situations and work productively with other people in situations of potential high danger and stress. One does not need to be abseiling down the side of a mountain to stimulate this element of risk; a totally new job in a setting which is totally new can present the same degree of perceived danger and challenge.

The value of the approach taken by those who run programmes designed on the principles of development training depends upon their skill in drawing out the learning. This is done by encouraging and facilitating active reflection, feedback between the participants and identification of ways in which the reflections and feedback can be tried out and used in practice. They put the learning cycle concept into practice.

This approach can be translated into everyday work. Perhaps there will not be the same dramatic impact of experience of outdoor development, but it can be used to contribute to normal working. To do this requires the manager to be forward-looking and to recognise which areas of work will present which members of staff with a 'risk'. On this basis, work allocation can be planned and individuals prepared. To be fully successful, the manager must be committed and disciplined enough to make sure that the preparatory briefing is thorough and that reflection and feedback sessions are held. This is an absolute prerequisite. If the manager cannot guarantee this will happen, the approach should not even be considered — it is unfair to expose staff to risk without the proper support being provided. However, if the back-up is available, the development and learning from real life experience can result in significant paybacks for everyone concerned.

Example 7.16

Elizabeth had never chaired a meeting before. Young, and limited in work experience, she knew that it was something she would eventually have to do. Learning about running meetings was part of her development plan and she had read widely about how and how not to do it. She had been to meetings as an observer and as a participant. There was little more she could do to prepare herself for the big day, but . . . .

Her line manager agreed. She had to take the big step and take it alone. The first opportunity would be the next production planning meeting the following week. The manager decided to be absent and asked Elizabeth to deputise. Together they went through the agenda and discussed the items and the people who would be at the meeting. Different techniques of chairing meeting were discussed and ways of handling the likely issues considered, Elizabeth was asked to voice her greatest fear. The manager worked through each aspect of the fear, step by step, asking Elizabeth how she would react if this or that happened.

The day came. Elizabeth was both nervous and exhilarated. The preparation had done its job, however, and the meeting went smoothly. No one misbehaved, the agenda was completed within the time allowed and clear decisions were made. Everyone left, still discussing the decision on a hotly contested area that had taken some time to reach. No one was interested in Elizabeth's conduct of the meeting. However, the meeting secretary whispered: 'Well done, that could have been sticky.'

The next day, Elizabeth and her manager went through the meeting point by point. Elizabeth was asked to relate how she had handled each stage and how the others had reacted. She was asked to record in a notebook the significant aspects of her own and others' behaviour, and to reflect on how she could have behaved in other ways in future. They planned to meet the following week when Elizabeth had had time to reflect more deeply. They both agreed to obtain some feedback from the other participants of the meeting.

When they met the following week Elizabeth was asked to express her reflections and to say where she saw strengths and weaknesses. These were recorded on a flip chart, so both her manager and Elizabeth could clearly see them. The manager summarised the feedback obtained and highlighted areas in which improvements could be made, according to others. The two sets of perceptions were compared, and from this a development plan constructed. The plan contained two elements – action to be taken to build up the perceived weak points, and action needed to be taken to maintain and reinforce Elizabeth's strengths.

LEARNING AS A NON-ACTIVE ACTIVITY

This section considers non-active development behaviours, the most important of which is *learning how to learn*. 'Education is the death of learning': the structured, constrained nature of our education system and the need to satisfy the requirements of a syllabus inhibit the individual's natural spirit of enquiry. The art of asking questions and challenging assumptions is neglected in favour of learning the accepted answers. As a consequence, in some cases before thinking about how best to help others to develop their skills, attention needs to be given to preparing them to learn. Megginson and Pedler (1992) say:

> The main task of the developer is to help the learner understand the learning process itself . . . that learning and action relate together . . . . This can help the learner 'learn how to learn', in that they begin to recognize what to do in order to act and learn in unfamiliar situations. The ability to learn how to learn is a key component of self-starters and, in a changing world, is perhaps the best insurance against the inevitable redundancy of our existing stock of knowledge and skills.
>
> The ability to learn how to learn is the real pay-off from the self-development process. Why bother to learn about, say, budgeting or a new technical skill in a self-developmental way when it can be easily instructed to operate by numbers? Because, only when you set out to learn because you want to, and in a self-responsible way, can you become aware of the actual processes involved in learning. Internalize these processes, make them part of your practice and, like riding a bicycle, you'll never forget them. This is the key role of the developer, not just to get this or that skill developed, but to help people to acquire that learning capability.

Teaching people how to relearn is not something that can be described in general terms. We all started life knowing how to learn, some people have just lost the skill. We are pressurised and conditioned into accepting the status quo as the truth. Learning is a process unique to each individual. Therefore some particular trigger mechanism is required to restore that skill and reawaken the spirit of enquiry. It may be a new challenge, it may be a chance question raised in that person's mind, it may be a dissatisfaction, it may be a shock. The role of the manager is to help foster the desire to learn with encouragement, support and by providing the facilities needed to help the individual continue learning.

Giving individuals the permission to ask questions may be enough to liberate them and spark off renewed interest. Formal education consists so much of 'sitting still and keeping quiet'. Despite the attempts to introduce new teaching methods (recently discredited), much conventional schooling discourages asking 'why?'. The normal practices at work also encourage people to 'keep their heads down and not to rock the boat', yet many of the people at the top of organisations are, in fact, the very people who asked the uncomfortable questions or made waves in their younger days. It was not their record of rebellion that led them to success, but their insatiable quest for knowledge and understanding. Not their ambition, but their desire to learn.

Another important feature of learning is the ability to *think*. Most of us do not think in any purposeful way. Our minds wander in an undisciplined way across the whole spectrum of the world as we each see it. Purposeful thinking is hard. Handy (1985) reports the work of researchers into the working patterns of managers. He cites Mintzberg, who identified in chief executives the 'ten minute itch', Stewart, who discovered that 'most of a sample of 100 managers spend only nine periods of more than half an hour without interruption in a four-week period', and Guest, who noted that 'a group of foremen averaged 583 incidents each day'. 'The job of a manager', says Handy, 'is that of brevity, variety and fragmentation'. If this is the reality, it is not surprising that most managers find concentrated thinking difficult. It is not a skill that gets much practice.

There is a great tendency to go from day to day, experience to experience without stepping back and reflecting on what is happening. This does not mean that people do not think about what and how they are working, but reflection is a more intensive process. It requires a distance, not in time or spatial terms, but a metaphysical separation from the events and people. This mental space facilitates the questioning and challenging process of self and existing practices that is not easy in the hurly-burly of everyday activity. Some people use such techniques as meditation or taking retreats as a way to help reflection. Others find that counselling or lengthy discussions with close friends can help, or that a round of golf or a long walk provides the rhythmic body motion that frees the brain sufficiently for it to be able to operate at the depth needed to reflect profoundly.

Like relearning to learn, learning to reflect is a skill which has to be acquired, practised and improved. There are some techniques that can help with the acquisition and development of the skill. The books by Pedler, Boydell and their associates (see references on p.250) perhaps contain some of the most useful. As well as discussing the concepts, they provide some instruments, such as questionnaires or areas for exploration with close colleagues, to help managers reflect on their behaviour and mind-set. They present ways of exploring contrasting views and suggest how to try alternatives. These guides are not intended to satisfy questions by providing answers; their main value is their encouragement to ask questions. Being books, familiar and easy to use, their physical format gives a manager a source of inspiration when needed. They can be a personal prompt, a resource of comfort and an uncomfortable prod into creativity.

Even though some reflection can only be done alone, there are times when it is useful to reflect in company. One of the reasons for 'away days' or 'time out' is to create the metaphysical space for colleagues to reflect together. The structure of such events should be designed to facilitate collective introspection and the examination of assumptions and constructs, resulting in a reframing of reality. Even though the reframing may simply be a new border around the existing perspective, the process followed can be strengthening. If values, approaches and goals have been challenged by change and put in doubt, reflecting upon them and reaffirming their position can be just as important as creating new paradigms. However, the danger of such events is that they do not progress beyond the introspective phase. Examining the collective navel can, in the short term, be beneficial, as insight can be gained into team dynamics. Eventually, however, it can become boring and unproductive. However, using a structure that enables active, purposeful reflection which is developmental (ie moving forward) can create a greater and clearer understanding of the current situation and solutions to problems which previously seemed intractable.

Such a structure can employ some of the techniques normally used for problem-solving or decision-making. Some of these are rational models, such as subjective expected utility and multi-attribute utility. These techniques allow the influencing variables to be weighted and the probability of an outcome occurring and the value of that outcome's desirability to be fitted into a matrix. The matrix allows a calculation to be made and a numeric result obtained, which can be used to indicate the 'best' solution. This sort of technique can be used during a group meeting to inform the debate and help make decisions. The thought processes that are needed to complete the matrix challenge preconceived ideas and assumptions. The remoteness of the calculation can make previously discounted options seem more attractive than hitherto, so giving apparently unthinkable solutions new perspectives that put them within the bounds of possibility.

Alternatively, a less rational technique can be used to stimulate and release the creativity of group members. Brain-storming is the most commonly used method of generating ideas. The weakness of this technique is its reliance on 'off the top responses'; in itself, it does not provoke any depth of thought. A more rigorous technique is called 'synectics'. Described by Nolan (1981), it is a way of 'making the strange sound familiar'. This is done by:

- forming a definition of a problem (make the strange familiar);

- putting that definition out of focus (make the familiar strange);

- using synectics (analogies and metaphors) to create this distortion;

- postponing the original definition while the analogy is analysed;

- using this analysis to consider the original problem.

This analysis is suitable for providing new insights into complex and difficult situations. It encourages those close to the problem to come at it from different angles. This technique can be particularly useful for situations that have been troublesome for some time. Some problems can create situations that become emotionally charged, which can make any attempt to resolve them doubly difficult. Not only is there a hard problem to solve, getting to it through the feelings is hard. Synectics gives the opportunity for ideas to be shared and compared in different ways from normal, thus helping to discharge some of the emotion.

Example 7.17

For the first time, the organisation was hit by industrial action by its administrative staff. This came as a shock, as this group of staff had previously been regarded as the non-militant section in a heavily unionised plant. During and after the strike the 'why' question was being asked. The answer that came back repeatedly was 'morale was low'. 'Fine', said the chief executive, 'did we know about this and what did we do? And more to the point, what are we going to do to ensure this does not happen again?'

The administrative section heads and specialists from the personnel and communications departments secluded themselves with a facilitator to answer the CEO's final question using synectics.

They defined the problem as *low morale*. The morning was spent generating analogies and metaphors. The facilitator asked prompt questions such as, 'What does it feel like?', 'What does it remind you of?', 'What is it not like?' These produced answers like:

- A grey November.

- Liverpool losing to Everton at home.

- Waiting in for a hospital appointment.

- Spending a week preparing for a party which turns out to be a huge success.

After lunch, the group was somewhat despondent, but on their return to the work room they found their reflections posted on the walls. The facilitator asked them to go back to the original definition and redefine it in terms of their analogies. The picture they saw was one with no clear goals, no feedback on performance, no sense of achievement, and a lack of success. However, having started with an intangible problem, they could now see aspects of it that could be tackled. Not easily, but at least the group left at the end of the day with some idea of what could be done to satisfy the CEO's 'It must not happen again.'

READING, LISTENING AND WATCHING

Despite the coming of the electronic era and the growth in more immediately responsive media, books still remain the principal store of human knowledge. Yet, in the busy world in which we live, how many of us take the time to read, reflect on the concepts and discuss them with our colleagues?. Guided reading is a well-known technique for self-development, but it is not used as much as it could be. This is reading with a purpose. Texts are selected, the reason for reading them is given, and conclusions are drawn as a result of discussion and consideration. Books are highly portable and easily obtained. They allow backwards and forward movement through the text, and readers are able to progress at their own pace.

Journals contain both up-to-date information of news and developments and articles which contain the experiences, reflections and ideas of others. How often are these simply skim-read and quickly confined to the waste-paper bin. The information explosion has been talked about for twenty years, and it continues to explode with greater and greater velocity. There is such a large quantity of printed material that it is almost impossible to keep up-to-date with it all, and managers' reading palates are jaded. However, there are some services, such as the abstracting services provided by MCB University Press, to help busy managers select essential reading. Reading should not be the first activity to go when things are busy. An article found serendipitously from regular review of journals could provide an answer that hours of toil over a hot desk would fail to produce.

Cassette tapes have been available for some time as a medium for learning new ideas and skills. Language tapes are a well-known and a respected method for acquiring and improving fluency. Cassettes are also available to help with other management skills. They provide an easily accessible method of learning which one can use at one's own pace and convenience. They can also be used during staff meetings or as a stimulus for focused group discussion. Their strength is in their ability to transmit ideas, stimulate thought and prompt experimentation.

Videos are increasingly available, both in the traditional TV form or now as interactive, computer-based learning aids. The former tend to be expensive, the latter are very expensive. Despite this they provide worthwhile means of developing skills. Their comparative cost is reduced if large numbers of people are to use the medium. Again, they can be used privately (and this can have much to commend it, especially for senior managers) or as part of staff group discussions.

Simple observation of human behaviour is perhaps the most readily available medium for learning. Always unique and inevitably unpredictable, other people can teach the watchful, thoughtful observer a great deal about people and about themselves.

There are also opportunities outside work for watching what sort of interaction is effective, or leads to trouble. Some techniques, such as transactional analysis and neuro-linguistic programming, can act as vehicles for understanding what is happening. One danger, however, in using such techniques is that they could be seen as giving simple answers, to all the nuances of human behaviour. Of course this cannot be so. The uniqueness of people makes their interactions extremely complex. Not even experienced psychologists pretend to understand all that is happening. Nevertheless, watching, listening and remembering can all help add to insight.

FEEDBACK

The art of giving and receiving feedback requires considerable interpersonal skills, as its potential for doing great good is matched by its ability to do great harm. Feedback is the mechanism that gives one person information about other people's perceptions of their performance and behaviour. It consists of rewards and punishments, it conveys assessments of achievement and failure, it motivates or it destroys the wish to learn. Because it can have such a powerful impact on an individual, this technique will not be treated as such here. The responsibility for its use and the ethics surrounding that use are clearly a key part of the manager's role, and so will be discussed as part of the next chapter.

SUMMARY

In this chapter, ways of stimulating and promoting the learning process and the development of skills have been considered. Various methods have been described, with examples, to show how managers can help themselves and others to develop their skills. The active methods that have been outlined include some that are familiar and others that are less so. The examples of methods have been given as suggestions to enable managers who are keen to help others learn some of these in operation for themselves. But before rushing into action, managers are encouraged to consider their state of readiness for development. For all the activities, if properly executed, will contain learning for the individual manager as well as those at whom the activities are targeted.

Much development can result from the use of the everyday as a learning opportunity. A main factor in turning work from routine into being a developmental event is the manager's attitude and approach to activities such as work allocation, delegation, project planning and assignment, deputising, and joint working. The manager's role in these activities varies from being the person in charge, to being a coach or mentor. To fulfil the requirements of the last role, the manager makes the effort needed to explain fully the purpose and context of the job. Mistakes and successes are analysed to identify the causal factors – not to attribute blame or reward, but to recognise and retain learning points. Faults in systems are used as vehicles for learning more functional and effective ways of working.

Many opportunities present themselves as part of normal working practice. For example, staff meetings are not uncommon and provide ready-made examples of opportunities for individual and team development. Most people, at some time in their working life, apply for other jobs. Most usually this is done in secret, but if applications can be made openly they provide the chance to engage in many development activities, such as focused discussion, feedback, skill recognition, self- and other appraisal. Depending on the way an appraisal scheme is operated, it can either produce much learning, or close the door. The outcome from a developmental scheme and the way it is put into practice is very different from a reward-based or performance evaluation appraisal scheme, even though the outline may seem the same on paper. The output from a development appraisal can include individual development plans or learning contracts. Learning logs may be used to chart the progress of these commitments, and help to record more general development. Planned long-term development activities can include career breaks and secondments, and attendance on short or post-qualification courses. To make the best of these opportunities, thorough preparation is needed and proper debriefing after the event is required. Another method that requires preparation and a disciplined reflection on the activity is the use of experiential risk. Using totally new and challenging situations to stimulate learning can be dangerous, but if properly conducted can be very rewarding.

Some opportunities for the development of skills and the gaining of greater insight do not require action. They are more concerned with modes of thought and ways of being. Learning how to learn and continuing to learn are critical skills that need to be acquired or relearnt by the manager and others if the more active opportunities are to be exploited to their full. The example set by a manager, the sort of questions asked and the ways in which problems are solved can influence and develop others' ways of working. A manager following a developmental path can encourage others to do the same without having to rely on huge stores of resources.

One of the most freely available resources and accessible vehicle for thought provocation is the common book. Purposeful reading is becoming a lost skill in this electronic age, yet books and journals can provide ideas, experiences and reflections to help focus thinking and introduce alternative ideas and ways of working. Books are comparatively cheap, are readily accessible and allow the reader to travel at a comfortable pace. Other media, such as cassettes and video are available to stimulate developmental thought for an individual or a group. Another easily obtained source of material is other people's behaviour. Watching and listening to what people do and how they interact can provide much food for thought.

Putting developmental methods into practice requires that managers become fully committed to this way of working. It can become so pervasive that it becomes normal and then, as with any learning, can be carried out with unconscious competence. The developmental manager assumes several different roles within the overall one. These will be described in the next chapter, whose starting-point will be the responsibility for and role in giving feedback. While some may consider this to be principally a method to aid learning, because it requires sophisticated and well-developed skills to be effective, feedback will be considered separately as a role element in its own right.

8
The manager's role

INTRODUCTION

One of the central roles of a manager is to contribute and enable the development of others. The others can be assistants, colleagues and peers and managers of the manager; in fact, virtually anybody with whom one works has the right to be helped with learning and development. After all, everyone is playing in the same team, aiming at the same goals. It follows that the development of the whole depends on the development of the individuals. Everyone should contribute to the process by taking responsibility for their own learning and for helping others.

The Framework shown earlier in Fig. 1.1 illustrates the five elements of the management role. *Working with people* shows how central the developmental responsibility for guiding, directing and enabling others can be to effective management. It is an inclusive role, encouraging team members to work together to reach shared goals, through helping, learning, listening and developing. The Framework indicates the actions needing to be taken by a developmental manager. Assuming these responsibilities requires the manager to act in a particular way.

Not only is the manager's role a collection of actions, it is also a matter of style. It is not just *what* but *how* things are done that is important. The manner in which individuals choose to act and the way in which they behave towards others sets the scene and influences subsequent events. Style is determined by personal preference and organisational culture. Even though the limits of choice are bounded by organisational norms, an individual manager will have considerable scope to decide which way they operate.

This chapter will examine some of the aspects of the manager's role and the skills needed to carry it out in a developmental manner. Some of the role's components have labels which embrace a number of skills, such as coaching; others are individual skills. Both will be described with examples, to demonstrate how the skills may be applied in typical situations. Some of the skills may seem to be common sense, others may be familiar. If this is so, the examples should be confirmatory at the least; at the best, they will provide some indication of other opportunities for their use or ways of improving on current practice. But while the skills may simply require common sense, they are not common practice.

It is possible that a manager is already acting in a developmental way without realising exactly what was being done, how, and what effect was being achieved. If this is the case, it is hoped that this chapter will provide due acknowledgement and reward. For some people, helping others learn is the *only* way to work. To others, the whole notion may be new. Managers taking this approach will confirm that, as a way of working, it really does result in the development of skills and improvements to the quality of working methods and the working environment.

THE USE OF FEEDBACK TO STIMULATE CHANGE AND LEARNING

The starting point for a discussion of managerial skills has to be the skill area that is elemental to the others. If a manager is not able to give and receive feedback in a positive way, using other skills which will be described below will be extremely difficult. Feedback in this context is the process of obtaining data to report on the state of a system, a reaction to an action, or to monitor progress between the current and desired states. The data exist in the system. Whether they are collected and used is a matter of choice. The data can be gathered and used in a purposeful fashion, or can be ignored. Ignoring the data may be a conscious decision; it may be unconscious. But the data will not go away. Since data are available, and since management is about making full and proper use of all available resources, it only makes sense to make the best use of feedback systems and the data they contain.

It was acknowledged earlier that individuals need information about their performance to motivate them, provide job satisfaction and to indicate areas where performance and skills may be developed. One function of a manager is to translate the raw data into information which can be used productively.

QUALITY FEEDBACK

Quality feedback is information that can be acted upon. It contains examples of behaviour which can be used in a way that enables the individual to see how the specific can be applied in general.

Example 8.1

'Mavis, when Fred asked you for the time of the last post, your answer was given abruptly. I have noticed that you have been short with him several times recently.'

The example gives data gathered from several different incidents over a period of time, and prepares the individual to explore the reasons for the behaviour. The wrong way to provide feedback would be to say:

'Mavis, why were you so rude to Fred?'

'Rude' is a value judgement. Fred may not have found Mavis to be rude. The point of giving feedback is to provide information that will allow behaviour to be changed. It should be given in a way that encourages and helps the individual to change. Passing judgements, focusing on aspects of appearance or personality, or trying to attribute motives and intentions, do not help the receiver to develop their skills in any way. Statements of this nature tend to say more about the giver than the person at whom they are directed.

Feedback needs to be specific and, to enable it to be acted upon, it needs to focus on behaviour. In the above example the crucial difference is between the word 'rude' and the phrase 'answer was given abruptly'. Using 'rude' does not give Mavis any information about her actions. If she is not aware of appearing to others as rude, how can she stop being rude? What does being rude mean? To alter her behaviour she needs to know what she is currently doing, as experienced by others, that limits her effectiveness in interpersonal interactions and what she could do differently.

The purpose of feedback

Feedback must be given with the sole intention of helping the recipient. Some messages sent to others are labelled as feedback, when their real reason is to allow the sender to express their own feelings. This may be a valid thing to do, but it is not feedback in the developmental sense. There are ways for two people to exchange information about one person's impact on the other. This should be a dialogue, structured to allow feelings to be expressed, and acknowledged in a way that enables a joint understanding to be reached. Assertiveness training helps to develop the skills needed to express one's own rights while respecting those of others. This is to enable feedback to be given and received.

When giving feedback, it is important to remember that the recipient has the right to refuse to accept or act on the feedback. Once given, it becomes the property of the recipient, who has *full* ownership. How they choose to use the feedback is entirely up to them.

Too much feedback can limit an individual's ability to hear it all or to decide which aspects need to be acted upon first. Usually what happens is that the person giving the feedback has had time to think about the message and to structure the way in which it is to be given. To the recipient, this will be new information. If the feedback is good, the receiver will need time to think about what is being said and to reflect on the implications of the contents. It may be that some of the effects the individual's behaviour has had on others are being reported for the first time. These messages could take the individual concerned some time to understand. It is important to gauge the pace being used to provide the information and the amount being given.

It is also important to assess the impact the feedback is having on the recipient. The message, or simply the process of receiving feedback can touch an individual's emotions. No matter whether these are feelings of joy or of despair, the degree of intensity of feeling can limit hearing and understanding. The provider needs to check the individual's emotional state.

It is useful to establish ground rules before starting to give feedback, so the individual knows in advance what is going to happen. It is also important for them to know their rights. For example, they have the right to stop the session or to challenge what is being said, or to ask for additional information if they cannot recognise the behaviour.

Using questions

The way in which the feedback is given influences its acceptance. Making statements or appearing to pass opinions can make the receiver feel under attack, and encourages a defensive response. Framing the message in the form of questions can help the recipient to accept the feedback in the spirit in which it is being sent. For example, saying, 'You were angry when I said I was going to hold a meeting' passes judgement on the other person's mood, assumes cause and effect and opens the way for the recipient to reply, 'No I wasn't'. An alternative approach would be to ask, 'What effect did my saying I was going to hold a meeting have on you?' This would be more likely to encourage the dialogue to be opened by the person being asked saying, 'I was angry'. This could then be followed with 'What caused your anger?'

The use of questions also allows the accuracy of the feedback to be checked.

The process of observing other people's behaviour is full of flaws and bias, which results in errors and the formation of inaccurate assumptions. No matter how careful an observer, their perception is influenced by their personal constructs and preconceptions. It is normal for assumptions to be made regarding cause and effect and for responsibility for an incident to be attributed to the person under consideration, rather than other people or the situation. Therefore, when giving feedback it is advisable to be ready to receive other information from the recipient that may alter the picture. Asking, rather than telling, creates an easy route for this information to be gathered.

The primary purpose of giving feedback is to help the receiver gain a better understanding of their behaviour and how it impacts on others, by giving information rather than providing read-made solutions. Ways of making improvements to the effectiveness of behaviour and building on strengths need to be acceptable to the recipient. The individual concerned must work out their own ways forward; the giver may be able to help that process but cannot do it on behalf of the recipient.

Being constructive

Part of the British culture encourages the focus to be placed on the negative and weak aspects of performance. We are not very good at being positive, yet being told that what one is doing is right is a necessary part of learning. We complain about what is bad; seldom, however, do we acknowledge what is good. Getting better, and working on areas in need of improvement, seem to imply the existence of initial flaws and weaknesses. Being told in which areas these improvements can be made seems like the attribution of blame for failure. Gaps in performance and the value of being challenged and stretched make it appear as though the individual is not trying hard enough, or is below par. There is a danger, in giving feedback, that an over-emphasis is placed on weaknesses in performance. Dwelling on the less strong aspects of performance does not always encourage the recipient of the feedback to rush out and find ways of getting better – sometimes just the opposite: putting people under unnecessary strain can reduce their ability and motivation to learn, rather than sharpening their awareness. However, sometimes this approach works. An individual can be stimulated by attack to accelerate their learning and increase their performance peaks. But this level of activity is hard to maintain, and it does not need to be like this. Work can be enjoyable and fun. Sadly, it seems to be normal to moan about the misery. Anyone who says they enjoy their job tends to be regarded as abnormal.

An alternative way is to see a perceived shortfall as being the difference between good and growing better. We are not very good at making genuine acknowledgements of strengths, especially in ourselves, nor are we very good at giving genuine praise to others. This contributes to a lack of self-worth which may inhibit confident and assertive behaviour. Many difficulties are caused by the clumsy handling of interpersonal transactions. These could be improved considerably if the parties were more aware of what they were doing right, rather than focusing on what they were doing wrong. Providing feedback is the opportunity for letting the recipient know, in factual terms, which aspects of their behaviour are effective. Skills, unacknowledged, become devalued; devalued skills do not get used. The under-use of skills leads to a decline in levels of proficiency, which leads to poorer performance – the downward spiral. On the other hand, the provision of quality feedback can help to reverse the trend. The celebration of worth and achievement does not necessarily lead to 'basking in one's own glory'. It could be the necessary spur to give the individual the courage to test and stretch their skills to make use of previously unrevealed potential.

Concluding feedback

After giving feedback, it is important to either summarise or ask the recipient to make a summary. The latter is the better option as it enables the giver to check the recipient's understanding and commitment to any agreed action. The summary also enables both parties to ensure that each part of the 'agenda' has been dealt with. Because of the sensitive nature of the process, it is possible for some issues to be forgotten or left unfinished. It is unwise to leave matters unresolved. They tend to fester in people's imagination if they are left. The sort of issue that falls into this category is the side-comment or chance remark.

Example 8.2

When discussing the successful way in which a project had been implemented, the provider of the feedback said 'Of course Pamela made several comments about your handling of her staff.' This remark was left there, as there were other, more important aspects of the project to discuss. But afterwards the recipient of the feedback was left wondering what Pamela had said and meant.

It is important that all matters are cleared. If it is not possible to do this at the time, then the way in which they will be dealt with at some other time should be agreed. The place for agreeing future action is after the summary and before the close. The close should also comprise a review of the process – feedback on the giving of feedback. This gives both parties material for reflection and some primary data to use when working on the skills of giving and receiving feedback.

Giving feedback requires skill. Done poorly, it can demotivate, or even harm the recipient. Giving praise in a genuine sense is difficult. It is not something that is done, often, at work. The giver of praise can be seen as ingratiating, even obsequious. Nevertheless, giving an honest appreciation of another person's efforts is as valid as pointing out weaknesses in their performance. When did you last tell a colleague or an assistant frankly what you appreciate about them? Try it as a way of developing your own skills of giving feedback.

There are other conditions that need to be met to ensure that the process is positive and one of quality for both parties. These are the aspects of the environment rather than the behaviour of the provider. Even though they can be influenced, some are beyond the direct control of the provider. These points will be addressed below, as it is important to distinguish between the physical and environmental needs and those which require the deployment of skills. The latter can be summarised into the 'golden' rules for providing quality feedback.

Rules of feedback

- Focus on behaviour that can be changed.
- Provide information that can be acted upon.
- Help the recipient see how the specific can be applied in general.
- Passing judgement should be avoided.
- The purpose for giving feedback is to help the recipient.
- The recipient has the right to refuse to accept or act on feedback.
- The quantity given should not be too great.
- The impact the feedback will have on the recipient should be considered.
- The impact the feedback is having during the session should be sensed and checked.
- Ground rules should be established at the start of the session.
- The way in which feedback is given should be planned.
- Questions should be used.
- The accuracy of feedback should be checked.
- The positive should be used more than the negative.

- A summary should be made before the session closes.

- Future action should be agreed.

- The feedback process itself should be reviewed.

Physical and climatic needs for giving quality feedback

Venue

The venue of the exchange of feedback is important – trying to conduct a feedback session in a corridor or cupboard will not necessarily be conducive to building rapport. The location should allow both parties to see each other, hear each other and to be close enough without invading personal space. Each person has a zone known as defensible space. The proximity of the zone's boundary to the body varies between individuals and cultures, and depends on whom they are talking to. It may be appropriate to conduct a feedback session sitting in armchairs, or either side of a desk, depending on the relationship between the provider and the recipient, and the nature of the session. The place selected should be conducive, and preferably private.

Confidentiality

It is possible to be private in a public space. Take the case where it is normal for the boss and an assistant to talk together in the office canteen. One day, it may be important for the boss to pass on some feedback to the assistant, and there is no other opportunity for it to be given. It would not be wrong for this information to be shared over lunch. However, if it is rare for the boss and member of staff to be seen together in public and the nature of the feedback is sensitive, exchanging this information in a public place would be very wrong. The location should be chosen on grounds of confidentiality rather than privacy. Confidentiality is essential, and agreement on this point should be reached during the establishment of the ground rules at the beginning of the session.

Ambience

The *ownership* of the site chosen should also be considered. Offices tend to belong very firmly to their occupier and reflect that person's personality. They also reflect elements of any power relationship that may exist. The way the furniture is arranged and its type also set the scene for the sorts of transactions that go on in the room. The type of furniture probably depends on what is provided by the organisation, which in turn reflects its culture. But it is also influenced by the room occupier's personality and preferred ways of working.

The nature of the relationship and the ambience of the room conditions the nature of the feedback session. If the relationship is informal and the room is set out in a casual fashion to facilitate relaxed, discursive meetings, it would be difficult to use it for a formal feedback session. It might be better to use someone else's room, or a more formal setting, if the feedback session were likely to be painful.

Time

The amount of time allowed for the session also should be given thought. It is not inaccurate to say that a session should last as long as it needs to, but modern-day business diaries do not really allow for such open-ended occasions. Therefore some prediction of how long will be needed has to be made. It is better to err on the side of the generous, rather than not allowing enough time.

The time of day also needs to be planned. Each organisation has its optimum time for work. Some are early morning organisations, some tea-time or early evening ones. And individuals themselves work better at different times of the day. These factors can influence the way in which the feedback is received. For example, if it is known that the recipient has commitments that require prompt evening finishes, it would not be\sensible to plan a feedback session to start at 4.00 pm. It is also worth considering the likely impact the message will have on the individual and what they would want to do afterwards. If the message requires prompt action, conducting the session at the end of the day would not be helpful. On the other hand if the message requires reflection before action is taken, holding the session later in the day could be better. It would not be wise to provide sensitive feedback just before the recipient is due to go into an important decision-making meeting. Their mind would then do neither subject justice.

If more time is needed than that allowed, how and when the remaining material is to be dealt with needs to be agreed upon. Having two goes at giving feedback is not ideal, but it does happen. If this has to be the case, the sessions should not be too far apart and every effort should be made to ensure that the second does not get moved. It is also important that the remaining feedback should be dealt with in the way agreed. Consistency is necessary, otherwise the recipient could easily get confused. Time distorts memory, so the opening of the second session should contain a brief recap of the first. But the issues already dealt with should not be reopened, unless there is new information or an exceedingly good reason for doing so. If the temptation to revisit is not resisted, it is possible that the second session will merely be a rerun of the first and that the outstanding material will remain unfinished. It is also likely that the messages will be altered, due to the passage of time.

Agreement on action

One aspect of the provision of feedback is the agreement on action. This action proposed may be for the recipient to take either alone, or with the provider. The value of giving and receiving feedback is the identification of what may be changed and how to do it. Change requires action. Even if the outcome of the feedback session is only increased insight, this too should result in some form of changed behaviour. Without resultant action the whole process is meaningless. However, action requires determination, especially if the timespan is likely to be protracted.

Effecting changes may be difficult, they may need the help of others less than willing to provide it, and the changes may be painful. Therefore it is important for both parties to be clear about who is going to do what, when. In addition, agreement should be reached on the help and resources required, and ways of monitoring progress established. It may be helpful to create a development plan or learning contract written in explicit terms. Examples of these were given in the previous chapter. Plans of this nature may seem to be mechanistic: they are, but these mechanisms are intended to facilitate development, not force it. If they do the latter they are being dysfunctional. The primary purpose of providing feedback is to help the individual understand and to want to develop their skills. Its purpose is not to oblige them to do so – other processes exist to achieve that aim.

WHAT IS NOT QUALITY FEEDBACK?

Quality, developmental feedback is not given as a part of a formal disciplinary procedure. (Feedback may, however, contribute to the development of an action plan drawn up as a result of the formal proceedings.) In the way in which the term is being used in this context, it would not be appropriate to try to give and certainly not to receive, feedback in a disciplinary setting.

Quantity

Giving more feedback does not increase the quality – in fact, the opposite is the case. Too much feedback can lead to overload, which will inhibit hearing and understanding. Overload can lead to distortion and misunderstanding, forgotten points and others which are not heard at all. The end result is confusion and, potentially, a situation that, in the longer term, could take more time and effort to sort out.

If all one's strengths and weaknesses are laid out as if they were the offering for a buffet, it would be difficult to know where to start, what to leave and when to finish. The end result is the same as any other over-indulgence — a wish that one had never started. The systems — emotional and cognitive — are unable to process an excessive quantity of information. The better way of giving large quantities of feedback is to plan its delivery by identifying priorities and those areas which will have most effect with the minimum expenditure of effort. Feedback should be given in appropriately sized chunks, at a pace that both the giver and the receiver can handle.

Time

It is neither possible nor desirable to set ideal times for feedback sessions. A rough rule of thumb, though, is to expect a minimum of half an hour and a maximum of two hours. Prolonging a feedback session can be worse than not allowing enough time. There can be a temptation to go over ground repeatedly, but repetition may lead to evidence being elaborated or invented inadvertently. It is better to finish when all the material has been dealt with and issues aired, rather than filling up the time.

Personality

Feedback should not make reference to an individual's personality or areas of behaviour that cannot be changed. It does not help anyone to improve their performance if all they are told is that they are too naive. This sort of comment on personality is judgemental and is based on impression and value judgement. The better way to give feedback would be to identify how that naivety was manifested, what the consequences of the behaviour were, and how the necessary skills could be developed.

Example 8.3

Ian was a well known maverick in the organisation. He always had an eye for the main chance. Unfortunately, his risks seldom paid off and had cost the company dear in the past. The only reason he had been kept on was because of his brilliant sales technique.

The most recent manager to be appointed had been warned about the way in which Ian tried to get other people involved in his wild schemes, but Martha was determined to make up her own mind about her new colleague. Within her first month Ian, true to form, made an attractive proposal to Martha about a promotional campaign for one of the products in her portfolio. The idea excited her, the campaign was mounted, the money spent, and it flopped.

Understandably, Martha's manager was disappointed and angry. Two choices were available to her. She could bawl Martha out, by saying she should have listened to the advice and not been so stupid as to be taken in by such a smooth talker; or she could unpick Martha's performance, helping her to work out what should have warned her of impending failure, how she could have checked on the reliability of Ian's proposals, why she was right to say she would make up her own mind about Ian and her other new colleagues, but what should have indicated caution – in effect, turning the incident into one which could be used to develop Martha's 'sensing' skills rather than being an embarrassing memory.

Appearances

Making comments on an individual's physical appearance can be regarded as improper on the part of the person giving feedback. In some circumstances, this could be tantamount to harassment, which in extreme cases can give cause for a justifiable complaint to an industrial tribunal. Unless the individual's appearance is having a detrimental impact on individual or organisationa performance, comments made on this subject should be omitted from feedback.

Similarly, comments about aspects of behaviour that cannot be changed should be avoided. For example, a speech impediment such as a stammer may cause irritation to colleagues, without impacting on the quality of an individual's work. Telling an individual that a stammer is irritating during feedback is not going to help the stammer go away – probably it would have the opposite effect!

Privacy

Giving feedback in public is not good practice. An individual has a right to privacy and confidentiality. Breaches of these two rights can do much to undermine the trust an individual needs to have in a manager's integrity. Without this trust, it is very difficult for an individual to accept what is being said. The only time when the giving and receiving of feedback publicly is acceptable is when the process forms part of another activity and all the parties have, knowingly, agreed to participate. Examples of this include team-building activities, assessment of collective strengths and weaknesses, and identifying team development needs.

Emotion

Giving feedback as a way of discharging one's own emotions is a common human practice. Because you feel bad about something, you take out your frustration, anger or negative sentiments on others, who may be innocent bystanders to the original incident. 'Kicking the cat' in this way does little for your reputation as a developmental manager, nor does it provide any information for the recipient. It may be common practice; this does not make it good practice.

Even when the negative feelings are a result of an individual's actions, giving feedback on the basis of reactive emotion is not as productive as feedback given on the basis of reflection. Neither the excitement caused by success, nor the disappointment arising from poor performance, provide a sound basis for assessment. Providing feedback in the heat of the moment does not allow other, perhaps important information to be collected, nor does it allow the full picture to be seen in perspective. However, timing is of the essence, for leaving the giving of feedback too long can reduce its value. The passage of time dims the memory and diminishes the importance of the message. A balance is needed. How soon or long after the event has to be a matter of judgement – a conscious decision made by the manager.

Bad news

Giving all bad news does not encourage the receiver of feedback to improve. Any human being has effective blocking mechanisms that limit the amount of damage negative information can have on the psychic well-being. Mental processes such as rationalisation, scapegoating, blaming and transference come into play. If the individual is overloaded with information about failure, mistakes and poor performance, they look for other reasons to explain the cause than themselves and their need to develop skills. The other possible consequence of excessive bad news is for the individual's self-esteem to be so badly damaged that considerable remedial action is needed before that person is ready to learn.

Generalised feedback does not help. Making broad comments and giving general information may seem a kinder way of helping the receiver learn. However, expecting individuals to work out for themselves where their performance could be developed is erecting obstacles and making the process into a guessing game. Expecting the receiver to draw inference can lead to wrong answers being given to wrong questions. It is better to provide factual, specific information that is based on evidence. This does not mean taking precise measures of every aspect of the individual's behaviour, but using specific examples over a period of time to highlight aspects of performance that can be developed.

The behaviours that diminish quality feedback are:.

- giving feedback as part of disciplinary procedures;

- giving too much feedback or spending too long on the giving;

- focusing on personality, or behaviour that cannot be easily changed;

- giving feedback in public;

- passing on bad strokes or discharging one's own emotions;

- always giving bad news;

- making generalised comments which cannot be evidenced or are not clear.

The provision of feedback is fundamental to many of the other developmental roles a manager can occupy. If it is not done with care and skill, the value of the manager's other roles is greatly diminished. Badly handled learning opportunities can quickly turn sour, becoming painful experiences that result in the recipient being taught to shy away from such encounters in future. The real purpose should be to show the individual receiving feedback that it can be a positive experience and to provide information to feed reflection and develop skills.

The feedback process should, ideally, be two-way. The giver, in the giving, should also be ready to receive. Obviously, the giver cannot give and receive at the same time, but at least the sensors should be operating. They should be ready to pick up cues which provide information about how the process is operating. The end of the feedback session should allow a review of the process and provide the receiver with the opportunity to comment on their perception of it.

INSTRUCTING

Sometimes it is appropriate for a manager to show how a particular task should be carried out. This does not imply that a manager needs to be an expert in every operation; rather, it acknowledges that in some areas the manager may have more skill or understanding to be shared. The need for a demonstration may also occur when a manager learns about a new approach and then 'cascades' the learning to others.

The Video Arts training video *You'll soon get the hang of it*, provides guidance on how to carry out good on-the-job instruction sessions. The key is preparation. Preparing to instruct requires consideration of two aspects:

- the content;

- the recipient.

The content needs to be arranged in a logical sequence – broken into chunks of a size that can be absorbed in one session, and put into context. The material to be used and the site where the instruction is to take place need to be prepared to ensure that everything required is to hand and in working order. Action also needs to be taken to ensure that the session will not be interrupted or disrupted.

References were made earlier to the need to think about the learner in advance, but to reinforce these points:

- thought should be given to what the learner already knows;

- what the learner is intended to get from the learning;

- what will make the learner come back for more.

Instructing someone how to carry out a task is full of pitfalls. When you know how to do something better than a learner, the temptation to do it yourself is very great. Standing to one side and letting the learner do it is not easy, especially when you can see the learner heading towards a mistake. But intervening means that progress will not be made – the learner never gets the opportunity to learn, the chance to get things wrong, to learn from their mistakes and develop their own approach and skills.

The simple mnemonic:

I hear and forget
I see and remember
I do and understand

provides practical guidance on how to provide instruction in a way that benefits the learner.

COACHING

Coaching has no different meaning in the work sense than it does in its more usual context of sport. It is a powerful way to help others learn and improve their performance (opportunities for techniques used are outlined earlier). Sadly, it has become one of the many management buzz-words. This over-use tends to obscure its true meaning, leading to a confusion between supervision, counselling and coaching. A coach is defined here as a person who has some knowledge about the tasks being performed and has some involvement with their execution. A manager in the coaching role would 'through direct discussion and guided activity help a colleague to solve a problem or to do a task better than would otherwise have been the case.' (Megginson and Boydell, 1979). A coach observes from outside the field of activity, is able to provide feedback on performance and to make suggestions on ways in which improvements could be made. The learner practises the task, with the coach monitoring performance, providing feedback and encouragement, rewards and indications of areas where further improvements can be made.

The four stages of the coaching process are identified by Megginson and Pedler (1992) as:

1. identifying the issue;

2. creating a forum for development;

3. carrying out the development activity;

4. developmental reviewing, ie reviewing to enhance learning, rather than to correct errors.

These stages can be elaborated and described in practical terms so that it is clear what the manager should be doing to occupy the role of coach.

Identify the problem

The 'problem' may be a performance weakness, or it may be an area in which improvements can be made, one in which additional skills are required or where a gap exists between the current and desired levels. (This should not always be seen in the negative; it could be the difference between good and excellent.)

The identification can be made as a result of appraisal, feedback received from customers, skill gaps identified in assessing business needs, or any of the many opportunities mentioned earlier. It could be that the issue has been identified during formal, structured analysis, or it could have emerged during normal operations.

Example 8.4

The company management team decided to slim down the volume of routine paper-work to improve efficiency. In future all reports were to be confined to four pages.

Peter was well known for writing interesting and informative reports, which were generally regarded as exemplary. He reacted with horror to the instruction. Never had he written anything so short. How would he cope . . .?

Creating a forum for development

Elsewhere, creating this sort of forum is referred to as establishing a learning culture, or developing a climate where mistakes can be made and learning can take place. How this can be done on an organisational sense will be discussed later. Individually a manager can do this within an operational unit, setting an example by:

- using learning opportunities personally;

- encouraging openness and honesty with oneself and with others;

- personally taking advantage of learning opportunities;

- using methods such as debate, questioning, reflection and reframing within the team, and challenging team members through delegation;

- deputising and making full use of the other techniques mentioned earlier.

Example 8.5

Peter's manager was a firm believer in turning every chance into a learning opportunity, and saw this latest decision in such a way. Peter and his manager agreed to meet and discuss the manager's and Peter's concerns about the impact the decision would have on Peter and try to find a way for Peter to change his style. They took his last offering as a typical example and examined its good points from the old perspective, and its 'weaknesses' from the new.

Carrying out the development activity

There is no point in deciding that a problem exists if no steps are taken to resolve it. Such inaction would rapidly destroy the forum for learning. Learning activities are rarely one-offs; they need to be planned in stages and efforts made to ensure that action is taken. This requires determination and follow-through. Broken promises lead to disappointment, which leads to demotivation, which leads to the death of enthusiasm for learning and virtually everything else.

Example 8.6

Peter and his manager saw several areas of potential weakness during their examination of the report.

Peter tended to:

- use examples of how other organisations approach similar tasks as a means of developing options;

- use long sentences and descriptive adjectives;

- discuss fully each available option;

- provide descriptions of background to set the scene of the report.

They decided that Peter should think about how other organisations present options, read about the use of simple, plain English and ways of report-writing, find out about other ways of comparing options and consider whether the full background was really necessary.

They agreed to meet a week later and draft a mock report together. The longer-term plan was to work on several joint reports, obtain feedback from another senior member and then for Peter to prepare a report alone in time to receive feedback before the next major report was due to be submitted to the management team.

Development reviewing

This means monitoring to make sure that the activities have happened and the required learning has been achieved. It is easy to set off on a course of action and half-way through lose sight of where it is intended to be heading. This is like setting off to go to the South of France for a camping holiday, but instead of going straight on at Calais turning left and finding yourself in the middle of the German industrial belt. It is important to keep the objectives firmly in sight. If things change during the course of the plan's implementation, there is nothing wrong with reviewing and modifying the plan, if that is the right thing to do. It would be wrong to carry on blindly.

Example 8.7

Peter and his manager were pleased with the reports they were producing, and the response they received was encouraging. The time for the next six-monthly section progress report was approaching, but suddenly a problem appeared in Peter's operational area of responsibility. Peter's manager thought through the implications and sadly concluded that Peter would have to be taken off the progress report to concentrate on his own area of work. They discussed it, and both came to the conclusion that what had been achieved was good enough. The reports Peter was now producing were shorter and more concise than those he had previously written. The final part of the plan would only have been the 'icing on the cake' – the objective had already been achieved.

A good coach is someone who is prepared to take time to work through problems with staff, who knows something about the task from experience and is able to sit outside the task in hand. A good coach does not rush in to do the task for the learner. Feedback is provided to help the learner understand how and in which ways their performance may be improved. The coach may demonstrate the correct or alternative ways of doing the task, but does not need to be better than the learner. The coach should know correct techniques, accepted good practice and alternative ways that have been known to work. Some of the best sports coaches are or were at the top of their field and have progressed into helping others develop their talents. Some, however, have never been and would never have been stars in their sport, but nevertheless they are stars in developing stars. The same goes for managers. The aim is to develop individuals who achieve more than their 'teacher'.

MENTORING

Coaching is intended to build on performance; mentoring goes deeper. Its purpose is to provide insight so that learning from performance can be translated and applied to other areas of life. (Opportunities for doing so are discussed above.) Another major difference between coaching and mentoring is that coaching tends to be focused on the now and soon. Mentoring is more long-term and can have whole (meaning length as well as scope) life implications. The impact a mentor can have was described earlier; it should not be entered into lightly.

Megginson and Pedler (1992) say that the role requires its occupant to 'act as a friend willing to play the part of an adversary'. This demands that the mentor is prepared to take risks with the relationship. Playing devil's advocate can sometimes provoke strong reactions. Challenging another's deeply held beliefs can lead to a vigorous defence of their values by that person. Megginson and Pedler go on to say:

> Effective mentors often seem to have a well-developed philosophy of life and to operate on a spiritual dimension as well as intellectually and emotionally. They ask a lot of questions and, whereas coaches focus on 'how?', mentors also ask 'why?' They are good at linking different bits of their learners' lives – home and work, success and failure, concrete and abstract, thought and feeling, hard and soft. They are happy to consider the long term.

Some organisations have started to appoint mentors for their trainee managers. It is questionable whether this can work in the longer term, however. The relationship between mentor and learner requires a high degree of trust and mutual respect. Liking each other is not a prerequisite but a high mutual regard is. For a relationship of this nature to develop into one of openness, maturity and honesty requires some degree of mutual selection and attraction. Whether this can grow from the intervention of an appointing third party is doubtful.

So much of the role's success depends on the personal characteristics of the mentor and of the learner. A mentor challenges and questions basic assumptions, helps to develop insight and understanding by sharing thoughts, experiences, mistakes and successes. The role demands friendship and enough affection on the part of the mentor to want to give, and of the learner to want to hear. The mentor will not be willing to give if the learner disregards or rubbishes the mentor's offerings.

Like any relationship, it may come to an end. If the relationship is successful, it is likely the two parties will eventually grow apart, sad at its demise but happy for each other's progress. It will become timely for them to go in their own directions. If the relationship has been profitable, both will have learnt from the other and will have gained mutual satisfaction from their interactions. The relationship may be comparatively brief, or it may last a lifetime. Regardless of its longevity, it will have been memorable and special. The individuals may have other similar relationships, but each will be a unique product of the people, the time and the situation. The mentor and learner form a close relationship that is a product of contributions from each. This makes it difficult to describe in concrete terms, and it is virtually impossible to prescribe a list of dos and don'ts. The only advice to be given here is if the chance to develop such a relationship presents itself, take it. It can be very rewarding and stimulating. If the chance is not offered – don't force anyone into being mentored or being a mentor. It can be extremely hard work, unrewarding, frustrating and even painful. 'Flogging life into a dead horse' achieves nothing more than a tired arm.

Mentoring can develop into a relationship of equals, in which both parties give and receive support, encouragement and act as sounding boards for each other. Friendship at work may be regarded with suspicion by those outside the relationship, but its foundations of trust and openness provide the forum for the exchange of personal feedback. This, as discussed above, is a major way of developing skills and performance, to the eventual benefit of everyone.

COUNSELLING

Coaching and counselling are terms which are often used interchangeably, but they are not one and the same thing. A counsellor occupies a very different role to that of a coach. A coach focuses on ways of improving performance, while a counsellor's role is to help individuals to solve their own problem. This may result in an improvement in performance, but it is not the primary reason for counselling. The goals of counselling are many and diverse, but they can include:

- gaining a better understanding of oneself;
- making important personal decisions;

- setting personal achievable goals;

- developing effective solutions to personal and interpersonal problems;

- changing ineffective behaviour to more effective behaviour;

- coping with difficult circumstances in life;

- dealing with negative personal emotions.

Some would argue that, as counselling frequently deals with personal difficulties being faced by an individual, a manager should not act in this capacity. The contrary can also be argued, however. Because personal problems can inhibit an individual's performance at work, a manager needs to be able to use the skills of a counsellor. But one of these skills is the ability to recognise when the problem is beyond the bounds of work. At this stage the manager should know enough to be able to pass the individual on to someone better able to help the individual.

Some managers are frightened by the prospect of having to help someone deal with a personal problem. Part of this fear may concern the possibility of the person who is being counselled displaying excesses of emotion – anger, distress, disappointment, ambition, excitement, fear. Any manager would be wary about going into a situation that is likely to be emotionally charged. Part of this wariness may stem from the manager's anxiety about reacting positively and handling their own emotions. Acquiring counselling skills helps to equip the manager to handle these eventualities but in reality, such extreme reactions from the person being counselled are rare, and fear of them happening is based on very slim odds.

Skilful counselling requires practice, and it is to be hoped that most managers will not get too many opportunities to carry out this role. However, the need can and does occur, and so it is as well to be prepared. Being able to counsel staff can be very productive and can be helpful to them in finding ways of dealing with difficult situations. It can also make a positive contribution to the development of the manager-assistant relationship. On the other hand, poor counselling can be counter-productive and may result in damage to all parties and to the relationship. It is as well to be prepared to refer the person needing help to someone better placed to provide it, rather than handling the counselling ineffectively.

Listening

Active listening requires a high degree of alertness and sensitivity. The words being spoken by the person being counselled need to be heard, but what they are not saying also needs to be picked up. The person may say everything is fine, but have a facial expression and demeanour of extreme unhappiness. Their body may be tense and their fingers fiddling nervously.

Recognising the presenting problem

The problem as initially described may not be the real problem, or not all of it. The counsellor needs to be able to recognise this and to know how to encourage the person being counselled to go deeper. This skill makes use of questioning technique, by using reflective and probing questions, for example:

'Are you telling me that you are having problems getting into work on time because of the traffic? Would you like to tell me more about them?'

Getting to the core problem

Using this sort of approach should help both the counsellor and the person being counselled get to the heart of the matter. However, to do this the person concerned needs to be able to trust the counsellor to deal with them ethically. This means that they and their problem will be treated with respect and seriously. Confidentiality is an obvious requirement, but credibility and empathy need also to be established. This may take time and require gentle exploration of the problem and surrounding issues. Statements such as the following may help:

'I can understand what you are saying'
'Does that cause you difficulty?'
'Do you find that hard?'

Recognising and admitting feelings

Part of the purpose of counselling is to help the individual get to the root of the problem. This is achieved through diagnosis and by exploring the individual's feelings about the problem. Feelings affect behaviour. If the intent of counselling is to identify the causes of ineffective performance, or the blocks which are preventing changes to behaviour, an examination of feelings may be required. This needs to be handled carefully by the counsellor and taken at a steady, step-by-step pace.

'How does being late every day make you feel?'
'How do you think your contribution to the work of the team influences how your colleagues see you?'
'Does that matter to you?'

Criticism

Criticism can be either destructive or constructive, depending entirely on how it is given. Destructive criticism can knock down any positive wish to change. If any incentive remains, it tends to be in spite of, rather than because of the criticism. Constructive criticism, on the other hand, can provide guidance on where improvements may be made and encourage the individual to take the first steps needed to get there. Contrast:

'I think the way you handled that interview was rubbish'

to:

'How do you think that interview went? Can you think of any way in which your performance changed so it may be improved?'

The problem-solving process

One basic principle of counselling is that the individual should find their own solution to their own problem. Usually, enacting the solution requires extra effort and determination, so it is essential that the person concerned is fully committed to the course of action. If this has been laid down by someone else, the sense of ownership will inevitably be less than if the solution had been chosen by the person themselves. This does not mean that the counsellor should not help the process of finding the solution, simply that they should not make the decision for the person they are counselling. Sometimes, it is necessary to provide information, or to question whether the apparently 'best' answer will, in fact, solve the problem. It is also worth checking with the person being counselled that they feel able to see the solution through to its end.

Influencing the direction

The counsellor will inevitably have some effect on the process and the outcome. A skilful counsellor will be able to check their own performance and modify it to ensure that the impact is contributing to a resolution of the problem. Ideally, the counsellor should have no preferred outcome to the problem, nor any opinion on what would be best for the person concerned. The role is to ensure that the person being counselled has established the core problem for themselves and has considered fully the available options. The choice of option is the responsibility of the individual alone. The process and the skills used to ensure a satisfactory outcome are the responsibility of the counsellor.

It is this point that causes managers problems when counselling at work. A manager must have some ideas about desired outcomes. For that reason it is essential that the manager is able to recognise when the person being counselled should be referred to someone with a different relationship and less vested interest.

From the above it can be seen how the role can be demanding, needing well-developed skills. There is no reason why a manager cannot acquire and make good use of these skills. The process of counselling can be a very effective way of helping someone develop their skills. This approach is particularly valuable for the development of interpersonal skills. However, no matter how well a manager is able to carry out the role, there are occasions when it is better to say that the manager is not the best person to help. These occasions tend to be those where an individual is carrying the scars of previous damage which is having an unfortunate impact on interpersonal relationships or is creating dysfunctional patterns of behaviour.

The positive outcome of counselling is a deeper understanding by the person being counselled of the nature of their behaviour, the impact it has on others and ways they may improve their effectiveness. They can also learn an approach to problem-solving from the experience of being counselled that will help in the future and also may be used to help other people in similar situations. The counsellor also gains from the experience by acquiring more insight into people, an opportunity to use and refine their skills, feedback from the person being counselled, and the satisfaction of knowing that another person has been helped.

SUPERVISION

This term has two meanings. In its more usual sense it means the process of giving instructions, providing direction and closely monitoring the work of others. In the caring professions, however, it is used to describe the process employed to help professional workers step back from the job and examine their approach, methods and reactions to their job with someone skilled as a supervisor and with an understanding of the work. Because carers work so closely with other people, it is not easy for them to detach themselves from their clients. Emotional involvement with clients is recognised as a block to effective performance, so regular supervision is used to help professionals check the way in which they are working with their clients.

Supervision is another way of obtaining support and allows the person being supervised to discharge their own feelings. Burn-out is a phenomenon that can occur when people are giving out constantly to others. The professions that are concerned with the provision of personal services are aware of this and employ practices such as supervision to avoid it disabling workers. Steps are taken to allow workers to discharge emotions and to receive emotional and practical support so they can continue to provide professional services to their clients. Some references have been made to burn-out in management journals, but its occurrence and the ways of avoiding it are not widely broadcast. Managers are constantly giving out to their assistants and colleagues, and tactics such as 'managing by walking about' and 'open-door policies' make managers readily available to others. But little advice is given to managers about drawing support for themselves from others.

Networks and mentors may provide succour and refreshment. Nevertheless, from the reported increase in the stress of a manager's job, it is possible to make a case for a more structured means of providing supervision to managers in a way similar to that described above.

There is no reason why a manager of managers should not provide this support during regular reviews of progress. How often do you discuss what problems your staff's employees are causing them, how they are developing, what they are achieving, what more they need to do to improve their personal and collective performance? Do you ask how situations affect your staff, how they feel about their job, what it is doing to them?

ROLE MODELS

A manager acts as a role model in two ways: as an exemplar and as a learner. The exemplar role may seem to be auspicious to the role occupier, but this is only so if the role is seen as being an example of a perfect version. Perfection is an impossible state for any human, but sadly, some managers believe they have or are likely to achieve that state. Believing they are there, their standards set for others are impossibly exacting. It is also impossible for them to make mistakes and, of course, there is nothing left to learn. If they are working to reach perfection, there is a chance that they will kill themselves (and others) in the process.

The way learning occurs as a result of copying the behaviour of others was described earlier. Instructors and coaches use this process deliberately. Social conditioning, script rehearsal and induction are frequently cited theories used to explain how role models 'teach' subconsciously.

Being a role model is not easy. Role models are aware of 'being on show' and that others are watching constantly. However, if a manager accepts that this is happening and recognises it as a very useful role to occupy, it can be transformed. On one hand it may seem like being on top of a pedestal with everyone waiting to see what happens when the mighty are fallen. On the other hand, they may see the 'hero' as infallible. Being held up as perfect by others can also place undue pressure on the manager. Alternatively, the role may be occupied by a normal, flawed human being who has some other, broader or wider experience to share but who has developmental needs of their own. The latter stance is the developmental one from which everyone can learn. The person placed at the top of a pedestal cannot learn. Learning requires an admission of imperfection – not knowing, not being able to, having room for improvement. The perfect manager is none of these things. A developing manager makes mistakes, gets into flaps, panics, worries, doubts and gets better. The perfect person is unlikely to help others – up there on the pedestal they are vulnerable. Sharing may make it possible for the people looking up to push the pedestal over. Zones of perfection are impossible to achieve but the developmental manager can achieve much.

The developmental role model

The role model sets an example by taking action to help others to develop and is committed to their own development. Their example demonstrates how self-development is put into practice. Learning habits are well practised and are clearly visible. The manager takes steps to ensure that debate is a normal way of working for the section. Ideas are considered and talked about. Ways of working are constantly questioned, not in a destructive way but to check that the best available methods are being used and systems remain effective. Staff are encouraged and helped to take risks; mistakes, on the rare occasions they occur, are welcomed as opportunities for learning. Assistants are expected to question and discuss their own work and to come forward with ideas for improvement. They are expected to innovate and are held to account for their own areas of responsibility. Developmental managers fully accept responsibility for their own development and are willing to share their own learning and insights with others.

Support

A developmental manager is generous, providing support to help others' learning. An assistant's increasing skills do not present a threat – just the opposite. Since managers are frequently judged on the basis of their staffs' performance, the overall development of skills and improved levels of achievement in a department are, in fact, a measure of a manager's success. Support amounts to more than the giving of permission and words of encouragement. It is about opening doors. Not doing for the learner, but making their development and learning possible. Support is about removing unnecessarily hard blocks, but leaving enough of a barrier for the learner to have meaningful obstacles to tackle. Support is about asking for regular reports from the learner and taking the time to monitor the progress being made, so that accurate feedback can be given. This may require the canvassing of other people's opinions so that accurate information about performance is obtained. Support, above all, is about trusting the learner – trusting them to make mistakes in a way that will not be damaging and trusting them to apply their learning to good effect.

Encouragement

A developmental manager provides encouragement continuously. True encouragement amounts to more than words of praise. The words contain critical appraisal of performance, feedback based on evidence and knowledge of actual achievement. Encouragement is sensed as well as heard. The learner knows that their manager is behind them, willing and able to provide support and help if it is needed and asked for. The learner also knows the manager is capable of recognising when interventions are necessary and when they are not.

Discipline

Discipline, in the form of firmness and determination, helps to keep the learner going when learning is difficult. The reason for the learning is kept clearly in sight. The worth of the end product is revalued regularly and the action being taken is checked against its purpose. This is to make sure that the reason for learning remains relevant. If not, the developmental manager has the courage and determination to change the action.

Whether they want to be or not, managers are role models. The actions they take – and those they do not – will be registered. Duplication of the manager's behaviour by the learner need not happen immediately; it may remain in the learner's subconscious for some years, emerging later in such a way that the learner cannot attribute its origins. Moreover, the standards and values of managers' unconscious actions will send clear messages to others about what is important and what is trivial. If a manager says that development is important and the organisation is committed to helping its staff learn, and then punishes staff for using their initiative, it should not be surprising that the staff respond more to the punishment than to the rhetoric. It is important, therefore, that, as a role model, the manager's words and behaviour are congruent.

DEVELOPING THE BOSS AND OTHERS

While developmental managers are responsible for their own learning and that of their direct reports, the role also carries the responsibility for facilitating and contributing to the learning of colleagues. This responsibility can be enacted through:

- participation in group activities;

- providing peer feedback;

- asking naive but intelligent questions during debate (like why?);

- promoting alternative approaches and new ideas;

- encouraging reflection;

- stepping outside the task in hand to consider the processes being used and the dynamics of the group.

Skills are needed to recognise when it may be appropriate to behave in this way, or when to get on with the task in hand. Some groups have been known to fail because they have spent time wallowing in the swamps of introspection and being concerned about personal issues, neglecting the group's real purpose.

Developmental managers are also responsible for the development of their own managers. This may seem strange in a traditional hierarchy operating according to the principles of bureaucracy and its reliance on a structure based on expert authority. Modern organisations, however, can no longer operate according to these principles. Teams need to group around projects rather than functional divisions, leaders should be selected for their skills rather than their technical knowledge, skills need to be developed continuously as environments and markets transform. They should not be seen as having been acquired at the beginning of one's working life and lasting thereafter. Development is a way of being. The main organisational value in managing its people is the belief that everyone can contribute to the learning of everyone else concerned within the organisation and to the organisation itself.

Helping one's manager learn may take more skill than those need to help reports. This form of manager–assistant relationship is founded on mutual trust and respect. Liking each other is not necessary, but acceptance of each other's motives, ethics and good intent is. Ways of contributing to the development of one's manager includes:

- offering articles for discussion;

- presentation of new ideas;

- suggestions, with reasons, for doing things differently;

- opening up a wider debate;

- asking naive but intelligent questions;

- arranging visits from and to specialists and experts;

- trying out and making experiments;

- admitting to mistakes;

- asking for help;

- accepting the boss as a valuable, unique but flawed human being who gets tired, stressed and who needs help and support.

Some of these tactics are high-risk, but only so if trust has not been fully established within the relationship. If there is an openness between the manager and the manager's manager, the above will become a normal way of working and will seem obvious. If the relationship is not like this taking actions such as those suggested above can help to establish it. Building a relationship, like any other form of development, has good days and setbacks – that is the process of learning. The pay-off, in this case, will be well worth the risk. Having a manager who is prepared to learn from staff means that the manager will be prepared to help their learning – a symbiotic relationship. Creating this kind of environment inside an organisation is one of the first steps towards building a learning organisation.

SUMMARY

This chapter concerns the ways in which a manager can contribute to the development of others. The fundamental skill of giving feedback has been described. The provision of feedback requires skills which, even though they are advanced, can be acquired and developed through learning and practice. In addition to giving feedback, the developmental manager should be capable of receiving and acting upon feedback as an example to others.

The manager creates the climate for development and, as a role model, provides behavioural examples of how learning and development can happen. The role of manager encompasses sub-roles, including being an instructor, a coach, a counsellor, a mentor and a supervisor. Each role has a different focus and skills. The reasons and occasions for their use are different. Consequently the developmental manager can choose from a range of approaches and can decide which to use for different situations and with different people as the need arises.

Equally so, the manager is a role model. Behaviour demonstrates examples of good and poor practice. The way in which a manager works is witnessed by those around and copied. It is important, therefore, that words and behaviour are consistent and congruent, and that the manager can be seen by others to be truly committed to development. This requires managers to take full responsibility for their own development, acting upon that responsibility, and accepting responsibility for contributing to the development of others.

Managers are responsible for contributing to and enabling the learning of their colleagues and their own manager, as well as their own staff. By assuming this role fully, a manager starts the process of establishing a learning organisation.

9
Learning organisations

INTRODUCTION

This chapter is both an epilogue and a prelude, completing what has gone before and introducing what may come next. Development, after all, is a continuous journey. The possibilities for introducing change and different ways of working and being are endless. Sadly, all too often, the individual manager feels alone and unable to have any impact. Nevertheless the manager's role is influential and powerful within an organisation. This chapter will explore what can be done by developmental managers, on their own and with their peers and reports, to instigate the search for alternatives and new ideas in the context of their own organisation.

Organisations are being told and appreciate that they need to be flexible and make full use of their available resources if they are to survive and prosper. The latest recession has seen organisations, which have done everything right, fail. Different solutions are needed to deal with unprecedented problems. To help achieve this organisations are being encouraged to look at new ways of working. The shortage of skilled workers has directed attention at the two aspects of the problem.

Firstly, as the 'demographic time-bomb' is still ticking, workers are being sought from non-traditional sources. Efforts are being made by initiatives such as Opportunity 2000 to increase the quality and quantity of women's participation in the workforce. There is also a growing awareness of the continued contribution older workers can make.

Secondly, the need to update existing staff, reskill the unemployed and retrain the workforce as a whole has entered the political agenda. The National Council for Vocational Qualifications owes its existence to the need to refocus on work-related training and to make sense of the panoply of qualifications. The Council was set up to simplify what was seen as an over-cumbersome system which did not pay proper attention to what people should be able to do. The previous emphasis of qualifications was seen to be placed on knowledge rather than skills. Investors in People is a government initiative aimed at encouraging organisations to engage in systematic training. To achieve the standard proposed, this approach should be an element in organisations' overall strategy and a normal way of working. Other systems draw attention to the need to ensure that staff are properly trained to do the job for which they are employed. For example, BS5750 looks at what procedures are in place to train staff in quality systems. And recently the term 'Learning Organisation' has entered the management vocabulary.

WHAT IS A LEARNING ORGANISATION?

This concept originated, in part, from the 'In search of Excellence' movement and was later referred to by Garratt (1987). Geoffrey Holland, Permanent Secretary of the Department of Employment, is reported to have said:

> If we are to survive — individually or as companies, or as a country — we must create a tradition of learning companies.

Early work was concerned to find examples of good practice so that the learning organisation might be replicated. What happened, however, was that some of the organisations held up as role models were subsequently found to be flawed. Almost as soon as descriptions of their excellence appeared in print, conditions had changed and their performance was no longer outstanding. This has served to diminish the importance of the concept in the eyes of those looking for cook-book solutions. People who are looking for the 'right way' have missed the point of the concept, however. The right way is as elusive as any other idealised state of being — there is no perfect organisation, for they are all peopled by fallible human beings; therefore, it is inevitable that organisations make mistakes, get things wrong and suffer setbacks. Mistakes and setbacks are elemental features of development and learning. It is the way in which organisations respond to the normal features of the modern world and the lessons learnt from the experience that qualifies them for the title 'learning organisation'. It is not what they do, but how they do it.

Pedler, Boydell and Burgoyne (1988) set out to:

> define and test the feasibility of the idea as an appropriate approach to business and human resource development strategies in the 1990s.

By a process of literature reviews, interviews and other investigations, they were able to produce a working definition of a learning company:

> An organisation which facilitates the learning of all of its members and continuously transforms itself.

In their report, Pedler *et al* take pains to stress the two-sided nature of the definition. A learning company is *not* one which merely engages in a lot of training. The need for the development of individual skills is embedded in the concept, equal to and part of the need for organisational learning.

Is an organisation an entity or a collective?

It is not possible to continue into the investigation of a learning organisation without considering whether an organisation has an existence of its own which is separate from those of its members, or whether it is simply a sum of the component parts. Organisations are an essential part of the way our society operates. They can be found at all levels of society and are involved in the bulk of the transactions in which we engage with other people.

Gibson, Ivancevich and Donnelly (1988) say:

> Organisations are, however, much more than means of providing goods and services. They create the settings in which most of us spend our lives. In this respect, they have profound influence on our behaviour.

Because of their importance to our everyday lives, the study of behaviour within organisations has become a discipline in its own right, concerning:

> The study of human behaviour, attitudes and performance within an organisational setting; drawing on theory, methods and principles from such disciplines as psychology, sociology and cultural anthropology to learn about *individual* perceptions, values, learning capacities and action while working in *groups* and within the total organisation, analysing the external environment's effect on the *organisation* and its human resources, missions, objectives and strategies.
>
> (Gibson, Ivancevich and Donnelly, 1988)

Life within one organisation may be similar to life in another, but it will also be different. Each organisation is unique. This uniqueness emanates from each organisation's culture, which grows and changes during the life of the organisation. It is influenced by its original and developing purpose, the people in membership and those with influence on the organisation. (The concept of organisational culture is described more fully earlier in this book and references are given for those who wish to explore it more fully.)

If organisations are merely the product of the people in them and their purpose, it would be reasonable to expect that those which are set up for similar purposes would have similar cultures. It would be reasonable to expect this to be especially so in those sectors where people move freely between organisations. In fact, this is not the case. The National Health Service provides an example that shows the opposite. Until recently, each health authority was run according to the same tight guidelines set down by central government. Doctors were trained using a rotation scheme that required the young medics to move between hospitals and specialities. If the argument about cultural commonality were correct, the doctors would have experienced no real difference between health authorities, but this was not so. Each authority had its own distinctive features that made the experience of each novel.

Therefore if each organisation is unique and has its own identity manifested in its culture, which develops and changes over time as a result of experience and influence, the organisation must be capable of learning. Learning, as defined earlier, is a purposeful activity aimed at the acquisition and development of skills and knowledge and their application. An organisation's skills are found in its accepted behaviour patterns and its collective knowledge in its shared assumptions. The organisational attitude exists in the core values. If these can be developed within an individual, there is no reason why this cannot happen for an organisation. It is more difficult and will take longer to achieve, but these factors do not reduce the possibility of organisational learning.

Pedler *et al* say 'A Learning Company is one in which learning and working are synonymous'. They concluded that, as a 'learning company' is really an idealised state, it is not possible to point one out as a visible entity. This is because the definition describes a way of *being*, which is more than *doing*. Nevertheless there are some features that can be used to distinguish between a company which is not learning and one which is. Many of these features concern the way in which the organisation's members *experience* the organisation and the climate within which they work. Pedler *et al* give 'glimpses' of a learning company, but as it is more important here to grasp the ideas rather than the actions, no examples will be given. Without the underlying understanding, there is a danger that, as with many other management techniques, the behaviours will be copied incompletely.

What is a learning organisation like?

According to Pedler *et al*:

a Learning Organisation is one which:

- has a climate in which individual members are encouraged to learn and to develop their full potential

- extends this learning culture to include customers, suppliers and other significant stakeholders

- makes human resource development strategy central to business policy

- is in a continuous process of organisational transformation.

The purpose of this process of transformation, as a central activity, is to enable the company to search within and without for new ideas, new problems and new opportunities for learning, to exploit a competitive advantage in an increasingly competitive world.

How to become a learning company

Megginson and Pedler (1992) provide a guide to the concept of a learning company. It is:

> an idea or metaphor that can serve as a guiding star. It can help people to think and act together on what such a notion would mean to them now and in the future. Like all visions, it can help to create the condition in which some of the features of a Learning Company could be brought about.

These conditions are:

- learning strategy;

- participative policy-making;

- informating (ie information technology is used to inform and empower people to ask questions and take decisions based on available data);

- formative accounting (ie control systems are structured to assist learning from decisions);

- internal exchange;

- reward flexibility;

- enabling structures;

- front-line workers as environmental scanners;

- inter-company learning;

- learning climate;

- self-development for all.

Doing all these things would not necessarily mean that an organisation is a learning company. To meet the standards of being an 'Investor in People', an organisation is assessed by independent assessors. This approach demonstrates the difference between doing and being. The assessors go beyond examining policy documents, procedures and records — the normal evidence used in quality assurance. Organisations are required to show what they do in practice. This means that they are open to a scrutiny that explores employees' experiences and understanding of training policy and practice. Being a learning company extends well beyond these. All the authors quoted above give systematic training a place within a learning organisation, but the concept goes deeper and is more sophisticated. It means, for example, that the learning strategy is much more than a human resource development strategy. In a learning company, this learning is a core part of *all* operations.

What does organisational transformation mean?

Organisational transformation is different from organisational development. The latter term was in common use in the 1960s and 70s to describe a process that relied mainly on the intervention of an external consultant. Most of the activities were aimed at exploring and improving the way in which organisational members worked together and responded to change. Techniques used included clarifying goals, negotiating roles, exploring group dynamics and gaining a better understanding of other members of a team, as a way of improving relationships. The economic recessions since then have switched attention from organisational dynamics to task/business requirements and the need to increase and improve skills. There is also a need to control change and to be proactive. Reacting and responding is no longer enough.

Organisational development typically focused on an area or point of time of change. The consultant would work with organisational members helping them work together and cope with change. Now, however, change is a part of normal reality. At one time, organisations moved in stages through periods of change into a steady state, and then again through a period of change. The strength of a bureaucratic organisation is its ability to accommodate changes of this nature. What happens is 'first-order' change. The organisation does 'more of' or 'less of' the same things, but this sort of response is not good enough. Life is no longer that simple. The changes occurring to organisations are now continuous:

> It is not just new kinds of problems and opportunities that we are facing, but whole new contexts within which these problems and opportunities reside . . .
> The ground itself is moving . . . . contexts have destabilised to the point where we can no longer assume that the basic structure of the context surrounding a situation will hold still long enough to make a planned course of action feasible
> . . . . In a destabilised context, you cannot know exactly what your problems are!

Perhaps even the metaphor of permanent white water is not adequate: we are not talking merely about a wild river; we are talking about an unpredictable wild river.

(Vaill, 1989)

The rivers have carried us into a world where second-order change is needed. This means 'doing different things'. In this world, there is no one who knows best, no experience of having done it before, and there are no consultants or experts who can show us 'how to do it good'. There is only us, with the untapped, unknown resource of our own potential and creativity. Sadly, the rigidity of most organisations' policies and procedures serve to deny them these resources.

The rational models of decision-making were not put forward as reflections of reality. Being normative theories, they describe how decisions *ought* to be made. As many organisations say they use the principles of rational decision-making, many people actually believe that decisions are made in this way. The notion of incremental decisions – 'the art of muddling through' – as described by Lindblom (1979) is probably a more accurate representation of what happens in practice. Rational decision-making suggests that an organisation decides its long-term goals, works out what needs to happen to get there, and then starts to take action. Muddling through implies that, even if such goals are set, the organisation starts from where it is and moves, incrementally onwards – perhaps towards the goals, but not necessarily so. Decisions are made on the grounds of expediency, rather than being goal-orientated.

Examples of both models can be seen to operate within existing organisational realities. The sort of decision-making required for the new reality in the world of permanent white water takes the organisation beyond these practices. The term 'sea change' has been used to describe the sort of fundamental shifts that modern conditions impose on organisations, but this notion is still limited to one-off changes. The world of organisations is now iterative; constantly moving and reshaping in unpredictable directions. To misquote Tom Peters, the American management guru: the unthinkable is no longer impossible, it is highly probable. Doing different things differently is the response required for organisations to manage and survive in their new world.

The nearest metaphor to be found to describe this new world is that of Brownian motion – the erratic random movement of microscopic particles in a liquid, gas etc as a result of continuous bombardment from molecules of the surrounding medium. If this metaphor is applied to organisations, the way currently used by an organisation to survive and prosper is for it to learn continuously from the nature of the medium in which it is moving and from its experiences in it. The concept of a learning company implies more than this.

The philosophy of continuous learning takes place in the organisation's larger system. This larger system actively involves customers, suppliers and stakeholders in a continuous unbreakable chain.

What is it like to be part of a learning organisation?

Being a member of a learning organisation is not necessarily an easy role. In fact it can be distinctly uncomfortable, depending on the individual's views of the world. To those who are excited by learning and development, who actively seek change and growth, the notion of continuous learning is very attractive – the prospect of being involved in a learning company is desirable. To others, the opposite may be true. The idea of change and challenge can be repulsive to those who prefer continuity and routine.

There is a belief among those who are committed to learning and development that this will be beneficial to all. This is not a correct assumption. Some people are content to go to work and do the same job, day in day out, for the whole of their working lives. They have as much right to take this view as those who believe differently. However, their wish for stability must not lead to stagnation, for stagnation brings death in its wake. As with people, some organisations prefer stability in their cultures and work actively to preserve the status quo. The existence of 'dynamic conservatism' must not be ignored.

The tendency to stagnation can be detected in statements such as: 'We can't do that, we have never done it before', which lead to paralysis and a systemic inability to change. The supposed effect of an ageing working population on organisations has not received much attention. The emphasis, recently, has been given to the positive contribution older people can make. However, there is a general assumption that as people grow older, they tend to be less experimental, becoming more risk averse and preferring the known to the unknown. If this assumption is true, the ageing nature of the workforce may affect organisations' abilities to learn, develop and transform, unless action is taken to counteract its influence. Therefore it will become even more critical for organisations to learn how to learn.

Living with change

Being a part of a learning organisation involves living in a state in which questioning and change are normal. Change of this magnitude is much more far-reaching than the stop/start first-order change of the bureaucracy. While changes which involve doing more of or less of something can be traumatic, in comparison to the sea-change implication of second-order changes, they are just storms in teacups. Sea changes involve mental shifts that require people (including those on the edges) to see their world in a totally different way. The term 'sea change' comes from Shakespeare's *The Tempest*:

> Full fathom five thy father lies;
> Of his bones are coral made:
> Those are pearls that were his eyes:
> Nothing of him that doth fade,
> But doth suffer a sea change
> Into something rich and strange.

In other words, even though structures may remain the same, their fabric is altered. While the basic shape stays constant, its very being is different. In terms of organisations, this level of change requires people to do different things and to see the world in different ways. Some of the changes that have occurred in the public sector since the introduction of privatisation are examples of sea changes. The same people are working in the same places, providing very similar services as before, but working in totally different ways for new reasons.

Living in an evolving world brings with it high degrees of uncertainty. Staff may know what the vision statement says because care has been taken to share its meaning. But 'what it means to me' may be unclear and likely to remain so until work starts to implement the vision. Even then, the full implications will only be revealed as the plans unfold. But, because the situation is evolving and the people and organisation are learning, the plans too will change. The vision, being a long-term dream, will be transformed. As some parts become clearer and move more sharply into focus, other parts will fade. The vision may not change in essence, but how it is seen may. It will be seen by different people from different perspectives at different times and be interpreted in different ways.

The nature of evolution may seem to be contradictory for some of the people involved – hence the cry of shifting goal-posts. However, it is not just the goal-posts that seem to move – the playing field changes into a swimming pool for water polo, to an ice rink for hockey, into an arena for horse-jumping and then to athletics. At least we stay with sporting analogies. Ambiguity to this extent requires managers and their staff to develop special sorts of skills if they are to continue to function effectively. Without these skills people can experience untenable levels of stress. Unchecked, this leads to dysfunctional behaviour or, in extreme examples, breakdown. A learning organisation takes action to help its members develop skills of managing in uncertain and ambiguous conditions.

Internal harmony

In the world of permanent white water, the changing nature of the organisation brings into question its internal harmony. The traditional view of politics has three strands: the Marxist belief that conflict between the owners or power holders of an organisation and its workers is inevitable and unresolvable; the pluralist view that it is possible for multiple agendas to be satisfied; and the unitary view that there is one correct overriding agenda that must be adhered to. None of these definitions hold good in a learning organisation. Encouraging questions undermines the unitary view and because there are no experts there is no right and wrong. Without extremes, consensus is possible but the developmental approach encourages healthy conflict as a means of synergising better, new solutions to new problems. How multiple agendas can coexist and be satisfied when there is one agreed and shared vision is dubious. Another theory is required to describe politics in a learning organisation.

Managing diversity

The term 'managing diversity' is increasingly used, mainly in a similar sense to equal opportunities. The new term implies facing up to contradictions and differences and finding ways, not of accommodating them as the pluralist approach would suggest, but of allowing them to exist together, each with equal validity and equal worth. The term implies that each individual has rights and is encouraged to make a unique contribution. The skills needed by those charged with managing in this context are very different from the control skills used in the past for managing groups of staff. Managing diversity brings conflict out into the open. Those used to having a quiet life in waters where the boat is never rocked may find this world of permanent white water a bit too exciting and dangerous.

It is little wonder that modern managers experience an exacting, tiring, stressful existence. The sort of satisfaction that can be obtained from working in these conditions is very different from that previously expected and regarded as normal. To some this sort of life may seem to be unacceptably pressurised and they may prefer a return to the old ways. However, we are in a new world, and need to find new ways of working with it. There are three ways in which we can respond:

- *It will never happen here* – the ostrich approach.

- *We must work harder* – the woodpecker approach.

- *We must work smarter* – the owl approach.

Sadly for the ostrich and woodpecker, if a pressurised existence is not acceptable, few options are open. The learning company offers a way of achieving the third option, that of 'working smarter'.

WHAT CAN ONE MANAGER DO ALONE?

It is not uncommon to hear senior managers say that they feel powerless to achieve change, and that their opportunities to develop are limited. This is, in part, due to the ease with which they become isolated from the rest of their organisation. Status, business, location, size of the organisation, different agendas and objectives, the difficulty of the task, perspective, time horizons and the perceptions of others all conspire to drive wedges between an organisation's senior managers and the rest of its workforce. As a result, the circle of people with whom senior managers transact is small. Also, and inevitably, they must rely on others to help effect changes and develop the organisation and its members.

Much of the attention given recently to management development has focused on the development of individual managers' personal skills and competence. The popular image of a manager is of a person in charge, working and deciding alone on tasks of herculean proportions. Success is possible and can be achieved by long hours, hard work and drive. Mixing metaphors and quotations mercilessly, the manager is a sole actor on the stage delivering a soliloquy to a hostile audience; the lone agent. This picture, of course, is false. The real role of a manager is to work with and through others, on objectives that are far too big for one person to achieve alone. This is done by the use of appropriate processes and techniques – and by treating colleagues and staff as respected individuals who each have a distinct and valued contribution to make.

If managers see themselves in terms of the popular image, it can be of little surprise to find them feeling disempowered and unable to achieve. The learning company philosophy provides a way of empowering oneself and others within the organisation. The term contains two concepts. The first, obviously, is that of learning; the second is not so apparent. Pedler, Boydell and Burgoyne (1988) do not use the word 'company' in its business sense. They are not describing a legal entity. Rather, they use the word in its older meaning – a group of companions, associates, friends, united by a commonality of purpose.

Developing this form of community is a means of reducing the sense of disempowerment and the overwhelming magnitude of the task. To misquote Benazir Bhutto 'the only way to eat an elephant is to chop it into small pieces'; sharing the task, by separating and distributing its elements reduces the strain on the individual. It can also improve the quality of the process of work and the outcome achieved. Involvement of appropriate others in appropriate ways can have a number of predictable outcomes:

- Group working avoids tram-line thinking.

- Individual assumptions are questioned by concerned others.

- Debate stimulates the creation of new ideas.

- Group members help each other stand back from the problem to reframe it.

- The available experience, knowledge, skills and brain capacity is increased.

- The vision or purpose can be restated and revalidated as a result of group discussion, challenge and debate.

- Group members can mentor and coach each other, and providing 'moral' support and encouragement.

- People are essentially social creatures and generally function better when working with others in conducive settings.

Thus, a group working on a common problem can produce better solutions than one person working alone.

To answer the opening question, one manager working alone cannot achieve a great deal; working with others can achieve much:

> No man is an Island, entire of itself; every man is a piece of the Continent, a part of the main.
>
> (John Donne, *Devotions*)

In the learning company, managers are not sole individuals. They are members of a professional community of co-learners, who help each other and provide support when the going gets tough. Collectively, they act as reflective practitioners, complementing each other, moving between action and thought as appropriate.

Viall (1989) describes the Chinese concept of Wu-wei — the art of non-action. This, he says, is about learning how to go with the flow, or follow the grain (of the wild river). This concept does not counsel passivity. It is a powerful idea and a way to learn the art of judgement, knowing when to intervene and when to leave well alone. Too many managers, led on by the decisive, driving 'I'm in charge' model, rush in, often making matters worse than they already are. Wu-wei suggests stepping back, examining what is happening, gathering ideas, listening to others' perspectives, considering options, thinking about the situation and, only then, deciding what action, *if any*, to take.

Stepping back in this way sometimes requires existing (preferred) approaches and ideas to be left to one side. It also means that assumptions and beliefs have to be abandoned while they are checked out with others. To be able to question one's assumptions and thought processes in this way requires a degree of self-doubt. However, to continue to function effectively, managers need to retain some confidence. The learning company provides the networks and trustworthy companions which help the process of questioning and reframing. It provides the context which allows this degree of risky self-challenge to be carried out in safety.

WHAT CAN A MANAGER DO WITH OTHERS?

Some of the above statements may seem to be highly idealised, impossible to put into practice in most organisations by most managers. This need not be the case. Even the isolated manager, striving to put these notions into practice, need not feel as though the task is too big. Much can be achieved by a single manager working with one or two peers and direct assistants. Many of the techniques described above do not need the permission of the chief executive; they are more dependent on the personal style and skills of the managers. Even though organisational culture can detract from the quality of learning, it is not a conclusive — it does not stop learning and development happening. It becomes a case of 'in spite of' rather than 'because of'.

The Framework shown in Fig. 1.1 is a vehicle for developing a cognitive model for managing organisations. Its elements can be used by managers as a guide to help them to develop 'learning companies' within their own sphere of influence. The components of each element are described below and some suggestions regarding possible courses of action are made. These suggestions are possible ways in which managers can act to develop a learning organisation within their own spheres of influence by working *with others*.

Guiding

Developing and sharing goals and ideas

This means that a vision is crafted and shared among the team members. The goals are debated and constantly restated as part of normal work activities. Questions such as 'How does this help us achieve?' are not regarded as being awkward or out of the ordinary. Retesting the goals does not imply that they are being changed; it is more a case of checking them out, validating them and reaffirming them. Nevertheless, this should not be automatic. If needed, the goals should be altered so the overall vision can take account of changed circumstances.

Sharing is important. Understanding requires explanation and time for thought. Commitment requires participation. If staff are not allowed a glimpse of the vision, how can they begin to understand it? How can they be expected to be committed to something they do not understand?

Monitoring progress is essential

The reason for having a vision and the purpose of goals is to enable you to know where you are going so you know when you get there. You also need some means of checking that you are going in the right direction and making adequate progress. Monitoring mechanisms are different from those which are used for control. The latter can be fences that, while keeping you on the right path, also hem you in. Monitoring helps you to test the environs and to obtain feedback. It should not be an end in itself.

Managing the parameters complements monitoring

If there are no fences to keep you on the straight and narrow, other means are needed to prevent the unwary from straying off the path. The edge is the area where the organisation, like a military operation, is vulnerable. A manager's attention is usually focused on those thrusting ahead and the laggards, trailing behind. The ones in the middle may seem to be all right, but they also need attention. If they are not reminded of the direction and not given feedback to help them monitor that they are doing the right things, it can be very easy for them to find themselves working very hard to no effect. The cause of ineffective working often is those tasks that sneak into the organisation from its side. To avoid this the manager needs to be positive in its management of the edges.

Taking responsibility

There are some tasks that a manager cannot delegate, and some decisions that a manager should not avoid. The very worst type of manager is someone who prevaricates. Staff get confused, they lose respect for their manager and either make decisions themselves or end up in a state of suspended animation where nothing gets done. Most tasks can be assigned to others, but some cannot move from managers' shoulders – hence their higher status and salary. For example, a manager cannot delegate the responsibility for developing staff. It is beholden on managers to accept all the responsibilities of their role willingly and to work at the skills needed for effective performance.

Setting examples

This is another role managers cannot avoid, no matter what is done and how others see. The manager can be either a good role model or a bad one. Sometimes the most valuable lessons are learnt from observing and experiencing the actions of a bad manager, but this is not to be recommended. It is far better to learn from a good one. No matter how hard it may seem, there is very little a manager can do to escape being seen. A manager who is a 'Do as I say but not as I do' manager is nearly as bad as one who does not decide.

Mentoring

Mentoring was described at length in the previous chapter. It may seem to be a time-consuming activity at first, but the benefits and pay-offs in terms of everyone's increased performance, commitment and productivity should more than repay the initial investment.

Collaborating

This may not come easily to managers who have been used to a highly competitive world. Collaboration requires trust and a sense of unity of purpose. Organisations that have encouraged internal conflict, believing it to be a way of stimulating higher levels of performance, will not have established a climate in which cross-boundary working is simple. The prevailing ethos will be to guard one's own patch from the robber barons and ensure that the control of one's own destiny is firmly in one's own hands. This breeds internal hostility, which makes the organisation very vulnerable to external attack. Everyone is so busy fighting each other that danger signs from outside are not seen.

Collaboration, on the other hand, means that organisational members help their colleagues, watch each others' backs and contribute to problem-solving. This increases the resource base of experience and enlarges the creative brain power. It is up to the managers to establish the climate in which collaboration can exist by demonstrating to their staff how they collaborate in practice. If staff see their managers working productively with each other, they will be more prepared to work jointly themselves.

Directing

Motivating staff

This means encouraging them, giving them feedback, rewarding them. They are given tasks that will stretch them and develop their skills, without over-challenging them. Staff need to be clear about what is being expected from them, what authority they have and what outcomes are required. While many sources of motivation come from within an individual, good relations with managers are important for performance to continue to give high levels of achievement and satisfaction.

Leading staff

Leading does not always have to be done from the front. The image of a sheepdog is useful here. A good dog knows that, to get a herd of stubborn sheep heading in the same direction, it is better to encourage them from behind, hurrying the slow, checking the wanderers and occasionally slowing down the bolters. The occasional nip at the heels of the renegades is the only discipline required. Only a foolish dog would yap from the gate expecting the sheep to organise themselves into an orderly file to pass through. The sheep have their own idea of who is in charge and prefer to follow their own social leader. People may have greater intellectual capacity than sheep, but sometimes less sense of collective direction. Leading groups of people requires the same sort of doggedness – quiet determination and strength of purpose.

Instructing, training and coaching

These were described earlier as a development method. They also comprise skills of leadership. Informing staff about the vision and goals is important, but the communication needs to be supplemented by demonstration and instruction to aid the understanding of the recipients of the message. Staff need to be shown how to do new tasks, and new patterns of behaviour have to be modelled. Sometimes, if the changes are radical, direct instructions need to be given for certain tasks to be stopped and new ones started. Support and coaching from the manager are necessary to help the new skills to be developed and practised.

Delegation

This is also a way of helping staff work in new ways, and to develop skills. Motivation can be increased by giving the responsibility for a new project to members of staff, providing they are helped to learn how to do it.

Providing discipline

Discipline complements delegation and is needed when the going gets tough. It is also needed to maintain quality. When standards drop below acceptable levels, proper disciplinary procedures should be used to ensure that people are treated with respect, given fair hearings and helped to improve.

Feedback

This can also be a part of discipline. Feedback processes were described at length in Chapter 8. Providing feedback is an essential aspect of the manager's overall role. A developmental manager is also prepared to receive feedback and to act upon it. Seeking and using information about performance is a normal way of working, isn't it?

Managing conflict

While this may not be easy or pleasant, the skills of dealing with conflict constructively are needed as all too often conflict seems to be an inevitable part of working life. Conflict can arise between managers and colleagues, between managers and direct assistants, between managers and staff from other sections and between managers and their managers. It also occurs within and between groups and with customers and suppliers. It is extremely rare for conflict to go away if it is ignored. Rather, it festers and waits for opportunities to break out, often in other guises. Then it is difficult to get to its source. This results in the managers dealing with symptoms, never being able to get to the roots of the problem. If conflict is faced up to early, the chances of resolving it are much greater.

Initiating change

This responsibility lies with a manager. It does not imply that the manager has to have all the good ideas and develop all the opportunities. But it does mean that a manager has a critical part to play in establishing the climate for changes to happen, encouraging staff to have good ideas and facilitating the seizing of opportunities.

Enabling

Managers are responsible for helping their staff to do their job. This goes beyond telling them what to do and expecting them to get on with it. Managers need skills to enable staff to do their jobs effectively. This includes helping (not doing for) them, opening doors and providing support.

Listening actively

This means more than hearing the words being spoken. The listener sits still, sets to one side their own thoughts and stops preparing the next question or a reply. Staying still and silent is hard work; concentrating on what someone else is saying is even harder. Try repeating verbatim what someone says to you, to test your abilities.

Supporting risk-taking

Staff are not very likely to take the chance of failing if they do not believe their manager is with them. Some will act in spite of their line manager, but these people are few and tend to be mavericks. It is better that everyone concerned knows that they are members of the team and that other team members, especially its leader, are willing to help if needed.

Trust

Trusting that the staff, in taking risks, will not be foolhardy is a prelude to giving support. But until the risk of letting staff members take risks is taken, the manager will never know whether they will repay the trust. This can be an unbreakable circle unless the manager is prepared to give the trust initially.

Recognising and developing potential

This is one way of minimising the chance of staff failing. Often staff fail because they are charged with a task that is not possible for them to carry out to the standard required, for a range of reasons. If managers are able to recognise the signs of potential and the indicators of ability, they are better able to plan and allocate work-loads and develop potential by means of calculated risks and experience, thus reducing the chances of failure.

Challenging tasks

Facing up to challenging tasks is a part of development. The tasks should not be so challenging, however, that staff are discouraged before they start. Being faced with Mission Impossible may be exciting for television characters, but not for mere mortals. Challenges need to be planned and scaled to match the assessment of the individual's potential. If the tasks are large or complex, it may be better to break them into do-able chunks, stages or mini-projects.

Facilitating learning

Facilitating is a word that is frequently used without reference to its true meaning. Its sense implies 'making easy'. Managers should not (and cannot) do the learning for their staff, nor should they remove its challenge. But they can help to make the process, rather than the content, of development and learning smooth and as trouble-free as possible.

Counselling

This is another process which can be used to help learning. Its purpose is to help individuals find ways of resolving their own problems. A counsellor uses skills to aid identification of the source of the problem and to help the person concerned to decide their own course of action. A manager must decide when it is appropriate to act in this role and when it would be better to refer the individual to someone better placed to help.

Giving positive encouragement

Encouragement is important when staff face difficult situations. Any new task or concept is hard, simply because it is new. If staff believe that their managers have faith in them, they will be able to meet the challenges more positively than if they feel that they are expected to fail. Positive encouragement is given by means of monitoring, feedback, praise and rewards. Sometimes silly gestures, such as buying staff packs of sweets at the end of a hard week, can tell them that their efforts are appreciated and valued and give them encouragement for the following week.

Nurturing

This term contains a sense of giving nourishment as well as training and encouragement. It implies care and tenderness – almost in a gardening sense, when a young trailing plant is coaxed around its support. Staff skills can be developed in a similar fashion, by being fed, supported and given shape as they grow.

WHAT DO DEVELOPMENTAL MANAGERS DO FOR THEMSELVES?

So far, much of what has been discussed has focused on the actions that can be taken by managers to help support and facilitate the development of their reports. Managers are also responsible for their own self-development. This sets examples to others and ensures that their skills, which otherwise can easily be neglected, continue to be refreshed and recreated. Managers can work with others in a learning community or as part of a network and they can work with themselves.

Pedler, Boydell and Burgoyne (1988) describe the value of learning communities and networks as a means of sharing information and ideas. Exchanging experiences enables participants to validate their approaches, test out alternatives by friendly questioning and obtain support. Collaborative working on problems presents the opportunity for assumptions to be explored, new solutions to be synthesised and the skills of helping other's development to be acquired.

Managers can also work on their own agendas. Texts such as Pedler,

Burgoyne and Boydell (1986) provide guidance on how this may be done. Other bodies, as disparate as the Institute of Personnel Management and the Engineering Council, recognise the value of continuing development for professionals. The IPM has issued a code which proclaims:

> Continuous development is self-directed, lifelong learning. Continuous (professional) development policies are policies first to allow and then to facilitate such learning at work, through work itself.

The Engineering Council has produced a practical guide, expressing the vision of:

> a joint commitment. By this [the Council] means individuals and the organisation may realise their full potential for excellence, for world class performance.

Both organisations attribute responsibility for development firmly with managers who 'must give regular and ongoing attention to subordinates' continuous development . . . [and] must promote their own learning about learning.' Individuals must also accept responsibility 'for their own CPD and should initiate discussions about CPD in their companies.'

The Framework set out in Fig. 1.1 also addresses the question of managers' self-development, and highlights four aspects of *knowing self*.

Applying Values

Re-evaluating beliefs

This is a way for managers to avoid Groupthink. It does not mean constantly changing one's mind. Rather, it suggests that managers should check their interpretation of assumed 'facts'. It also provides a way of exploring stereotypes and preconceptions.

Maintaining ethics and values

Even when beliefs have been examined and re-evaluated, it does not follow that they have to be altered. It is important that managers know what they believe and why, act consistently in accordance with their values and stand by them. Adopting ethics in business is perceived by some as a sign of weakness — some managers genuinely believe that all is fair in love, war and the world of work. This attitude does not foster a climate for development, and will not be found in a learning company.

Challenging assumptions and prejudice

This is part of the re-evaluation of beliefs and application of values. If other managers are operating from positions of prejudice and are using stereotypes or misinformation as bases for decision-making, the ethical, developmental manager should offer a challenge. This should not be done to oppose the other but, through friendly questioning, to help the other reframe constructs and enlarge their thinking and widen perspectives.

Accepting and respecting differences

Every manager has the right to their own opinion — providing it has been formed on the basis of evidence and consideration, and is not used to prejudice others unfairly. A developmental manager accepts these differing views and respects the right of their holder to have them. It does not imply that the first must agree with the second. It does mean, however, that the uniqueness and individuality of each person is appreciated and valued.

Managing self

Self-development for managers starts from the premise that, before anyone can manage and develop others effectively, they need to be able to manage and develop themselves. Most of the written work produced to describe the techniques and processes of self-development has been produced by Pedler, Boydell and their associates. To complement their published guidance, the Framework offers the suggestions set out below.

Asking for and receiving feedback

Asking staff to comment on behaviour could be perceived as a sign of weakness, making the manager vulnerable by threatening their status and authority. In fact, the reverse can be the case. People tend to respond to the way in which they have been previously treated. If the manager has been giving feedback to staff in a way that respects the individual, and has provided actionable information, the staff are likely to treat the manager in a similar way. Moreover, if the manager has been sensitive and responsive, the feedback messages should hold no surprises. Asking for feedback and listening carefully can provide a manager with useful information. It is important that staff have confidence in the manager's willingness to act on the feedback, and that it will not be used for other purposes. Feedback from staff can be a source of support and reaffirmment. Managers can be lonely people. The sense of support and backing from one's own staff is important, especially in times of stress, rapid change and uncertainty. Asking for feedback, receiving and reflecting on its contents and being seen to act upon some of the messages can be a very positive way of securing staff trust and gaining their respect.

Organising self

How many times have you heard the phrase, 'They couldn't organise a xxxx-up in a brewery' used to describe managers' organisational abilities? Being able to organise oneself is a prerequisite for effective management. It is possible to be efficient without being effective, but not the other way round. Effective managers are able to use time, organise their desks and papers and plan their own work. They create time and space for thinking and their own development and they are able and have the time to give due attention to the development of their staff.

Developing personal and professional skills

The effective organisation and use of time and space are skills that can be learnt. Professional skills of management are those evidenced by the use of appropriate management processes, tools and techniques. For example, interviewing, coaching and giving feedback are professional skills. Effective listening and communication require personal skill. Both personal and professional skills need to be used in conjunction. However, it is not uncommon for attention to be given to one set, to the neglect of the other. Both balance and feed each other, and so should be developed together.

Balancing work and personal needs

This concerns the effective use of time. No matter how great a workaholic an individual manager may be, there are still domestic duties that need attention. If these are neglected, work life does not run as smoothly as it could. (Many senior female managers wish desperately for the life of their male counterparts.) In addition to the maintenance of domestic well-being, a variety of thoughts, agendas and activities can provide the refreshment needed for continued effective work performance. The exhausted manager does not give the necessary degree of attention to problems, does not think clearly, makes mistakes and is not able to learn. Recreation is essential to maintain the alertness and freshness required by the brain so it is able to access the deeper cognitive levels and memory stores.

Being flexible and able to adapt

Being able to accommodate multiple activities and demands can demonstrate a clarity of vision and purpose. The sharpness of definition this clarity brings enables a manager to decide whether an activity is within or beyond the parameters of the organisation's portfolio. Knowing when to stick and when to bend to meet the demands and aspirations of staff, customers and suppliers demonstrates skills of judgement. Finding solutions which satisfy apparently conflicting agendas gives evidence of imagination and creativity. The ability to say 'No' positively can be a demonstration of firmness, not rigidity.

Being resourceful and playful

Resourcefulness is about using one's creativity and imagination to find solutions to problems. It implies the ability and willingness to act on initiative and make appropriate use of others' resources to take action and encourage them to use their own initiative. It also suggests a preparedness to keep on going – not stubbornly, but with determination – and knowing when to stop when progress is really no longer possible.

Playfulness suggests having fun while working. A lot of the research into job satisfaction and motivation refers to the importance of the social side of work. There is no good reason why this should not be true for managers as well as other staff. People are more prepared to take risks when they are happy. They are more prepared to work co-operatively with people they like and respect. When the brain is both stimulated and relaxed, they are able to learn. Playfulness also allows the brain to be imaginative and creative. Dreaming up daft ideas is one of the ways used deliberately as a means of finding new solutions to new problems. (Can you imagine the next board meeting making use of Nolan's synectics (as described earlier) to solve the cash flow crisis, or the board members giggling at the outrageousness of the finance director's metaphors?)

Using conceptual abilities

Having daft ideas is not an end in itself. Its purpose is to access some of the brain's unused and untapped resources. Psychologists are aware that the brain is not used to its full capacity. For most of the time, only a small fraction of our potential mental capabilities are used. It is possible to learn how to extend our brain capability and learn cognitive skills other than those we use every day. Buzan (1977) offers some ideas on how to increase creativity. Other ways of extending the brain's capacity and improving its functioning are as follows:

Using vision and creating opportunities

A vision is a view of the future which is more than the organisation five years older. It means that unthinkable options are thought about and implausible possibilities considered. Deciding which scenario is the most desirable is followed by an identification of what needs to happen for it to be realised, what steps need to be taken, what needs to be avoided and what sorts of opportunities need to be grasped. The creation of a vision develops managers' abilities to think in abstract terms over an increased time horizon and to bring those thoughts back to the present via the steps that have to be taken to get to the desired future.

Assimilating and reflecting

These develop the breadth of the mind's capacity. Learning techniques such as speed reading can help a manager learn how to cope with large quantities of written information. Another useful skill to aid assimilation of information is learning how to access and use data bases and information sources. The ability to sense and pick up ideas and messages from the ether of the organisation is also worth development. The ability to reflect has already been referred to many times. This skill is mainly the ability to concentrate and to be disciplined.

Questioning, reframing and redefining

Questioning helps the manager to decide whether to reframe and redefine or not. Sometimes the only way through a problem is to reframe it. At other times, the way through is to stick with the existing definition and simply work at it. How many times do managers search for new answers and seek new ideas, attending course after course, reading book after book and engaging consultant after consultant, only to be faced at the end with high expenditure, a brainful of concepts and the same old problem?

There are occasions when new learning or the development of new skills are not needed. What is needed is the application of those which have already been acquired. Perhaps they have not been fully developed, but this is no excuse for their rejection – more the reason for their application.

Being innovative, creative and enterprising

Managers should stand back from their existing assumptions and beliefs. Being innovative means that impractical, impossible ideas are considered. Being creative means that unthinkable options are thought about. Being enterprising involves managers and their staff in new activities, using new or alternative ways and thinking other thoughts.

Being logical and intuitive

Most techniques for decision-making have been developed by the rational school and based on the belief that individuals work to maximise their gain at the least personal cost. Logical processes have been developed to enable choices to be made and appropriate action to be taken. Even though it is well known that people do not behave according to the normative principles of rational decision theories, this popular image of the managerial decision-maker continues to be portrayed. In reality, a skilful decision-maker is someone who is able to make use of these rational models to think through options logically, stage by stage *and* use intuitive decision processes.

Intuition has two forms (at least). One is the gut feeling; a sense of rightness or wrongness of a particular decision. The feeling cannot be attributed to any one cause. Some call this sixth sense, some experience and judgement, and others describe it as 'having a nose'. The other form of intuition can be attributed to past learning that has been stored so deeply in the cognitive store that its very existence has been forgotten. It has become 'unconscious competence'. Experts learn how to exercise their professional judgements from acquired knowledge and experience of its application. They do not just 'become' experts. Probably they cannot describe what they know or how they came to know it.

Thinking strategically and with confidence

Different sets of skills are used to develop a vision than those needed for strategic thought, even though the terms tend to be used together. Thinking strategically is about breadth and shorter time horizons. Having decided where to go, the next step is deciding how to get there and what needs to be done to ensure that the journey is as trouble-free and easy as possible. Strategic planning identifies the resources available and those which are needed. The strategic plan breaks down into action plans, with specific responsibilities assigned to individuals.

A manager needs confidence to draw up a strategic plan. It means making choices and closing down options. A plan that takes account of all eventualities is not strategic. A manager who does not have the confidence to allocate responsibility to others and hold them accountable is not effective. The plan needs to be based on a realistic assessment of strengths, weaknesses, opportunities and threats. Resources are allocated, obtained and done without on the basis of the assessment; confidence comes from knowing the plan is based on reality and has been drawn up skilfully. Moreover, everyone concerned expects that mistakes may be made or that other factors will influence the execution of the plan. These are not to be feared – they are the opportunities for future development.

Using personal power

The degree of powerlessness experienced by senior managers is very worrying; yet it is not an uncommon phenomenon. One way in which they can reduce this sense is to view their organisation's power bases through the perceptions of others. An analysis of who has the power to decide whether or not to allow a decision to be made, can help identify just how much perceived and actual power different individuals, including themselves, may actually hold.

Recognising and valuing personal power

Very often, managers do not appreciate just how much power they have. The sense of powerlessness tends to pervade all levels of an organisation facing turbulent conditions and rapid change. Senior managers can only act through the middle managers. Middle managers can only act with the permission of the senior managers. The people at operational levels are left wondering what is happening and who is deciding what.

A learning company is one which is all-powerful. All its members know the limits of their existing power and that of others, yet they are able to push at the boundaries. Because they are all learning together, power is not finite. If one member of staff gains more power, it does not imply a decrease in power for someone else – it simply increases the total power of the company.

Using interpersonal skills

These skills allow the value of other peoples' power to be recognised and are essential for harmonious and smooth working, and for everyone's learning. Interpersonal skills involve respect being given to others, helping others develop and allowing space for learning, trying out, practising and action. Denial of others' power restricts their abilities to act and learn. Disempowered people do not develop; they diminish. People who are not treated with respect tend not to be able to respect others. The deployment of interpersonal skills is very akin to acting assertively – respecting one's own rights while giving full acknowledgment to those of others.

Allowing for the rights of others

The denial of others' rights causes discontentment, jealousy, inter-sectional disharmony and bitterness, fuelling destructive conflicts which can distract the organisation from its true purpose and inhibit development. Allowing for the rights of others encourages collaboration, risk-taking and joint development.

Caring

Caring is not a soft option. It involves the expenditure of emotion and energy. A member of staff who does not care is perhaps one of the most difficult types of poor performer to deal with, as it can be hard to find ways of making an impact on them. Caring is about having beliefs and conviction – caring about individuals and equally about the effective completion of task and the organisation. One does not take precedence over the others.

Taking risks

A developmental manager knows that to enable organisational learning to take place, calculated risks must be taken. These risks are made with the organisation's resources, involve other people (with their agreement) and draw on the individual manager's personal resources. A learning company recognises the need to take these risks, makes allowances for them, and is prepared to support its managers fully. If the risk goes wrong, the manager is not reprimanded; the learning is abstracted and value is given to the experience.

Taking challenges positively

If change and its inherent challenge is avoided or ignored, development cannot happen. If, however, the challenges are seen as opportunities, they can be exploited for their potential pay-offs and possible learning.

Being aware of the impact of one's actions on others

This awareness is necessary on the part of both individual managers and the total organisation. Acumen usually applies to financial awareness, but it can also mean awareness of the broader effects of actions. Often steps are taken, things are said or plans set in motion without thought being given to their wider consequences. Part of the development of cognitive skills aims to extend the thought processes beyond the immediate and the obvious. It is not expected that a manager will consider every eventuality before making a decision or entering into a new venture. However, it is anticipated that likely and various cause and effect outcomes will be considered. Moreover, if the unthinkable is possible, then the potential outcomes must also be given attention. This process can be similar to that used for reframing. Extending the chain of cause and effect scenarios in all directions is a useful way for managers to learn how to develop their thought processes.

SHAPE OF A LEARNING COMPANY

It is not possible to construct a diagram of a learning company. There is no predetermined structure that can be laid out on a page. Neither is there a flow chart of systems and processes which can act as a formula for other organisations to replicate. Learning companies are not like that. Pedler, Burgoyne and Boydell (1986) give some glimpses of organisational and managerial behaviour they have seen which fulfil the requirements of being called a learning company. But they are not simply the actions taken by the managers of those organisations. It may be easier to draw a picture of a learning company than to show its structure. A picture can communicate feel as well as give form to an organism, for a learning company is more than *doing*; it is *being*. It is important that managers who want to develop such an organisation appreciate that they need to believe. To become a learning company an organisation must be more than one with a policy. Commitment and beliefs only become real when they are translated into the actions and approaches taken by the organisation's managers and others with leadership or power roles. These people need to base their actions on the belief that people throughout the organisation have the right to be treated in a developmental way.

A total organisation can be a learning company. Alternatively it is possible for a small section of a larger organisation to become a learning company, even though the rest of the wider organisation would not meet the conditions. This is because the actions and approaches taken by individual managers can foster and nurture a developmental climate. Equally, they can inhibit one. Even in an organisation striving to be a learning company, an individual manager can sabotage the intent by the attitudes adopted and actions taken towards other staff. Being a developmental manager requires determination, commitment, effort and belief. Being a contra-developmental manager is easy. You expect nothing, give nothing and get nothing.

FINALE

This chapter and the whole book has attempted to provide guidance to managers on how they can act to be developmental for themselves, the others around them and the whole of their organisation. Many of the concepts discussed have been drawn from the belief that learning is a life-long activity. It should be normal and easy, in theory and practice. All that is needed are the prerequisite conditions. Sadly much of what happens within organisations positively serves to discourage risk-taking and experimentation. Change is seen as a threat to the status quo, rather than an opportunity to improve.

Managers can act to alter these typical scenarios. They may be required to start in a small way within their own zones of influence. With practice and the growing confidence that comes from the development and subsequent increase in skills levels, they can widen those zones and ultimately influence their whole organisation. After all, behaviour is largely learnt from repeating the patterns that are seen to work for others. It is well known that nothing succeeds like success, and aspiring managers learn their behaviours from the successful role models around them.

This book has aimed to draw together practical ideas to help managers develop their skills to develop those of others. This is not just a pious wish. Development of individuals, self-development and the development of others, is an investment which is vital to the well-being of the country. This does not just concern the country's ability to produce the wealth it needs to sustain itself. It also concerns the quality of working life, and this has a direct effect on the rest of the quality of workers' (and managers') lives. Therefore investing in people at work and their development is an investment in the quality of their whole life. This investment is not for short gain. Its return, albeit long-term, is an incremental spreading in a virtuous spiral. As the quality of skills develops, performances increase, which enhances the quality of the output, which satisfies consumers, which encourages repeat business, which provides the funds for more investment in skills enhancement, which adds to job satisfaction, which increases productivity and reduces stress-related illness, and so on.

It is appreciated that in a difficult economic climate, it is not easy to convince a hard-pressed company accountant to spend time and money on development. When redundancy payments have to be incurred and plant maintenance pared to the minimum, it may seem almost bizarre to talk about investing to increase skill levels. It may seem to be a totally impractical irrelevancy. However, a case can be made to show that this sort of investment can actually be extremely relevant. Recession, decline and redundancy damage morale so significantly that the motivation level of the remaining staff stays chronically low, even after any recovery has started. At the very time the company needs extra effort the staff are still wondering whether it will be worth the energy. Investing in skill development at the lowest point can help maintain the staff through difficult periods and equip them in readiness for the upturn. When an organisation is moving forward, making investments in the development of people can bring forth untold benefits for individuals and the whole company. If this book adds anything to this process it will have achieved its aim.

Bibliography

Bevan S and Thompson, M (1991) 'Performance management at the crossroads' *Personnel Management* November.

Blanksby M (1988) *Staff training: a librarian's handbook* AAL, Newcastle-under-Lyme.

Bloom B S (1956) *Taxonomy of education objectives. Handbook 1: The cognitive domain* Longmans, Green, London.

Boyatzis R E (1982) *The competent manager* Wiley, Chichester.

Boydell T H (1992) *Developing the developers: improving the quality of the professionals who develop people and organisations* AMED, London.

BTEC (1990) *National Vocational Qualification at Level 5 in Management. Part 2: Standards* BTEC Publications, London.

Buzan T (1973) *Use your head* BBC Publications, London.

Buzan T (1977) *Make the most of your mind* Pan, London.

Cascio W F (1987) *Applied psychology in personnel management* (third edn) Prentice Hall, Hemel Hempstead.

Cattell R B, Eber, H W and Tatsuoka M M (1970) *Handbook of the sixteen personality factor questionnaire* NFER, Windsor.

Chambers C, Coopey J and McLean A (1990) *Develop your management potential: a self-help guide* Kogan Page, London.

Constable J and McCormick R (1987) *The making of British managers* BIM, Corby.

Dale M and Iles P (1991) *Assessing management skills* Kogan Page, London.

Day G S and Wensley R (1988) 'Assessing advantage: a framework for diagnosing competitive superiority' *Journal of Marketing* 52.

Eitington J E (1989) *The winning trainer* (second edn) Gulf Publishing, Houston, Tex.

Fayol H (1949) *General and industrial management* Pitman, London.

Fletcher S (1991) *NVQs, Standards and competence* Kogan Page, London.

Garratt B (1987) *The learning organisation* Fontana, London.

Gibson J L, Ivancevich J M and Donnelly J H (1988) *Organizations* Business Publications Inc, Homewood, Ill.

Hackman J R and Oldham G R (1975) 'Development of the job diagnostic survey' *Journal of Applied Psychology* 60.

Handy C (1985) *Understanding organisations* Penguin, London.

Handy C (1987) *The making of managers* NEDO, MSC and BIM, London.

Handy C (1990) *The age of unreason* Arrow, London.

Harrison R (1989) *Training and development* IPM, London.

Herriot P (1987) 'The selection interview' *in* Warr P *Psychology at work* (third edn), Penguin, Harmondsworth.

Hertzberg F (1966) *Work and the nature of man* World Publishing Co.

Honey P and Mumford A (1982) *Manual of learning styles* Honey.

Inhelder B (1962) 'Some aspects of Piaget's genetic approach to cognition' *in* Society for Research in Child Development, *Monograph* 27(2).

Janis I L (1972) *Victims of group-think* Houghton-Mifflin, Cambridge, Mass.

Johnson G and Scholes K (1989) *Exploring Corporate Strategy* (third edn), Prentice Hall, Englewood Cliffs.

Kelly G A (1980) *The psychology of personal constructs* W W Norton, New York.

Kolb D A (1974) *Organisational psychology: an experiential approach* Prentice Hall, Hemel Hempstead.

Lewin K (1968) 'Group decision and social change' *in Readings in social psychology* (eds by E E Maccoby, T M Newcomb and E L Hartley) Holt.

Lindblom C (1979) 'Still muddling, not yet through' *in Decision making: approaches and analysis* (eds by A G McGrew and M J Wilson) (1982) Manchester University Press, Manchester.

Mager R F (1984) *Goal analysis* (second edn) Pitman, London.

Mansfield B (1989) 'Functional analysis – a personal approach' *Competence and Assessment* Special Issue 1: the analysis of competence: current thought and practice (Training Agency, Sheffield).

Mayo A (1992) *Managing careers – strategies for organisations* IPM, London.

Megginson D and Boydell T H (1979) *A manager's guide to coaching* BACIE, London.

Megginson D and Pedler M (1992) *Self-development: a facilitator's guide* McGraw-Hill, Maidenhead.

Mintzberg H (1973) *The nature of managerial work* Harper & Row, London.

Nolan V (1981) *Open to change* MCB University Press, Bradford.

Parker, Ferris and Otley (1989) 'The broadening accounting constituency' *in Accounting for the human factor* Prentice Hall, Hemel Hempstead.

Pedler M J and Boydell T H (1985) *Managing yourself* Fontana, London.

Pedler M, Boydell T, and Burgoyne J (1988) *Learning company project report* Training Agency, Sheffield.

Pedler M, Burgoyne J G and Boydell T H (1986) *A manager's guide to self-development* (second edn) McGraw-Hill, Maidenhead.

Piaget J (1953) *The intelligence in the child* W W Norton, New York.

Plant R (1985) *Managing change and making it stick* Fontana, London.

Powers E and Cane S (1989) 'AMED conference on the competency approach to management development and assessment', Association of Management Education and Development, London.

Reason J (1990) *Human error* Cambridge University Press, New York.

Revans R (1980) *ABC of action learning* (second edn) Chartwell-Bratt, New York.

Rosenhead J (ed) (1989) *Rational analysis for a problematic world: problem structuring methods for complexity, uncertainty and conflict* Wiley, Chichester.

Skinner B F (1971) *Beyond freedom and dignity* Knopf, New York.

Smith M (1988) 'Calculating the sterling value of selection' *Guidance and Assessment Review* 4 (1).

Sternberg R J (1988) 'Sketch of componential sub-theory of human intelligence' *Behaviour and Brain Sciences* (3).

Stewart V and Stewart A (1982) *Business applications of repertory grid* McGraw-Hill, Maidenhead.

Stewart A and Stewart R (1982) *Managing poor performance* Gower, Aldershot.

Training Agency (1989) 'Development of accessible standards for national certification' *Guidance note 2: Developing standards by reference to functions* Training Agency, Sheffield.

Vaill P B (1989) *Managing as a performing art: new ideas for a world of chaotic change* Jossey-Bass, San Franciso, Calif.

Whetten D A and Cameron K S (1991) *Developing management skills* (second edn) HarperCollins, New York.

Woodward J (1965) *Industrial organisation* Oxford University Press, Oxford.

Zoll A (1974) *Explorations in management* Addison-Wesley, New York.

Index

Groupthink 107–9

Hackman, J R and Oldham, G R 97
Hawthorne Studies 109–10
Hertzberg, F 96, 97
Honey, P and Mumford, A 103, 113
human resources
  accounting 53–4
  as assets 53–4
  management 23, 54
  valuing 59

imagination 241
induction 123–4
inhibitors
  see blocks
initiative 241
innovation 242
instructing 202–3, 234
intelligence 76, 78, 86, 103
interpersonal skills 244
intuition 85
  see also decision making
investment 23, 51, 52, 54, 68
investors in people 219

Jacques, E 102
Janis, I L 107
job analysis 42–3, 47
  see also job design
job definition 134–5, 155
job description 120
job design 141–5
job enlargement and enrichment 154
job satisfaction 97–8, 241

Kelly's personal construct theory 39–40, 41
  see also constructs
knowledge 32–3
Kolb's learning cycle 103–4, 152–4
  see also learning style

leading 234
learner, unmotivated 98
learning 12, 67, 222
  abilities 104–5
  adults 76

blocks, 95–105
  see also blocks
company 25
  definition 220, 229–31
  see also learning organisation
communities 237
  definitions 229–31
contracts 172–3, 198
culture 204
curve 66–7
cycle 178
  see also Kolb's learning cycle
definition 222
facilitating 236
from mistakes and successes 165–6
inhibitors
  see blocks
logs 174
organisation 217, 219–47
  features 222–4
  membership 226
process 75, 76–87, 153
  adult 76
  early 78–9
  style 87, 103–4
  taxonomy 78, 163
  to learn 87–8, 180
  see also development
listening 184–5, 209–10, 235, 239
Luddites 101

maintenance decisions 67–70
Management Charter Initiative 27
management functions 19
management, professional skills 240
manager
  alone 229–31
  as a learner 213–4
  as role model 213–5, 232
  behaviour 112–3
  competent 13, 229
  developing the boss 215–7
  personal skills development 229, 240
  relationship 112
  role and responsibilities 22–3, 98–9, 152–4, 190–218, 229, 232
  self development 151, 153, 237, 238, 239–41